D1553128

BARCELONA AND BEYOND

BARCELONA AND BEYOND

THE DISPUTATION OF 1263 AND ITS AFTERMATH

ROBERT CHAZAN

University of California Press

Berkeley • Los Angeles • Oxford

University of California Press
Berkeley and Los Angeles, California

University of California Press
Oxford, England

© 1992 by
The Regents of the University of California

Library of Congress Cataloging-in-Publication Data

Chazan, Robert.
    Barcelona and beyond: the Disputation of 1263 and its
aftermath / Robert Chazan.
        p.   cm.
    Includes bibliographical references and index.
    ISBN 0–520–07441–6 (alk. paper)
    1. Barcelona Disputation, Barcelona, Spain, 1263.
2. Naḥmanides, ca. 1195–ca. 1270. Vikuaḥ ha-Ramban.
3. Judaism—Relations—Christianity.   4. Christianity
and other religions—Judaism.   5. Jews—Spain—History.   6. Spain—Ethnic relations.   I. Title.
BM590.C48   1992
296.3—dc20   91–35284
                                                           CIP

Printed in the United States of America

1   2   3   4   5   6   7   8   9

The paper used in this publication meets the minimum
requirements of American National Standard for Information Sciences—Permanence of Paper for Printed Library
Materials, ANSI Z39.48–1984 ⊗

Contents

Preface

For more than a decade, I have researched and written of the famed disputation that took place in Barcelona in 1263. Two chapters in my *Daggers of Faith* were devoted to that important confrontation, and I little dreamed that my work would continue and expand into a book devoted solely to it.[1] To be sure, on concluding *Daggers of Faith*, I was well aware that there were underlying questions about the 1263 encounter that I had not undertaken, and I was also cognizant of a number of related matters that I had purposely held in abeyance. These latter issues involved particularly some of the postdisputation activities of Rabbi Moses ben Nahman. Because my purpose in writing *Daggers of Faith* was an investigation of the new-style missionizing that developed in western Christendom (preeminently in its southern sectors) during the middle decades of the thirteenth century, I was leery of devoting excessive attention to the 1263 disputation, out of a fear that undue focus on Barcelona would seriously unbalance my account. On those grounds, I left some of the follow-up activities of Nahmanides for what was projected as a series of fairly brief studies. In the process of undertaking these studies, two factors contributed to the extension of my investigation. The first was external—an invitation to present a paper on the Barcelona disputation at an international conference, "Religious Disputations in the Middle Ages," sponsored by the Herzog August Bibliotek of Wolfenbüttel. Participation called for reexamination of the Barcelona material and the issues.[2] Equally significant was an important internal development in my own work—the growing conviction that the most interesting postdisputation activity of Rabbi Moses ben Nahman was the remarkable record that he composed of the encounter and his role in it. As a result of these twin influences, I was drawn once again into an examination of the Barcelona engagement and of some of the underlying issues I had heretofore skirted.

What were these issues, and why had I chosen to bypass them in my earlier treatment? Let me begin with the latter question. My early interest in the encounter had emerged from the sense that it was a major milestone in the new-style missionizing that developed during the middle decades of the thirteenth century. I was convinced that the Barcelona disputation was the great testing grounds for this new-style missionizing and the key to understanding it. I was of course aware of the extensive and highly polarized literature that had developed around the confrontation, a literature divergent in its assessment of the event, its outcome, and the extant sources that depict it. It was my desire, to the extent possible, to avoid that extensive scholarly debate, focusing rather on the information that could be reliably gleaned from the extant sources and that would shed light on the development of the new missionizing techniques and argumentation. I was aware that inevitably I was making judgments about the sources and was drawing conclusions as to the outcome of the confrontation. Nonetheless, I attempted, within possible bounds, to stay outside the polarizing issues and treat the confrontation only insofar as it contributed to an understanding of my topic, the emergence of the new missionizing techniques and argumentation. My reinvolvement in the Barcelona disputation and, in particular, my projected study of the narrative of Nahmanides drew me ineluctably into many of those thorny issues that I had previously avoided.

The result has been a full-scale treatment of the Barcelona disputation, in which the contentious historical literature surrounding it has been fully confronted and in which the basic issues of what happened at Barcelona, what was the outcome of the engagement, and how the conflicting sources are to be evaluated have been fully treated. I have undertaken this study out of the sense, first of all, that the event remains a major one, well worth careful treatment. As we shall see shortly, there is broad agreement that the disputation was, from a variety of perspectives, the most important such Christian-Jewish encounter during the Middle Ages. Such a crucial event deserves the fullest possible attention. There is more. Since conflicting reports, Christian and Jewish, have given rise to a polarized secondary literature, there is considerable methodological importance to a reinvestigation of the divergent medieval sources. I believe it is possible to develop guidelines for the treatment and resolution of such divergence, resolution that can and will move beyond labeling one or another of the accounts as deceitful and lying. There is, it seems to me, more than enough guidance available in recent social science literature and literary criticism to move us beyond such partisanship and into more productive modes of confronting perspectival clash. A fundamental examination of the Barcelona disputation offers the possibility of introducing into the historiography of the medieval Christian-Jewish conflict new stances that hold the promise of more productive insights.

The focus of this book, as it has developed, moves inevitably beyond the disputation itself. I have been much concerned to delineate the activities undertaken by both sides in the wake of the 1263 encounter. My attention to these post-1263 developments is clearly skewed toward fuller treatment of the activities in the Jewish camp. The reason for this is, on a simple level, the availability of richer source material from the Jewish side. To be sure, the disparity in source material is in itself hardly accidental. It was the Jewish side that was most heavily invested in aftermath activities, as it sought to minimize any potential damage from the new missionizing campaign. In particular, close investigation shows a series of remarkable compositions by the Jewish protagonist, Rabbi Moses ben Nahman. These valuable writings, which have long been known but not sufficiently analyzed, enable us to chart major intellectual and spiritual developments in the Jewish community of Catalonia and, at the same time, to discover new aspects to this highly creative thinker and leader.

Understanding of the Barcelona disputation and its aftermath has surely been advanced by new research on the mid-thirteenth-century Roman Catholic church and its policies vis-à-vis the Jews of Western Christendom, the thirteenth-century Crown of Aragon and its complex stances toward Aragonese Jewry, and the internal dynamics of Jewish material and spiritual life on the Iberian peninsula at this critical juncture.[3] This research can significantly augment our appreciation of both the disputation and its aftermath. Conversely, fuller and better comprehension of what transpired at Barcelona and in its aftermath promises to deepen our knowledge of evolving ecclesiastical policies, of the realities of Aragonese history, and of the vicissitudes of Aragonese Jewry during the middle decades of the thirteenth century. Beyond illumination of broad developments during this important period, the detailed evidence for a series of individuals helps us to achieve fuller insight into the class of new converts represented by Friar Paul Christian, the complex and fascinating King James I, and the gifted and multifaceted Rabbi Moses ben Nahman. On all these scores, a renewed and fuller probe of the important event of 1263 and its aftermath seems sufficiently warranted.

I would like to thank a number of colleagues who have read drafts of the manuscript and offered me their constructive criticisms. Joseph Shatzmiller of the University of Toronto and Michael Signer of the Hebrew Union College-Jewish Institute of Religion read the entire manuscript and made many useful suggestions. One of the joys of teaching in the Skirball Department of Hebrew and Judaic Studies at New York University has been the companionship and intellectual camaraderie of a number of gifted colleagues and friends. Since this work cut across a number of their fields of interest, my associates Yael Feldman, Baruch Levine, Lawrence Schiffman, and Elliot Wolfson read segments of the manuscript and shared with me their expertise. While all of these friends have had a positive impact on this work, the shortcomings that remain are of course my responsibility alone.

The staff of the University of California Press has, once more, been kind, caring, and efficient. I would like to thank, in particular, Stanley Holwitz, who has become both editor and friend, Shirley Warren and Michelle Nordon, who guided the production of this volume with thoroughness and concern, and Sheila Berg, who provided skillful and thoughtful editing. As always, *aharon aharon haviv,* my wife and family have extended their usual unflagging support. Despite my wife's heavy professional responsibilities, including her own publications, she manages nonetheless to afford constant encouragement and advice. Our children, embarked on their own academic careers, still find time to discuss their father's projects and offer valuable suggestions. My appreciation is profound.

Introduction

On Friday, July 20, 1263, a remarkable assemblage was convened at the royal palace in Barcelona, consisting of King James himself, royal officials, barons, ecclesiastical dignitaries, leading burghers, and Catalan Jews. The gathering was surely impressive, colorful, and—for the Jews involved—somewhat frightening. The purpose of this convocation was to witness an unusual public colloquy between a Dominican friar and the rabbi of Gerona. The Dominican, Friar Paul Christian, had been born a Jew, had converted, had entered the Dominican Order, had taken a role of leadership in considerable anti-Jewish activity, had in particular been zealous in developing a new line of Christian argumentation to be used against the Jews, and had won ecclesiastical and royal backing for convening this public debate. Friar Paul's opponent, Rabbi Moses ben Nahman of Gerona, was by this time a recognized authority in Catalan Jewry and, indeed, beyond the boundaries of Catalonia. He was, in fact, one of the giants of thirteenth-century Jewish life, distinguishing himself as a talmudic authority, a central figure in the rising mystical circles on the Iberian peninsula, and a communal leader of sensitivity and acumen.[1]

The public discussion that was undertaken that July day, amid the pomp and splendor of the royal palace, was not intended by its instigators, the Dominicans, as an open exchange of views concerning the superiority of one of the two faiths. Rather, the encounter was rigidly circumscribed: it was to serve as a test for the new missionizing argumentation developed by Friar Paul, which utilized rabbinic texts as the basis for proving to the Jews that their own talmudic tradition in effect recognized fundamental truths of Christianity. Confronted with such proof from their own tradition, Jews were supposed to recognize the error of their ways and to follow the path of the friar into the Christian fold. In the course of the public debate at Barcelona, Friar Paul was to advance a series of such Jewish texts in an effort to prove rabbinic recognition of Christian truth. The rabbi's role in the encounter was to be rigorously limited to disproving the friar's contentions. Disproving the friar's reading of rabbinic texts and their implications did not mean casting aspersions on the truth of Christianity. In the course of his defense, the rabbi was forbidden to say anything that might be construed as offensive to the Christian faith or to the sensitivities of his Christian auditors.

We shall never know precisely what transpired on that July day in Barcelona or on the succeeding three days of public discussion. Two reports on the engagement have come down to us, one written from the Christian perspective and one from the Jewish point of view. It is of course not surprising that Christian and Jewish observers might see the selfsame events in remarkably divergent ways. It is surely safe to say that the friar did advance his rabbinic texts, while the rabbi denied the meanings attributed to them. Some of the broad lines of the exchange can be reconstructed, but the full details are lost to us. How long did each speaker hold forth? While the friar was clearly accorded the first word, who had the last word? What was the mood of the gathering—solemn, festive, raucous, ominous? What was the feeling among the ecclesiastical instigators of the encounter? What of the king? How did he view the proceedings? What was the sense of the Jews who witnessed the discussion? Were they delighted with their spokesman and his responses? Were they comfortable that the new missionizing argumentation was devoid of all meaning? Were they secure in the protection of the monarch? Did they experience some anxiety over the spiritual challenge? Were they apprehensive that royal support for this engagement presaged new political pressures and dangers? So many of these questions cannot be answered. The perceived significance of this debate was so strong in 1263 that each side set about creating its own version of what transpired. That sense of significance has hardly abated, moving historians of the nineteenth and twentieth centuries to turn their attention time and again to those balmy days in thirteenth-century Barcelona.

THE ENCOUNTER AND ITS SIGNIFICANCE

Unten allen Disputationen, welche in mittelalterlichen Abenlande Christen mit Juden hatten, ragt jene hervor, die in der Gegenwart des Königs von Aragon, Jakobs I, zu Barcelona am 20. Juli 1263 zwischen den von Judentume bekehrten Dominikaner Pablo Christiani und dem beruhmtesten Rabbinen Spaniens, Mose Nachmani aus Gerona, stattfand.[2]

Of the Judaeo-Christian disputations which were staged publicly from time to time during the Middle Ages, perhaps none was of greater interest, and certainly none was recorded more intimately, than that which took place at Barcelona in the summer of 1263.[3]

Of the disputations which took place during the Middle Ages, there are only three of which any detailed record survives: the Paris Disputation of 1240, the Barcelona Disputation of 1263, and the Tortosa Disputation of 1413–14. Of these the most celebrated is the Barcelona Disputation of 1263.[4]

The three scholars whose sense of the importance of the Barcelona disputation of 1263 seems almost interchangeable in fact represent three widely divergent views of the event, its outcome, and the extant sources. Indeed, they have differing reasons for assigning significance to this debate. Nonetheless, their agreement on the importance of the Barcelona confrontation is valuable in alerting us to the widely held conviction of the special significance of this event.

When we ask why this event holds such significance, we are confronted with a plethora of explanations: because it was such a signal Christian victory and Jewish defeat; because it was such a signal Jewish victory and Christian defeat; because it heralds the onset of new pressures on European Jewry; because it represents a new line of missionizing argumentation, one destined for considerable impact on European Jewry; because of the drama of the occasion; because of the exciting source materials bequeathed to posterity. There is, of course, no need to argue these considerations; it is enough to note that from a variety of perspectives, the Barcelona disputation has been viewed, since the event itself, as a major Christian-Jewish encounter, worthy of recollection, investigation, and consideration.

Like so many aspects of Christian-Jewish engagement over the ages (and indeed interreligious conflict of all kinds), the Barcelona confrontation has given rise to considerable polarization in points of view. It represents almost a classic case of divergent perspectives, and to the modern historian that characteristic as well makes the encounter of special interest. The question posed to the modern researcher is whether such an event can be treated in a manner that proceeds beyond a simple taking of sides. To frame this methodological issue properly and, in the process, to lay bare the procedures of this study, it will be necessary to portray in some detail the prior disagreements with respect to the Barcelona disputation.

THE PRIOR HISTORIOGRAPHY

Almost immediately after the Barcelona disputation, there was concern on both sides for portrayal of the encounter, portrayal in a manner deemed appropriate by each of the two parties. This concern eventuated in a Christian-Latin account that proclaims repeatedly the superiority of the Christian protagonist, Friar Paul Christian, and the humbling of his Jewish opponent, the renowned Rabbi Moses ben Nahman. This Latin account portrays a Jewish spokesman badly discomfited and confused, disparaged as a result by his coreligionists, and forced eventually, out of desperation, to flee the circumstances of his humiliation. While not formally a declaration of victory, this Latin report in effect asserts the success of the Christian side and the humiliating failure of the distinguished Jewish protagonist.

Similarly, from the Jewish side, the public spokesman himself, Rabbi Moses ben Nahman, undertook a Hebrew narrative account of the confrontation. Here, too, while no overt statement of victory is made, the account is intended to assure its Jewish readers of the remarkable achievement of its representative and the ignominious failure of the Christian protagonist. This portrait of Jewish success is achieved first and foremost by the extensive depiction of exchanges that, for all their drama and unpredictability, always end with the rabbi enjoying the last and decisive word. No issue is left dangling or ambiguous. For each Christian thrust, the rabbi provides a definitive response. This general impression is reinforced powerfully by depictions of two meetings between the rabbi and the king of Aragon. The first portrays a meeting that took place on the very day of the closing session of the formal disputation; it has the king congratulating the rabbi for defending brilliantly his incorrect cause. Given the constant picture of the king as a loyal and devoted Christian, such praise is the highest to which the Jewish spokesman might legitimately aspire. This image of royal approbation is reinforced by Nahmanides when he tells his readers that, some days later, after further argumentation in the synagogue of Barcelona, the king formally dismissed him with a considerable gift. The sum total of the impression created by Nahmanides was of a remarkable Jewish achievement, an impression thoroughly in opposition to that created by the Christian account.

Not surprisingly, the polarization of the mid-thirteenth century has been absorbed by later observers as well, on both sides of the Christian-Jewish schism. For many centuries, these polarized views existed comfortably within each camp, with no real concern for bridging the impasse. Christian writers, particularly of the Dominican Order, continued to trumpet, for internal consumption, the victory of Friar Paul Christian. Likewise, Jewish authors depicted glowingly the achievement of Rabbi Moses ben Nahman.[5] Christian authors wrote for a Christian audience and Jewish authors for a Jewish audience, and never were the twain intended to meet.

Comfortable adherence to these polarized perspectives was disturbed by the emergence of a new middle ground, the realm of purportedly disinterested scholarship, a development first notable already in the eighteenth century but of accelerating significance during the nineteenth century. In the case of the Barcelona disputation, the outbreak of hostilities on this new battleground took place during the closing decades of the nineteenth century.

The opening salvo was fired by one of two learned Heinrichs, Heinrich Graetz, the learned historian of the Jews, or Heinrich Denifle, the learned historian of medieval Christendom; again, even this matter can be viewed in a variety of ways. Graetz, in his depiction of the Barcelona disputation in the monumental *Geschichte der Juden*, leans heavily on the Nahmanidean account. He portrays a decisive Jewish victory, accurately sketched in the rabbi's narrative. In Graetz's account, there is no room for doubts or subtleties: the rabbi overcame his foe decisively, and the rabbi's account is the one to be trusted.[6] This forthright declaration of Jewish victory and reliability—now no longer written for internal Jewish consumption only—enraged Denifle, who took Graetz and his Jewish source to task severely. While some of the criticism involves Graetz's lack of awareness of key source materials, the real force of Denifle's attack involves the twin issues of victory versus defeat and the reliability of the Christian versus the Jewish materials. For Denifle, the trustworthy source is the Latin account, validated, as it were, by the royal seal. The conflicting Jewish source is therefore mendacious. The divergent assessment of sources— one true and reliable and the other false and deceitful—leads inevitably to a precise sense of the event and its outcome. The true and reliable source—for Denifle, the Latin account—portrays the event in its proper perspective; the portrait painted by the rabbi must be resolutely rejected.[7]

The battle had been fully joined. The medieval divergence of views had been transported into the somewhat different arena of modern scholarship. No longer could members of two differing communities write comfortably for internal consumption. The arena was now a larger one, with the stakes significantly high. The old two truths in two circles were now to be replaced with one truth only, the objective truth provided by historical research. The only problem—and it was a mammoth one—was how to arrive at that elusive objective truth, which all observers would have to acknowledge. In an ironic way, the old theological battle was transformed into a new historiographic battle. While it would be unseemly for moderns to argue over who possessed religious truth (the ideals of new egalitarian society precluded such argumentation), it was possible to argue over the rectitude of historical sources and figures and relative victory and defeat at an earlier time when such argumentation was in vogue.

To be sure, historians of Western Christendom or—more narrowly—the medieval Crown of Aragon and the Dominican Order have hardly been obsessed with the issue of the Barcelona disputation in the way in which historians of the Jews have.[8] The concern for rectitude of sources and the actual outcome of the Barcelona disputation has been far deeper among historians of the Jews. We shall pursue this issue a bit further, again as an introduction to the methodology to be followed in this study.

Denifle's assault on Graetz, and indeed on Nahmanides himself, was met head on by a major French student of the medieval Jewish experience, Isidore Loeb.[9] Loeb's treatment of the Barcelona confrontation affords interesting evidence of the transformation of medieval issues into a modern format. Unlike Graetz and Denifle, Loeb was not deeply concerned with claims of victory or defeat.

As a historian of religious debate, he was quite accepting of divergent assessments of the same event. "Le P. Denifle ne sait donc pas ce que c'est qu'une controverse religieuse? N'est-il pas de règle que, dans ces joûtes, chacun des partis s'attribue sincèrement la victoire et la gloire d'avoir réduit l'ennemi en poussière?"[10] While the divergent assessments of the event cause Loeb neither grief nor astonishment, he is deeply distressed by Denifle's assessment of the sources, in particular, by his negative views on the Nahmanidean report. The ground of disagreement for Loeb lies with the intellectual accuracy and moral probity of the divergent sources. Loeb in effect reverses Denifle's assessment. For him, the Hebrew account is true and reliable, the Latin untrustworthy and misleading. While two of Loeb's arguments have to do with objective details, such as the time of composition and the presence or absence of charges of lying in subsequent sources, the brunt of his argument focuses on issues that are far more subjective. For Loeb, the Latin report is untrustworthy because it is obviously a work of propaganda; because it came out of the circle of Raymond of Penyafort, "dont on connaît l'esprit violent"; because it involved centrally a convert from Judaism, "dont il est permis de dire le plus grand mal sans être injuste"; because the Dominicans revealed their lack of reliability by first promising Nahmanides freedom of speech and then pursuing him on charges of blasphemy.[11] Contrasted with this negative assessment of the reliability of the one side is his portrait of the other. For Loeb, "Nahmani est un homme vénérable et sans tache," a man who would not in fact have dared to lie with respect to the events of 1263.[12] The shift from the ground of religious truth and falseness to the ground of moral reliability and shortcoming is striking but not at all surprising. Issues of morality had come, by the late nineteenth century, to dominate the field of enlightened Christian-Jewish relations.

Only three twentieth-century figures will be considered, although many more have written on the issue. The first of these is Yitzhak Baer, perhaps the most probing of all twentieth-century historians of medieval Jewish life. In the early 1930s, Baer wrote a major article on the disputations of 1240 and 1263, an article that set the agenda for most of the subsequent work on these two key events.[13] While Baer treated both events in his fairly brief study, he emphasized sharply the difference between them. The Bar-

celona disputation is examined carefully within the framework established by the Denifle-Loeb debate, that is to say, with heavy emphasis on the sources and their reliability. While eschewing Loeb's
ad hominem attacks on the circle of Friar Raymond and Friar Paul,
Baer subjects the Latin account to painstaking criticism, drawing
up a catalog of its shortcomings. Still offended by the Denifle remarks, Baer concludes, "It is a historical responsibility not to cover
up the truth, as Loeb did, but to say explicitly that the report as
written before us in the Latin account is a lie."[14] What Denifle had
charged against the Ramban has now been turned by Baer against
the Latin account.

To be sure, Baer went far beyond this negative assessment of
the Latin report. While praising the narrative of Nahmanides, he
also indicated some of the shortcomings of that source as well. His
strictures on the Hebrew narrative are all valuable, as we shall subsequently see. In a striking reflection of Loeb's claim with respect
to the Latin report, Baer concludes, "In my view, I have proven
that the Ramban's composition is not a reliable account, but rather
simply a work of propaganda."[15] For Baer, this conclusion involves
neither a reassessment of the outcome of the disputation (in his
History of the Jews in Christian Spain, he depicted the confrontation
as a success for the Jewish protagonist)[16] nor any sort of moral condemnation of the Jewish sage. Rather, for him, the tendentious
quality of the Hebrew narrative is simply a reality that must be
acknowledged and that must be recognized in careful utilization
of this important source. Thus, Baer evaluates the two sources in
more nuanced fashion than his predecessors. For him, the Latin
account is a lie, the Hebrew account a work of propaganda.
Clearly, the latter must continue to be the primary authority, but
one to be utilized with more care than exercised heretofore.

In 1964, Martin A. Cohen wrote an insightful and provocative
study of the Barcelona disputation that is distinguished by its sensitivity to a variety of methodological issues.[17] Cohen argued, at the
outset of his essay, that despite the scholarly attention focused on
the Barcelona disputation, "we still do not know the real significance of the debate." He proposed a series of critical questions for
further investigation:

> Who was responsible for calling the debate? How was its agenda
> determined? What strategies of attack and defense did the an-

tagonists employ? Who won the debate? How was the disputation related to the subsequent anti-Jewish legislation which emerged from the royal palace? What was the purpose of the debate? Why did Nahmanides publish his record of the disputation nearly two years after it was held? Was this publication responsible for his emigrating from his native Gerona and seeking the solace of the Holy Land for the remaining days of his life?[18]

These are important and well-formulated issues. Inevitably, Cohen was drawn to a discussion of the sources, and here, too, he had useful contributions to make. He emphasized the paucity of documentation and, in particular, "the inadequacy of the two extant accounts of the debates." For Cohen, the Latin record is in no sense a lie; its major shortcoming is its brevity and terseness. "By comparison, Nahmanides's account inundates the reader with its torrent of details and the celerity of its motion." This contrast leads Cohen to a well-founded warning:

> The only danger which besets the reader of Nahmanides' account is that the dazzling realism of his narrative, contrasted with the pall and laconism of the Christian version, will blind him to its numerous shortcomings, and impede him from using this text cautiously in reconstructing the torrid events of that far-off July.[19]

For Cohen, the strengths and weaknesses of the two sources preclude decisive contrasts, and the effort to reject one in favor of the other is misguided. "The effort to reconstruct the reality of the Disputation of Barcelona from the sparse relics in our possession demands a recognition of the inadequacy of both texts and therefore, *faute de mieux* and no evidence to the contrary notwithstanding, the utilization of both with caution and without prejudice."[20]

The provocative aspect of Cohen's study lay in its reconstruction of the event. Still absorbed by the issue of victory or defeat, he proposed an innovative theory that in many ways shifted the ground of prior discussion. The key finding is enunciated early on: "The texts of the disputation point to one inescapable conclusion, that the debate was not an open discussion, but rather a demonstration of Christian intellectual superiority contrived in advance."[21] For Cohen, careful utilization of both sources leads to the conclusion that, indeed, the Christian side emerged victorious. He then proceeds to locate the basis for Jewish collusion in what was a preordained defeat outside the realm of intellectual and spiritual encounter. According to Cohen, Nahmanides, for political reasons, agreed to participate in an encounter that could only lead to a public defeat in order to aid the king of Aragon in his purposes. The reward for such painful collusion lay in royal benefits conferred on the Jews of the realm.

For most subsequent observers, the Cohen thesis has raised more problems than it has solved. I find particularly difficult the derailing of the event from the intellectual-spiritual realm into the political arena. The root problem, it seems to me, lies with a rigidly limited sense of victory and defeat or—to use already more flexible terminology—achievement and shortcoming. Despite the problems in the Cohen thesis, for methodological purposes, I would emphasize the important contribution of this study to both identification of the issues and adoption of an evenhanded approach to the sources. On both scores, Cohen broke valuable new ground.

The third twentieth-century figure to be discussed here for the methodological perspectives provided is Hyam Maccoby.[22] Maccoby must be introduced for at least two reasons. The first involves the length and fullness of his treatment of the Barcelona disputation. He has provided us with a new English translation of the Hebrew report (a translation that is the best available),[23] with a detailed commentary to the text (the fullest yet undertaken), and with a lengthy introduction to the Hebrew narrative. In addition, he articulates in clear fashion some of the issues that any methodological investigation must address. To be sure, Maccoby's study rejects many of the advances (from my perspective, at least) embodied in the Baer and Cohen essays. Again, however, because of the fullness of his treatment of the Barcelona confrontation and because of the sharpness with which he treats key issues, we must devote attention to his work.

Like Baer (and unlike Cohen), Maccoby is firmly convinced of the Jewish victory at Barcelona. Like all his predecessors, he is deeply concerned with evaluation of the twin sources. His assessment of the Latin report is, not surprisingly, thoroughly negative: "There can be no doubt that the brief and badly composed Christian document is a travesty of the disputation."[24]

The Hebrew source is treated by Maccoby in far greater detail. To do so, he examines at some length the earlier views of Baer,

Cecil Roth, and Cohen. This analysis is introduced by the following curious statement:

> Once the battle for the superior truth of the Jewish account was won, Jewish scholars turned their attention to the possible deficiencies of the Jewish account too. Here they have had some just things to say, but have also, in their search for painful objectivity, sometimes succumbed to the pleasures of masochism.[25]

A careful look at the strictures of Baer, Roth, and Cohen leads in a somewhat surprising direction:

> The attempts by Baer, Roth, and Cohen to diminish the stature of Nahmanides in the Barcelona Disputation must be judged to have failed. Despite the unequal conditions of the debate (which were nevertheless fairer than in any of the other disputations), Nahmanides managed to make some far-reaching statements of the Jewish standpoint vis-à-vis Christianity. While his opponent, Pablo Christiani, sought to confine the discussion to trivial points, so that he could catch out Nahmanides in "admissions" the importance and relevance of which he could then exaggerate, Nahmanides continually sought to turn the discussion to matters of real importance, in which the fundamental differences between Judaism and Christianity could be displayed.[26]

I have called this a somewhat surprising direction because Maccoby had promised the reader a look at the purported deficiencies of the Hebrew account. His summary statement, on concluding that investigation, turns unexpectedly away from the reliability of the account and to the actual achievement of Nahmanides. In a closing paragraph, Maccoby does turn his focus to the Hebrew narrative but only to praise its remarkable style and then to reiterate the importance of the confrontation itself. Despite the lack of a formal recapitulation of his arguments with Baer, Roth, and Cohen, it is clear, nonetheless, that he believes he has laid out a case for the thorough reliability of the Nahmanidean account. In a real sense, Maccoby has taken us back full circle to our modern starting point, Graetz. Like Graetz (though more articulately so), Maccoby is convinced of the rectitude of the Jewish source and the nullity of the Christian account. This leads ineluctably to espousal of the stance of the Jewish source itself—indisputable Jewish triumph over an ill-equipped Christian foe. Again, I emphasize that I have cited Maccoby for the fullness of his treatment of the disputation and for the clarity of his stances, not out of any agreement with his conclusions.

THE METHODOLOGY OF THE PRESENT STUDY

The foregoing survey of the contention that has surrounded the Barcelona disputation has its own intrinsic interest as a reflection of Christian-Jewish controversy and of shifting patterns of modern Christian-Jewish relations. I have traced this picture, however, to serve, first of all, as a backdrop to my study and, more important, to isolate several methodological issues that are best clarified at the outset of this investigation.

Let me begin with the matter of orientation. I quoted just now a curious comment by Maccoby about "Jewish scholars" turning "their attention to the possible deficiencies of the Jewish account too" and, in the process, succumbing "to the pleasures of masochism." What precisely does Maccoby mean here by the term "Jewish scholars"? This designation must be understood in the context of the previous sentence, which reads, "When the Christian scholar Heinrich Denifle championed the Christian account as the truth, he was well and sufficiently answered by the Jewish scholar Isadore Loeb." Thus, for Maccoby, the adjective "Jewish" in "Jewish scholar" is clearly neither an innocuous reference to field of research (a scholar who studies the Jewish experience) nor a pointless reference to ethnic or religious identity (a scholar who happens to be a Jew); rather, the term clearly indicates some kind of partisanship, that is, a scholar who represents the Jewish cause. I have some doubts as to whether Loeb would have been happy to find himself designated a Jewish scholar in that fashion; my own reading of Loeb suggests that he would have been offended rather than gratified. More important to the purposes of this study, I would wish to emphasize at the outset that, although I am a "Jewish scholar" in the sense of field of research and in the irrelevant sense of ethnic and religious identity, I make no effort—indeed, I reject the effort—to serve as champion of a partisan cause. I am not disavowing the possibility that my personal identity may play a role in shaping my scholarship; I am avowing, however, that I begin with no partisan cause, and I make every effort to assure that my analysis remains free of partisan perspectives. The issue under study is one beset, as we have seen, with partisanship from its very inception. The purpose of my investigation is to analyze as rigorously as possible the available evidence and to reach conclusions that would make sense to readers from every quarter. I explicitly eschew the kind of modern extension of medieval partisanship reflected in the Maccoby comment.

Turning to more substantive matters, there are six basic principles that underlie this investigation:

1. In any serious study of the Barcelona disputation, both extant sources must be utilized. Rejection of one in favor of the other will inevitably skew the results. The issue is not to determine which source is accurate and which mendacious; the issue is to understand each source in its own right. What were the purposes of its author? What was the organizational pattern that he adopted to achieve these purposes? Wherein lie the special strengths of each record and wherein its particular weaknesses?

2. Proper analysis of the Barcelona disputation can only be conducted if the organization and conduct of the confrontation is clearly established and firmly borne in mind. While I will make the case more fully at a later point, it must be recognized that the engagement was engineered by the Dominican Order as a missionizing exercise and was conducted throughout for that purpose. While there are many efforts, ranging from Nahmanides himself down through the Maccoby study just now cited, that lose sight of this basic structure, obfuscation of the fundamental organization and conduct of the engagement can only result in confusion.

3. In Barcelona, during the summer months of 1263, a series of exchanges took place which can no longer be precisely reconstructed. These exchanges were public, heated, tense, lengthy, and undoubtedly somewhat amorphous. The Latin report on the confrontation makes no effort to portray in any significant detail the ongoing engagement. The Hebrew record does purport to do so but can clearly not be taken as a stenographic account of the fluid event in question. The Latin account, the Hebrew narrative, and modern analysis all make one or another effort to recapture the essence of that fluid and amorphous event, each from one or another perspective. The recapturing

of the supposed essence of the encounter cannot obscure, however, the complexity and confusion of the original event.

4. Evaluation of the available partisan sources must be undertaken out of an awareness of the brute fluid and amorphous reality. Let us begin with the issue of mendacity, a charge leveled by Denifle against the Hebrew narrative and by Baer against the Latin narrative. To call either source "a lie" means that its author recognized the truth and chose consciously to obscure that truth and create a false picture of the event. That is to say, Denifle's allegation is that Nahmanides honestly knew that he had been vanquished by Friar Paul and purposefully wrote an account designed to mislead his Jewish readers. Similarly, Baer must be understood as charging that the author of the Christian account recognized deep down that the rabbi had won the day and fabricated a report designed to create the opposite and patently false impression. While neither scenario is utterly unthinkable, I would argue that there is sufficient evidence—the royal seal, on the one hand, Nahmanides's general stature, on the other, and above all else, the public nature of the event— that makes such out-and-out lying unthinkable. There is a far simpler and more sensible explanation for some of the discrepancy in the sources, and that is merely the conflicting perception of what has already been established as a lengthy, tense, and fluid confrontation. It is the nature of public partisan engagement to generate polarized perceptions. If we consider, for a moment, the contemporary political debates aired before huge television audiences, we are struck by two phenomena. The first is the immediate and predictable divergence in reactions to the debates. Democrats wax poetic over the victory of their candidate, and Republicans are enthused with the unqualified success of theirs. Some of this reaction is disingenuous, to be sure, but much of it is sincere. More important for our purposes, the subsequent polls always show a relatively even split in viewer perception. It is clearly possible for large numbers of viewers to divide fairly evenly over the results of a televised debate. Similarly, it is thoroughly conceivable—indeed, highly likely—that the thirteenth-century partisans, the Christians on the one side and the Jews on the other, saw the same set of events and evaluated them in diametrically opposed fashion, the one side

seeing a Christian triumph and the other a Jewish success. One cannot brand one perception a lie and the other the truth. It is possible to investigate the divergent views as such, attempting to ascertain the basis for both the Christian and Jewish sense of success.

5. Not all the divergence between the two conflicting sources can be attributed to alternative perspectives on a fluid and shifting reality. It must further be acknowledged that both sources embellished the truth through overstatement and exaggeration. Again, I shall argue this case more fully in the body of the study. For the moment, however, let me indicate that the Latin account's depiction of a hopelessly confused Rabbi Moses ben Nahman seems to be more than simply a perspectival disagreement; it seems likely to be a gross exaggeration. Similarly, I propose that the Nahmanidean portrait of a supremely confident Jewish protagonist, ranging far and wide in both defense of the Jewish position and attack on central Christian views, is more than simply an alternative Jewish view of the affair; I argue that there are, in this portrait, elements of embellishment and exaggeration. Here it may well be that the notion of mendacity is appropriate, although the charge seems a bit harsh. Neither author, it seems to me, intended to write an objectively accurate account of the proceedings; each account was intended to serve a significant communal purpose. That these purposes may have led to some embellishment and exaggeration does not seem to me to warrant the accusation of lying. If readers prefer that label to embellishment and exaggeration, so be it.

6. Accurate evaluation of the outcome of the fluid and amorphous encounter in Barcelona must go well beyond the divergent statements composed in the wake of the encounter. To achieve proper understanding of the results of the confrontation, considerable attention must be focused on the subsequent actions and behaviors that were set in motion. Both the Christian and Jewish sides will reveal most tellingly their true perceptions of the Barcelona disputation through the actions subsequently undertaken. Here again, of course, there is no reason to anticipate a united vision. It may well be that the two sides will reveal themselves once again to hold polarized perceptions of the outcome of the public confrontation.

These methodological observations have involved us in some fundamental—and for many readers, rudimentary—observations on historical events and human perceptions. It may well be argued that the principles outlined are simple enough and widely acknowledged. However, we have already seen the polarization in both medieval and modern views of the Barcelona disputation. Clearly, this is an area of interreligious conflict into which some of these simple assertions as to events and perceptions have not yet penetrated. As I indicated earlier, the challenge of encountering and overcoming centuries of polarized perception, in quest of a more nuanced understanding of a dramatic, fascinating, and important medieval encounter between major representatives of Christianity and Judaism, is a significant element in the motivation for writing—and, hopefully, reading—this analysis.

1

Setting and Dramatis Personae

The historic disputation between Friar Paul Christian and Rabbi Moses ben Nahman in Barcelona in 1263 can only be properly understood and appreciated in its rich and complex setting. While a host of factors conditioned this important engagement, three major features of the period must be discussed to set the stage properly for our detailed analysis of the event and its aftermath. Moving from the broadest canvas to the narrowest, these three crucial elements are the policies and programs of the Roman Catholic church during the middle decades of the thirteenth century, the achievements and aspirations of the Crown of Aragon at that crucial juncture, and the situation of the Jewish communities of the Crown of Aragon in general and of Catalonia more particularly during these important years. Since the focus of this study is a specific event involving specific personages, I shall, in each case, begin with a discussion of general developments and then highlight one of the three major protagonists in the drama that unfolded in Barcelona—Friar Paul Christian, King James the Conqueror, and Rabbi Moses ben Nahman. In this way, I hope to afford both the requisite broad background and, at the same time, introduce the dramatis personae and the mood of this study, which is highly particular.[1]

Before approaching the three critical elements that form the backdrop to the Barcelona confrontation, let us focus briefly on the general mood of the period. A striking designation of the thirteenth century, particularly the middle decades of that century, has been provided by Robert I. Burns in his introductory essay to a collection of papers on James the Conqueror of Aragon and Alfonso the Learned of Castile:

> The thirteenth century, whose decades our two Spanish kings nearly fill, was not "the greatest of centuries" in human and cultural terms, as is often said (the fourth and twelfth, for example, have

17

stronger claims to the title); but it was perhaps the most startling and dramatic century, a chiaroscuro of achievement and failure, the promise and threat of Western civilization's future directions.[2]

Burns's emphasis on the ambiguous combination of achievement and failure, of promise and threat, serves as a useful starting point for our investigation. In whatever direction we turn, a baffling combination of countervailing forces awaits us: in the stances of the Roman Catholic church, with its simultaneous emphasis on protection and limitation of the Jews and with the reflection in its missionizing of both arrogant self-confidence and underlying anxieties; in the policies of the Crown of Aragon, with evidence of both strong encouragement and support of the Jews tempered by a commitment to assist the Church in both its limitation of the Jews and its proselytizing endeavors; in the personal stance of King James the Conqueror, at one and the same time (on occasion, as we shall see, seriatim as well) respected and honored friend of the Jews and supporter of antipathetic programs; in the circumstances of the Jewries of the Crown of Aragon in general and of Catalonia in particular, living through what has been depicted sometimes as their golden age and sometimes as the onset of their lengthy decline; in the rabbi of Gerona, assertively maintaining his supreme confidence in his tradition and in himself, yet surely concerned enough to bend all his creative energies toward assuring his beleaguered community of its present hold on the truth and its future realization of salvation. If there is anything this close look at a particular incident and its aftermath should provide us, it is a feel for the complexities of historical experience, rather than an urge toward oversimplification.

THE ROMAN CATHOLIC CHURCH AND
FRIAR PAUL CHRISTIAN

The thirteenth century was surely a great century in the history of the Roman Catholic church, yet it was a period that, viewed retrospectively, reflects vigor, confidence, and creativity intermingled with considerable anxiety and uncertainty.[3] On the one hand, the century saw the flowering of an administrative structure that was the most well developed in the Western world. The local parishes of Western Christendom were increasingly subsumed into larger and more effectively controlled dioceses and archdioceses. The papal court became the bustling center of European society, with emissaries heading out into the far reaches of Western Christendom on papal missions, while, in a rich counterflow, litigants from far and wide sought out the jurisdiction of the papal court. The newly organized mendicant orders, directly controlled by the papacy itself, served as yet another avenue of expanded centrist ecclesiastical governance. There was much more happening than merely bureaucratic maturation. This was also the great age of intellectual synthesis. In a number of critical areas, the Church strove energetically toward fuller and clearer exposition of the goals of Christian living, on both the societal and individual level. Perhaps most fully symbolizing this drive were the magnificent *summae* of the period, capped by the brilliant works of Saint Thomas Aquinas, a tribute to the impulse toward full and coherent definition of the norms of Christian behavior and thought.

On the other hand, all was not well in the Church. With all the splendid achievements of the period, there were, first of all, the normal negatives associated with such achievements: the constriction that regularly flows from administrative and intellectual system building and the venality that all bureaucracies breed. The more powerful the ecclesiastical structure became, the more strident were the voices of criticism. Some of this criticism reinforced the internal deviations that, from the perspective of the Church, were perceived as heresies. While the problem of heresy antedated the thirteenth century, it became more obvious and more acute during this glittering period. The concern with internal enemies was more than matched by a deepening awareness of the range and power of Christendom's external enemies, particularly the world of Islam. Gone was the heady exuberance of 1099. Thirteenth-century Christendom had a surer and more realistic sense of the true dimensions of the Muslim world, the depth of its resources, and the profound challenge that it posed. Fuller awareness of the extent of the Muslim world and its resources engendered new tactical initiatives for combating the threat, particularly a new commitment to missionizing among the Muslims. Yet alongside the confident plans for a new-style assault on Islam, there was also a measure of unease over future confrontation.

The critical question for our purposes is the stance of the thirteenth-century Church toward the Jews living within the boundaries of Western Christendom.[4] These Jews constituted neither a new nor a particularly threatening problem. Yet—not surprisingly—there was recurrent concern over the Jewish issue and a series of significant initiatives aimed at the small but readily identifiable Jewish population of Western Christendom. By the thirteenth century, a well-defined position had emerged on the part of the Church with respect to Jewish life in Christian society. That position, traceable in its boldest outlines all the way back into the fourth century, stipulated for the Jews a complex combination of legitimacy and limitation, protection and encroachment. On the one hand, the thirteenth-century Church continued to proclaim the right of Jews to live openly and unimpeded as Jews within the borders of Christendom. This right included protection from physical violence and undue impingement on Jewish religious life. The Church did more than simply proclaim that stance; when occasion demanded, it attempted to intervene on behalf of Jews threatened by illegitimate forms of violence. Perhaps most striking in this regard were the efforts of the Church to examine the new slanders raised against the Jews and to denounce these new slanders as fabrications. Yet, on the other hand, there were traditionally two further facets to the Church stance vis-à-vis the Jews. The first involved the notion of responsible Jewish behavior, the sense that the right of the Jews to live legitimately in Christian society was balanced by a Jewish responsibility to live in such a manner as to bring no harm to the Christendom that served as the host society. The second involved the conviction that Jews, while permitted to live as such in Christian society, should be exposed—in proper manner to be sure—to the truth of the Christian vision. Never to be brought into the Christian fold violently and unwillingly, the Jews should nonetheless remain important targets of missionizing ardor. Let us examine each of these two important conditions to the Jewish right of existence in Christian society in a bit more detail.

The demand for responsible Jewish behavior, for limitations intended to ensure that the Jews bring no harm to the Christian society that hosted them, has a long history. What is striking about this underlying stance toward the Jews is its inherent elasticity. It could be, and was, interpreted diversely over the ages. What we observe during the thirteenth century is heightened ecclesiastical concern with the potential for harmful Jewish behavior. More specifically, we note new techniques for meeting traditional Christian fears and novel perceptions of the dangers flowing from Jewish presence.

The oldest and most persistent concern with respect to the potential harm that Jews might inflict was the possibility that they might attract Christians away from their faith. To obviate such danger, the Church had long insisted that Jews not be permitted to enjoy positions of superiority with respect to Christians, positions that would enable them to wield undue influence on those Christians under their control. Such legislation included stipulations against Jews holding Christian slaves, against Jews occupying political office, against marriage of Jew and Christian. The thirteenth-century Church continued to assert these traditional demands. At the same time, the perception of heightened dangers moved the Church to introduce more stringent limitations designed to minimize further the potential for Jewish influence on Christian neighbors. The most extreme and striking manifestation of this new stringency was the demand, first voiced at the Fourth Lateran Council in 1215, that Jews be forced to wear distinguishing garb that would enable all who met them to identify them immediately as Jews and to relate to them accordingly. This drastic new demand serves as a perfect illustration of the intensification of traditional concern with potentially harmful Jewish behavior.

The Church perceived, during the course of the thirteenth century, a series of new dangers as well. One of these newly perceived dangers was related to the increasing attraction of Jews to the money trade during the previous century. As the economy of Western Christendom expanded and, at the same time, the Church vigorously pursued its campaign against Christian usury, Europe's Jews enjoyed considerable advantage in the developing money trade. In fact, both the Jews and the secular authorities who were their sponsors and protectors came to realize the potential for mutual profit in Jewish moneylending. As Jewish moneylending business increased, the ecclesiastical authorities began to perceive a new threat emanating from the Jews, the threat of economic harm to Christian society, particularly to the less fortunate in

Christian society. During the thirteenth century, the Church lob-
bied intensely for restrictions on this set of Jewish behaviors, calling, for example, for limitations on the rate of interest that Jews
might charge, on the penalties that might be imposed for default,
and on the range of borrowers with whom the Jews might be permitted to do business.[5] Again, what we find here is an enhanced
sense on the part of the Church of potentially harmful Jewish behavior and a new set of limitations designed to thwart such harm.

A more traditional concern of the Church was the possibility of
Jewish harm not to Christians but to Christianity—through blasphemous expressions of insult against the Christian faith or its central symbols. Such blasphemous insult was, of course, prohibited
to the Jews.[6] What is new during the thirteenth century is not the
concern with Jewish blasphemy but heightened awareness of this
blasphemy. The wide-ranging expansion of knowledge that is one
of the hallmarks of the period expressed itself, inter alia, in new
information concerning the traditional sources of rabbinic Judaism.[7] While Christians had long been aware of the existence of rabbinic tradition and literature, it had largely remained closed to
direct Christian knowledge. It is not at all surprising that the thirteenth century should have produced the first in-depth medieval
Christian familiarity with the Talmud and, concurrently, the first
major medieval assault on it. The Talmud was the object, during
the 1230s, of a series of allegations, central to which were the
charges that it included extensive blasphemy against the major
symbols of Christian faith.[8] The traditional concern with Jewish
blasphemy took an intensified new form, in the process leading to
expanded efforts to control aspects of internal Jewish life. This
serves as a clear illustration of the inherent elasticity of the notion
of limitation of harmful Jewish behavior. The condition that Jews
comport themselves in a responsible manner had the potential to
lead in a variety of directions and to result in wide-ranging and
unanticipated new legislation concerning Jewish life.[9]

One more point deserves to be noted with respect to the anti-
Talmud campaign, and that is the central role played by a convert
from Judaism to Christianity. The allegations against the Talmud
were first raised by this convert, Nicholas Donin, and it was he
who led the campaign to translate the allegations into a course of
action. Donin was sent forth from the papal curia to the courts of

Western Christendom on a mission involving substantiation of the allegations and stimulation of the rulers of Western Christendom to take requisite action. It was out of this mission that Donin conducted an inquisitorial procedure against the Talmud in Paris in 1240, the result of which was a massive burning of the Talmud in 1242. We know little of this Donin—who he was, what his motivations in converting were, why he chose to take the offensive against his former coreligionists, and what his subsequent fate was. Nonetheless, the phenomenon of a convert with some measure of Jewish learning taking a position of leadership in a campaign aimed against the Jewish community is well worth noting.

Thus, the thirteenth century saw enhanced efforts at limiting the potential harm that Jews might cause to Christian society, through innovative forms of segregation, new programs designed to restrict Jewish economic activity, and an assault on the postbiblical literature of the Jews. At the same time, the inclination toward missionizing among the Jews, in prior centuries scarcely noticeable in Western Christendom, suddenly burst into full flower.[10] To be sure, the drive toward proselytizing among the Jews was not an isolated phenomenon; it can only be understood as part of a larger context in which the Church committed itself to a profound effort to convince dissidents within its own ranks of its normative vision of the Christian way and to convince nonbelievers of all stripes of the superiority of the Christian religious vision. The Jews were hardly the chief target of this overall commitment to missionizing. There were, however, a number of factors that combined to make the Jews attractive targets to at least a small group of (predominantly Dominican) missionizers. These include (1) the ready identifiability and availability of the Jews for missionizing confrontation—unlike the heretics, Jews were easily identified; unlike nonbelievers living outside the pale of Christian domination, Jewish presence could be forced at missionizing sermons or debates; (2) the historic sense of the Jews as a gauge for the success of a new missionizing endeavor—since the Jews had for so long resisted the argumentation of the Church, they came to serve as a useful acid test for innovative missionizing enterprises, for it was felt that successful conversion of the Jews would serve as stunning evidence of the unique strength of the new missionizing endeavor; (3) the personal interest of former Jews in such proselytizing. What moved former Jews to attack their former coreligionists, as did Donin, or to seek to bring them into the new faith community, as did Friar Paul Christian, can only be surmised but cannot, given the state of our evidence, be verified. The reality of the central role played by such converts is nonetheless patent.

Elsewhere I have labeled this mid-thirteenth-century missionizing the first serious Christian proselytizing among the Jews during the Middle Ages. My criteria were three: (1) the commitment of significant resources to the campaign; (2) the establishment of regular channels for confronting Jews with Christian argumentation; and (3) the adumbration of new lines of argumentation, lines of argumentation that were specifically designed for effectiveness in a Jewish audience and that were based on an awareness of Jews and their thinking. All these criteria are, in fact, identifiable in the new missionizing activities aimed at European Jewry—particularly southern European Jewry—from the 1240s on.[11] The disputation at Barcelona can only be understood against the backdrop of this new proselytizing endeavor.

Thus, in many ways, the thirteenth century shows us the Church involved in traditional lines of pro- and anti-Jewish activity, all at a highly accelerated pace. The key Church spokesman in the Barcelona disputation, Friar Paul Christian, reflects in his own activity many of the central thrusts of ecclesiastical policy during this period. In focusing briefly on Friar Paul's pre-1263 activities, we will illustrate some of the campaigns identified just now and at the same time provide a background sketch of the central ecclesiastical figure in the Barcelona confrontation.

A word about the sources at our disposal. Curiously, although Friar Paul was extremely active in Dominican activities related to the Jews over a number of decades, he has left us no writings of his own that might help us understand him more fully. While we do know much about Friar Paul, all of our information is provided by others—court scribes, royal decrees, Jewish testimony. Much of this material focuses on the Barcelona disputation of 1263. We have no Christian evidence whatsoever for the friar's previous activities; we possess only a brief comment in Nahmanides's narrative account of the disputation, a fourteenth-century note on Friar Paul's Jewish origins, and a detailed letter penned by a contemporary of the friar, seeking to dissuade him from pursuing some of those actions perceived by the Jews as highly deleterious. Clearly, the last of these sources is by far the richest for reconstructing Friar Paul's pre-1263 activities.[12] I have provided elsewhere a detailed analysis of the authorship and circumstances of this unusual letter.[13] Let me here only summarize my conclusions. This letter was written, I suggest, prior to the disputation of 1263 by a Spanish Jew intimately familiar with the friar. This author, Jacob bar Elijah, may have been Jacob ben Elijah de Lattes, scion of a distinguished southern French family, forced to leave his home and resettle in Spain.

What do we know of the early years of Friar Paul? From the letter of Jacob bar Elijah, we learn that he came from a pious Jewish family and was born with the name Saul.[14] One of the later copyists of the letter tells us that he was related to the author; another tells us that he was, prior to his conversion, a student of the author.[15] A fourteenth-century source tells us that he was a student of Rabbi Eliezer of Tarrascon.[16] All of this suggests that we are not dealing here with a fringe member of Jewish society but with a man who grew up in the center of a major European Jewish community, probably one of the communities of southern France. Given this background within the organized Jewish community, how knowledgeable was Friar Paul in Jewish matters? The Christian praise of the friar's Jewish erudition has been much overshadowed by Nahmanides's lively portrait of a man who was notably deficient in serious Jewish learning. At a later point, we shall consider some of the purposes of this depiction.[17] Comprehension of Nahmanides's goals in sketching Friar Paul in this fashion vitiates the trustworthiness of his portrayal. Unfortunately, we have at our disposal no reliably disinterested perspective on the Jewish learning of the friar. Let me advance tentatively a number of suggestions. The specific sources advanced by Friar Paul do not indicate any special depth of Jewish learning. There is in the material he utilizes none of the richness that we encounter a bit later in the writings of Friar Raymond Martin.[18] However, a student of Rabbi Eliezer of Tarrascon was unlikely to be the kind of ignoramus portrayed by Nahmanides. In his epistle, Jacob bar Elijah certainly assumes that his addressee, seemingly Friar Paul, was thoroughly capable of reading a flowery Hebrew text and understanding the rich allusions that normally permeate such texts. In a general way,

then, I might propose that Friar Paul was somewhat better informed than Nahmanides allows, while not reaching the status of
an outstanding student of Jewish halakhic and aggadic texts.

The circumstances of Friar Paul's conversion are not at all clear
to us. From the letter of Jacob bar Elijah, we know that the Jew
Saul's conversion was the action of a fully mature adult. The author speaks of the anguish the conversion caused Saul/Paul's
Jewish wife and of the fact that her anguish was augmented by the
loss of their children, whom the newly converted Paul took from
her and introduced into his new faith and community.[19] Our author gives us no clear-cut explanation for Saul's conversion or his
subsequent decision to join the Dominican Order. He does indicate
that the conversion was related to internal stresses within the
Jewish community. In some fashion or other, this internal strife influenced Saul's decision to convert.[20] Subsequent to this conversion, Friar Paul involved himself in a number of activities related
to his former fellow-Jews, all of them viewed by the Jewish author
of the epistle as unfair and harmful. Indeed, the purpose of the
letter was ostensibly to dissuade the friar from continuing these
activities.

The harmful activities depicted by the writer of the letter involved, as noted, a number of the major thrusts in mid-thirteenth-
century ecclesiastical policy. Particularly striking are Friar Paul's
purported concern with Jewish moneylending, described rather
cryptically in the letter, his assault on the Talmud, and his missionizing efforts. Despite the unfortunate lack of details, it is clear
that Friar Paul immersed himself in the contemporary ecclesiastical
effort to limit what was perceived as the harmful impact of Jewish
moneylending on Christian society. Precisely how he was involved
is not detailed for us.[21] Friar Paul followed the lead of the earlier
Nicholas Donin in taking a hand in the effort to ban the Talmud.
This was surely an area in which such converts might play a central
role, partially as a result of their detailed knowledge of the Talmud—a number of sources speak of Saul/Paul as a student of the
Talmud—and partially because the Talmud was clearly at the
center of the Jewish life they were abandoning. It is interesting that
Friar Paul's attack was directed at an aspect of talmudic teaching
other than that focused on by Donin. Friar Paul's concern, to judge
from the material presented by Jacob bar Elijah, was centered on

seemingly irrational material in the Talmud. While this issue had been raised by Donin, it was not at the core of his allegations. In the case of Friar Paul, it was this aspect of talmudic teaching that he seems to have brought most stridently to the attention of ecclesiastical authorities.[22] The third major thrust of Friar Paul's efforts involved missionizing, the activity for which he is indeed most renowned. The letter of Jacob bar Elijah speaks of the convoking of Jews to hear the sermons of Friar Paul, and similarly, early in his account of the Barcelona disputation, Nahmanides indicates that the new argumentation, based on exploitation of talmudic materials, had been utilized by Friar Paul in a preaching campaign that predated 1263.[23]

Thus, in sketching the pre-1263 activities of Friar Paul, we have familiarized ourselves with this central figure in the drama we shall be investigating, while, at the same time, reinforcing our sense of some of the main thrusts of thirteenth-century ecclesiastical policy vis-à-vis the Jews. Friar Paul was very much in tune with the ecclesiastical temper of the period. He is clearly a fascinating figure, of whose personality we know unfortunately far too little. Since our sources come almost exclusively from the Jewish side, there is little desire to present him in all his complexity. We do not know him nearly so well as we might wish.

One last word with respect to the ecclesiastical policies outlined above. It is important to bear in mind that, except for those few areas in which ecclesiastical authorities directly controlled Jewish communities, the policies adumbrated by the Church had to be introduced by those secular rulers who were the overlords of the Jews. Thus, it is reasonable to move on to a discussion of the Crown of Aragon and its ruler, for it was ultimately the needs and mood of the realm and its sovereign that would affect most immediately the Jews of those lands.

THE CROWN OF ARAGON AND
KING JAMES THE CONQUEROR

The mid-thirteenth century was a glorious period in the history of the Crown of Aragon, on the Iberian peninsula at least, and King James the Conqueror, complex figure though he was, was subsequently a revered monarch in the historic recollections of Spanish society.[24] Crucial to our understanding of the situation of his Jews in general and of the Barcelona confrontation in particular is an awareness, from the outset, of the patchwork quality of the territories King James ruled. Like his Angevin, Capetian, and Hohenstaufen contemporaries, King James ruled over vast and heterogeneous lands; in James's case, these lands stretched across the Iberian peninsula and on into southern France. As was true for his distinguished contemporaries, James's effort to carve a unified kingdom out of such disparate territories was only partially successful. While he expanded substantially the holdings of his kingdom both on the Iberian peninsula and on the Mediterranean islands, he lost control of considerable southern French territory; it was his Capetian rivals who were to prove the eventual rulers of these valuable lands. For our purposes, the key Jewish communities that James controlled were those of Aragon proper and the larger and more important Jewries of Catalonia. It is on the latter that our attention will focus.

The name by which James is most commonly designated, James the Conqueror, attracts our attention immediately to the most significant achievement of his reign. On September 5, 1229, James and his fleet set sail for Majorca, landing on the night of September 8–9. By the end of spring 1230, James's forces had completed their conquest of this important island. The Muslims of Minorca recognized James as their sovereign in 1232, and the king ceded the islands of Ibiza and Formentera to the archbishop of Tarragona, who completed their occupation in 1235. These military achievements, important in their own right, served also as a prelude to the yet more striking conquest of Valencia. James took his crusading vow at Monzon in 1232. The conquest of Valencia was no simple matter, and, distracted by other issues, James was not able to devote all his attentions to it. Eventually, in 1236, the king renewed his vows and pressed more strongly for successful conquest. A lengthy siege finally brought about the capitulation of the city of Valencia on September 29, 1238. A large and rich domain was added to James's holdings.

The military successes of James should not obscure other aspects of his lengthy reign. James was more than simply a successful warrior. Indeed, on more than one occasion, he proved himself a man of peaceful compromise as well. More important, successful absorption of the newly conquered territories required administrative skill and imagination, both of which James was able to provide. In his essay on James of Aragon and Alfonso of Castile, Burns suggests a broad overview of the achievements of James and his contemporary, Alfonso the Learned of Castile. Burns focuses on five major developments that characterize the lengthy reigns of the two sovereigns:

(1) Both societies [Aragon and Castile] had just acquired vast territories from Islam, and repercussions in each colonialist homeland were immediate and far-reaching. Administrative innovation and colonization became priority activities for both.

(2) Each society was experiencing a surge of pride and local consciousness one might term protonationalist. If Alfonso's masterworks were deliberately written in Castilian, James composed his autobiography in Catalan rather than in Latin, and James's archives and actions reflect this regional emphasis.

(3) Each society, throughout its legal stratum, was a prime mover in introducing Roman Law into Europe. James's *Furs* had more practical Roman effect than such celebrated secular codes as the Melfi constitutions of Frederick II, while Alfonso's collections would in time not only reshape Castilian life but have wide impact in later contexts abroad.[25]

(4) Each society faced the problem of confrontation between the mercantile way of life and the baronial. The urban-commercial element assumed some prominence in Castile. But in Aragon-Catalonia the conquests fortified the already dominant urban-commercial interest and thus hastened a confrontation with upland Aragon's barons, while simultaneously redistributing and diffusing the urban bases of power.

(5) Each society entered the wider political stage of Europe. Alfonso long campaigned to become Holy Roman Emperor, to a degree that precipitated domestic crises. James fell heir to the collapsing Hohenstaufen cause, and by marrying his heir to its heiress paved the way for the conquest of Sicily by the realms of Aragon within a few years of his death. Both monarchs opened an African front, commercial as well as military.[26]

This convenient summary of the major developments of the middle decades of the thirteenth century in the Crown of Aragon provides us with a secure point of departure from which to view the situation of the Jewries of the Crown and—eventually—to understand better the Barcelona disputation. Most of these major developments had significant implications for the Jews living within James's diverse realms. In particular, the extensive conquests, with all that they implied, the clash of urban and baronial interests, with the former gaining the ascendancy, and the increasingly European orientation of royal policy and activity explain much of royal policy with respect to the Jews and, in addition, help us to understand some of the internal dynamic of Jewish life.

The addition of further territories, the need for greater bureaucratic sophistication, and the growing ascendancy of the urban-commercial interests combined to offer dramatic new opportunities for the Jews of Catalonia. To be sure, these positive developments (from the Jewish perspective) were balanced somewhat by the increasingly strong ecclesiastical commitment to careful limitation of Jewish activities and by the growing surge of local pride identified by Burns. Given the complexity of these developments and the undisputed role played by King James in Jewish affairs in general and in the Barcelona confrontation in particular, it becomes imperative to provide some sense of the monarch himself. Fortunately, substantial evidence is available. It is provided, in part, by the copious archival data left by the royal chancery and, in part, by the king's own autobiographical sketch—a most unusual and fortuitous source.

In a sense, the rich complexity of King James is reflected in the diverse developments of his reign. Clearly, the broad tendencies highlighted by Burns impinged on King James and were, in turn, influenced to a considerable degree by his own direct involvement in the affairs of the diverse domains he ruled. Burns's assessment of King James's many-faceted impact is worth citing: "James was truly a *stupor mundi*: a formidable administrator; a central figure in the evolution of Europe's universities, public finance, and the legal renaissance; a brilliant winner in the endless military debate on land and sea with Islam (when the crusades elsewhere were declining from bad to ever worse); and in his own way an imposing literary presence."[27] Many of these royal interests and achievements had potent implications for the Jews living within his realm.

Particularly important for our purposes is some sense of the religiosity of the monarch. Royal support for the new missionizing campaign had to flow, above all else, from a genuine desire on the part of the king to foster the aims of the Church. What sort of spiritual figure did King James cut? Burns has provided, in addition to his broad assessment of the reign, an interesting look at the monarch's spiritual life, based heavily on the king's memoir.[28] Burns begins his analysis by noting the value of the royal memoir for understanding the king's spiritual life and, at the same time, its limitations. It was hardly intended as a thorough portrait of a multifaceted man; it focuses, rather, on the military side of the man and his achievements in that key sphere of his activity. Burns notes specifically the lack of concern in the memoir with the urban and commercial aspects of the reign and the man, those areas that most directedly impinged on the Jews of Catalonia. Nonetheless, even from this rather one-sided source, Burns has succeeded in eliciting considerable clarification of James's spirituality.

The first point that emerges from Burns's analysis is the spiritual complexity of King James. No simple depiction will do. He was hardly a saintly character, and neither his own efforts nor the efforts of some of his admirers have been successful in erasing some of the considerable stains that mar his spiritual image. Nonetheless, Burns insists that the spirituality of King James cannot be simplistically dismissed: "Unlike the contemporary rulers St. Ferdinand of Castile or St. Louis of France, James was no saint, but he did have a spiritual life. It lay coiled at the center of his being and activities, never wholly in hibernation."[29]

For our purposes, two tendencies identified by Burns are most important. The first is the king's devoted support for the Church. This is reflected in a kind of personal religiosity, for example, his constant concern with mass and confession, and in a more royal religiosity, for example, the concern with establishing new churches in conquered territory. Particularly striking is his respect for and involvement with members of the new mendicant orders. Burns notes that, at a truly critical juncture in his life, James, feeling a desperate need for confession, bypassed the bishop of Barcelona in favor of the Franciscan Arnold of Segarra (an important observer at the Barcelona proceedings). The relationship of the king to the yet more important Dominican Raymond of Penyafort is well documented. Thus, the king was more than simply committed to pious purposes: his view of the Church was heavily conditioned by the attitudes of the mendicants who stood in the forefront of many of the most important new ecclesiastical initiatives, including the innovative missionizing campaign among the Jews.[30]

Balancing that facet of the king's personality was his concern for his word and his decency toward those under his protection. Both of these attributes are demonstrated in his memoir with respect to his Muslim military foes. Instances of his protection abound, as do occasions on which he actively prosecuted followers who broke faith with subjugated Muslims. The implications for the Jews are considerable. King James certainly saw them also as subjects of another faith who had every right to enjoy the protection that was due them.

These seemingly contradictory aspects of the king's spirituality—his full commitment to the programs of the Church, especially as adumbrated by the leaders of the new mendicant orders, coupled with a chivalric sense of honorable responsibility toward those who had the right to royal protection—will explain much with respect to the king's complex stance at the Barcelona disputation. This stance, amply reflected in both the Christian and Jewish source materials, involved, on the one hand, unswerving royal backing for the new Dominican missionizing effort and, on the other hand, an effort at requisite protection of his subject Jews. Most striking is the reflection of this duality in the Hebrew source, which makes no effort to gloss over the king's full support of the forced dispute, yet continues to speak respectfully of the monarch and to claim him as a devoted friend of the Jews and of the Jewish spokesman. In undertaking our analysis of the Barcelona confrontation, the broad interests of the king and the sometimes contradictory thrusts of his spirituality must be firmly borne in mind.[31]

THE JEWS OF ARAGON AND
RABBI MOSES BEN NAHMAN

How did the conflicting tendencies of both the ecclesiastical and secular establishments play themselves out in the lives of the Jews of the Crown of Aragon or, more narrowly, of Catalonia? More accurately, how did the secular authorities responsible for the Jews of the realm balance the conflicting pressures imposed by the realistic needs of the times, on the one hand, and the demands of ecclesiastical policy, on the other?[32] Not surprisingly, there is some divergence of opinion. Clearly, there were developments that can be construed as highly positive from the Jewish perspective and others that can only be viewed as detrimental. A balance sheet of these contradictory developments has not been convincingly drawn up, and the likelihood is that no such overall assessment can ever be realized. A perceptive statement of the ambiguities of the period was provided by Yitzhak Baer.

> The traditions of the glorious days of the early Reconquest, including the liberal policy toward the Jews, were carefully cultivated by James I (1213–1276), the Conqueror. After his accession to the throne, the young ruler retained in his service members of the same Jewish courtier set which had served his predecessors, Alfonso II and Pedro II. With the resumption of the Reconquest the influence of these men increased.[33]

> The public careers of the Jewish functionaries, brilliant though they were, nevertheless represent only isolated instances of individual Jews rising above the generally modest station of their coreligionists. In our previous discussion we defined the conflicting forces which shaped policy toward the Jews, namely, the needs and objectives of the Reconquest and a rising tide of anti-Jewish feeling. The influence of the latter is clearly apparent in the legislation of James I.[34]

To put the matter in the perspective provided by Burns regarding the major developments of the reign of James the Conqueror, we might amend Baer's statement to suggest that the needs of the Reconquest and the accelerating ascendancy of the urban-commercial element in royal policy were balanced by the growing sense of national identity and by an enhanced emphasis on the introduction of ecclesiastical norms.[35] Clearly, the king was forced to play off these divergent tendencies, pursuing a policy of both support for and limitation of his Jews. Added to this, the king's own religious contacts (particularly with the new mendicant orders) and proclivities made him susceptible to the influence of new thinking in the Church and, at the same time, conscious of his broad responsibilities to those non-Christians whose protection remained his obligation. Many of the vagaries of royal policy and behavior with respect to the Barcelona disputation can only be grasped against this background of complex royal policy and personality.

Baer documents in considerable detail some of the positive implications of the renewal of the Reconquest for the king's Jews, including the role played by Jewish courtiers during the military conflict itself and, more lastingly, during the efforts to administer the new territories and to maintain urban life during the period of adjustment. But Baer also follows the introduction of a series of Church-inspired limitations on Jewish activity, particularly in the areas of Christian-Jewish social contact and Jewish economic activity. As we have seen, these issues were in the forefront of mid-thirteenth-century ecclesiastical concern with the Jews, and it is no surprise that there should have been efforts at introducing such limitations into the laws of the Crown of Aragon. It is similarly no surprise that these limitations were pursued only fitfully by a monarch who was, on a number of grounds, ambivalent about such issues.[36]

During the reign of James the Conqueror, the Jewish communities of the Crown of Aragon maintained their powerful institutions of internal authority, aided by royal policy. As had been the case heretofore, power in the Jewish community continued to be exercised by the community's elite of wealth and political power working in tandem with those bearing religious authorization for their leadership role. The precise relationship of these two power elements is far from clear, but of their independent authority and mutual interaction there can be little doubt. One of the intriguing questions concerns the level of interpenetration of these two power groups. More specifically, it would be interesting to know more than we do of the family background of Rabbi Moses ben Nahman and the extent to which he was more or less integrated into the wealthy leadership caste of Catalonian Jewry.

While the focus of this introductory discussion has been the impingement of external realities on the Jewish communities of the Crown of Aragon, it will be necessary, to understand properly the Jewish response to the Barcelona confrontation, to have some sense as well of the cultural atmosphere within this Jewry. Baer is insistent on these decades as a period of significant cultural transition.

> As in general European history so in Jewish history, and especially in the history of the Jews of Spain, the thirteenth century marks a cultural turning point. This period ranks in importance with the Golden Age of Judaeo-Arabic culture. During the latter period Jewish tradition, aided by Graeco-Arabic rationalism, had received its classic formulation. The centers of Jewish culture were at that time to be found in the courts of the autocratic Moslem princes. In the thirteenth century, this cultural heritage, nurtured and fostered by an enlightened aristocracy, was transplanted to a different social scene agitated by new conditions and currents.

For Baer, this transition was of abiding significance.

> The work of the Spanish reformers may be compared to that of the sages of the Mishna, who had sought to save their people from sec-

ularization and disintegration. A generation which witnessed so great an effort must still have possessed considerable vitality and could be led to appreciate the decisive role history had placed upon it.[37]

While there may be considerable disagreement with aspects of Baer's analysis, the reality of major transition is beyond dispute.[38] The important findings of Bernard Septimus accord well with Burns's emphasis on an increasing integration of Spanish society into the fabric of western Christendom and Baer's sense of radical transition in Spanish Jewish culture.[39] Septimus has argued convincingly in his studies of both Rabbi Meir ha-Levi Abulafia of Barcelona and Rabbi Moses ben Nahman of Gerona, that the Jewry of Christian Spain was, during the thirteenth century, brought into fruitful contact with both the attractive Jewish culture fashioned in Muslim Andalusia and the newer but equally vigorous Jewish culture of northern Europe. Eschewing simplistic alignment of the Jewish cultural leaders of this period with either of the competing influences, Septimus argues for a nuanced understanding of the synthesis effected in such areas as Catalonia. Clearly, this major cultural disturbance and movement toward innovative cultural synthesis must be borne in mind as we undertake our investigation of the Jewish response to the new missionizing thrusts.

This sense of cultural and spiritual orientation leads us ineluctably to the third major figure associated with the Barcelona disputation, the rabbi of Gerona. Rabbi Moses ben Nahman was a major figure on the medieval Jewish scene and has been widely cited and studied. It is clear from the Barcelona engagement itself—as well as from other evidence—that he was a highly respected figure in Catalonian Jewry of the mid-thirteenth century. In the early fourteenth century, Rabbi Yom Tov ben Abraham Ishbili, a leading rabbinic authority in Aragonese Jewry, depicted the special circumstances of the scholars of his area: "We have received [our knowledge] from one faithful shepherd, whose hand was great and able in all things."[40] The reference is clearly to Nahmanides, who is recognized as having had both unusual abilities and wide-ranging impact. With the passing of the centuries, the sense of the importance of Rabbi Moses ben Nahman has not abated; if anything, it has grown. He is surely, at this moment, one of the most carefully studied figures in medieval Jewish life. A number of traditional biographies are available, but all of these efforts focus on the Jewish literary sources and the rabbi's literary activities. None makes any attempt at integration of the rabbi into his milieu.[41] Of late, the interest in Nahmanides the author and spiritual leader has taken on new dimensions.[42] We have noted already the efforts of Baer and Septimus to locate the Ramban on the cultural map of thirteenth-century European Jewry. Considerable attention has focused on identification of the major lines of Nahmanides's thinking.[43] In particular, recognition of his important place in the development of the kabbalah has given rise to a spate of studies of his mystical teachings and their place in the rapid emergence of the mystical movement to a position of eminence in European Jewish life.[44]

Unfortunately, we know little of Nahmanides's socioeconomic circumstances. As will be argued later, he was clearly not a member of the famed de Porta family.[45] To what extent he was part of the Catalonian Jewish aristocracy cannot be determined. There is reference to a considerable royal grant to him prior to the Barcelona confrontation.[46] Similarly, the seal ring discovered in Israel (if authentic) would seem to suggest a man of wealth and standing.[47] Finally, an interesting letter, ostensibly written by Nahmanides to one of his sons, indicates that son's entrance into royal service and warns him against the enticements of an aristocratic life-style.[48] All this suggests—not definitively, to be sure—that the rabbi may well have enjoyed comfortable circumstances and may well have been part of the Catalonian Jewish aristocracy. However, at the present time, we cannot be sure of his socioeconomic standing.[49]

Less problematic is the sense of his manifold religious and spiritual interests. Commentary on the Torah, commentary on the Talmud, halakhic treatises, important formulations of spiritual doctrine, mystical speculation, communal leadership during a number of periods of crisis—all this constitutes the remarkable creativity of Rabbi Moses ben Nahman.[50]

A central issue in recent study of Nahmanides concerns the environment or environments that affected him. Previously, Baer had depicted the Ramban as ranged in opposition to Andalusian rationalism, a spokesman, as it were, for the alternative style of Jewish thinking that had developed in northern Europe and that was—in Baer's own view—more authentically Jewish than the rationalism of the south. This fairly simple picture of Nahmanides has been challenged of late, as already indicated, by Septimus, who has argued for a more nuanced view of Rabbi Moses, for setting him at a critical cultural crossroad and for portraying him as a figure sensitive and receptive to the variety of cultural influences striving for dominance in mid-thirteenth-century Jewish life. Septimus has argued quite convincingly that Nahmanides can only be understood properly when seen against the complex backdrop of a Jewish world in ferment, a Jewish world in which a variety of intellectual and spiritual strains were meeting and competing against one another. Specifically, Septimus identifies as potent cultural forces the rationalism of Andalusia, which reached its apogee in the writings of Rabbi Moses ben Maimon; the mysticism of Provence, which had begun to unleash powerful mystical inclinations throughout southern European Jewry; and the Tosafist revolution in talmudic study, destined for enormous impact on patterns of Jewish teaching and thinking. He makes his case for a more positive stance toward Andalusian tradition on the part of Rabbi Moses in a number of ways: from Nahmanides's attitude toward *aggadah* and its authority; from his relationship toward the giants of Andalusian tradition, ibn Ezra and Maimonides; and from his protective posture toward Andalusian halakhah.[51] I shall suggest, toward the end of this investigation, that the Nahmanidean stance toward messianic calculation adds yet another dimension to the argument for the positive impact of Andalusian thought.[52] All this is not intended, of course, to diminish the impact of the other currents. As argued by Septimus, Nahmanides stood at a remarkable spiritual crossroad and absorbed productive influences from a number of directions.

Little is known of the personality of Rabbi Moses ben Nahman. Perhaps the most salient feature extrapolated from his writings and his activities is a sense of moderation and conservatism. Moderation is ostensibly reflected in his accommodationist stance during the eruption of controversy over the writings of Maimonides.[53] Conservatism is ostensibly reflected in two purported characteristics of the Nahmanidean kabbalistic stance—his insistence on esoterism, with an unyielding commitment to maintaining kabbalistic knowledge in a close and closed circle of disciples, and his refusal to innovate, relying only on teachings authoritatively communicated from tradition.[54] My analysis of the Barcelona disputation and its aftermath introduces a few further aspects of this multifaceted personality, including fuller appreciation of his remarkable literary abilities and awareness of his flair for the radical, at least in his messianic speculation. As we shall see, the man who was so conservative in his kabbalistic teaching was far more open and radical in his reassurance of messianic deliverance.[55] All of this will enhance the available portrait of the rabbi of Gerona.

The Barcelona disputation took place at a point of considerable transition—in Western Christendom altogether, in the Crown of Aragon in particular, and in European Jewish life. The staging of the disputation reflects new sensitivities and aspirations in Christian society; the Jewish response alerts us to a changing Jewish community. With this background in hand, we can now proceed to our analysis of the event and its aftermath.

2

The Disputation of 1263

The first step in undertaking the kind of analysis I have proposed involves a careful evaluation of the two conflicting sources. On one point there can be no disagreement whatsoever. Of the two accounts, the Hebrew is the lengthier and fuller. This implies no qualitative superiority. It is a simple observation—but one that is worth making, nonetheless. We shall want to ask at some point why the author of the Latin account chose to make his report so cursory and why the writer of the Hebrew record chose to make his so lengthy. For the moment, however, we have simply begun with an obvious statement with no immediate implications.

Let us open our investigation with the briefer Latin account.[1] The defenders of this record emphasize, above all else, its placement in the register of the king of Aragon and the appending to it of the royal seal. The official character of the Latin document, according to its defenders, affords more than ample testimony to its validity. To put the matter more fully, King James I would hardly have signed a document that was a crass fabrication of the confrontation to which he had been an eyewitness and in which he had actively participated. Objections to the Latin account have flowed from two directions. The first, noted in our résumé of Loeb's attack on Denifle, involves simply an attack on the credibility of the Dominicans, who were responsible for both the disputation itself and—seemingly—the Latin record of it.[2] This assault on credibility is of no real significance at all. Even if one were to take it seriously, Loeb is still left with the problem of recognition of this account by a king whom Nahmanides continually extols as a model of probity and fairness. The serious attack on the Latin account is that mounted by Baer, who argues that a careful look at the report reveals it to be superficial and terribly confused. It is on these grounds that Baer comes to his negative conclusion with respect to its validity. Baer subjects the Latin account to careful point-by-point inspection and reaches the following conclusion:

> One who examines punctiliously this order of things [as depicted in the Latin account] will see that this [account] is not the work of a narrator who was himself an auditory witness at the time of the disputation and failed to understand the issues properly, but [is rather] the work of a writer who took his account from a full report that was before him. Out of an intention to delete and to advance matters that seemed worthy of it, he destroyed the entire account, to the point where we have before us only fragments ripped out of place and reintegrated without any meaning.[3]

For Baer, a close look at the Latin text itself suffices to indicate its inadequacies; indeed, for him, this is the only legitimate way to disclose its inadequacies. To be sure, Baer's assault on the Latin account still leaves a gnawing problem. How could the royal chancery, a relatively professional organization, have included in the king's register such a jumbled mess, and how could the king himself, with credibility as a literary figure, have appended his seal to such a sham? While not insuperable objections to Baer's negative portrait, these questions are troubling.

Let us examine carefully the negative assessment made by Baer of the Latin text, not on any external grounds but in terms of a close rereading of the text itself. Is it, in fact, true that the document is the kind of hopeless jumble depicted by Baer? My answer is that it is not. It seems to me that Baer was unfair in his judgment of the Latin account in one fundamental way. He made his negative assessment in a comparative manner. That is to say, he took the two accounts, compared them, and found the Latin record wanting. More precisely, he established the narrative sequencing of the Hebrew report as the standard and judged the Latin account as deficient in comparison. This seems to me a mistaken procedure. Why must we assume that the two compositions should have been organized in parallel fashion? Perhaps differing purposes occasioned differing principles of organization.

If we begin, then, by asking what the purpose or purposes of the author of the Latin text were, we would, I believe, emerge on firmer ground. To be sure, the author of the Latin account regrettably does not explicitly inform us of his purpose. In seeking to uncover inferentially his goals, we can comfortably begin with a negative statement: This account was surely not intended to serve any broad public purpose; it was not intended to be widely read. This lack of broad public purpose explains a number of characteristics of the report, in particular, its brevity and its sketchiness. It is important to note also that the author eschewed the narrative format. There is clearly no effort here to supply an extensive narrative record of the disputation. All these observations are negative, focusing on what the author of the Latin account was not interested in providing. Why then did he compose his report, and what was he concerned with providing? Given the placement of the document in the royal register of Aragon, the best guess is that this account was intended to serve as a summary statement of the disputation that would in some fashion serve to undergird the royal orders for ongoing Christian missionizing, along the lines essayed in Barcelona. For this bureaucratic purpose, neither length nor engaging format was required. What was needed, rather, was a brief analytic résumé of the major elements of the event, an overview that summarizes thematically the Christian thrusts and the Jewish responses (or lack thereof). There is, in this analytic résumé, no effort whatsoever to provide a running sense of the dramatic encounter. Rather, the author was clearly interested in providing a set of conclusions, a sense of the overall goals and results of the disputation.

Viewed without prejudgments, the document actually divides nicely into five major sections: (1) a clear and accurate depiction of the setting; (2) a clear and accurate description of the agenda; (3) two comments on the Jewish participant in the disputation; (4) the issues discussed and the results of the discussions; (5) depiction of the general discomfiting of the rabbi, eventuating in his flight from Barcelona. The organization of the report, rather than being confused, is actually clear and cogent.[4]

The first two sections present no problems whatsoever and are widely cited in the literature. In particular, there is widespread recognition that the itemization of the agenda in the Latin account is quite carefully formulated. According to the Latin text, the following items were to be proven, all on the basis of rabbinic texts: (1) that the messiah, who is called Christ, whom the Jews anticipate, has surely come already; (2) also, that the messiah, as prophesied, should be divine and human; (3) also, that he suffered and was killed for the salvation of mankind; (4) also, that the laws and ceremonials ceased and should have ceased after the advent of the said messiah. Indeed, it is generally agreed that this Latin version of the agenda is more accurate than that found in the Hebrew account. Put differently, it is clear that Nahmanides's rendition of the agenda is a distortion (the purposes of which we shall discuss in a later chapter) of the items scrupulously recorded in the Latin document.

The problems raised by Baer with respect to the Latin account derive almost exclusively from the third and fourth sections as described above. The third section includes two comments on Nahmanides. The first notes that it was proven to the Jewish protagonist that he ought not be designated "rabbi," since the term should not have been utilized after the passion of Jesus, and that the rabbi conceded that this was so for at least the previous eight hundred years. For Baer, this is a prime example of the manner in which segments of an original account were meaninglessly ripped from their proper context. The proper context, for Baer, is the narrative account of the flow of the debate, in which the issue of the title "rabbi" was introduced tangentially during the discussion of Gen. 49:10 and its rabbinic interpretation. Now, it may well be that this was in fact the point at which the issue of the title "rabbi" was raised; however, there is nothing shocking or untoward in the author of a résumé noting, prior to his summary of the results of the deliberations, that the Jewish protagonist suffered from a number of liabilities, one of which had to do with his very title and qualifications as a Jewish leader. Similarly, the second observation introduced at this juncture, reference to an earlier discussion between Friar Paul and Rabbi Moses, which Baer similarly finds misplaced, is intended by the author to point once more to the weaknesses of the Jewish spokesman, who had been purportedly bested once before by the same Dominican missionizer. While one may argue that these points are slight and that the author of the résumé was ill-advised to introduce them into his account at this or any point, introduction of two negative observations on the Jewish disputant hardly suggests a lack of coherence.

The critical section of the Latin account is the fourth, in which the actual proceedings at Barcelona are depicted. This breaks down into the following five segments: (1) Christian posing of the key question of whether the rabbi believed that the messiah had already come, the rabbi's negative response, and a further comment by the rabbi that, were it proven to him that the messiah had already come, then that messiah perforce would have had to be Jesus;[5] (2) reference to a series of rabbinic texts that speak of the messiah as having already come and the rabbi's responses; (3) brief reference to the argument that the messiah was essentially human, to which the rabbi is portrayed as unable to respond;[6] (4) a return to the first agenda item, the prior advent of the messiah, with the Christian argument based on Gen. 49:10 and its rabbinic interpretation; (5) discussion of the Servant of the Lord passage in Isaiah, clearly intended to reflect consideration of the third agenda item. All of this is again hardly disorganized or incoherent.

The final section of the Latin account portrays the rabbi in greater and greater desperation, led finally to repudiate the authoritative texts cited by Friar Paul. Moreover, the rabbi is depicted as increasingly confused and as eventually rebuffed by his fellow-Jews. In the end, according to this Latin account, he was forced to flee, clearly for the author of the Latin account the ultimate sign of his incapacity to respond to the new missionizing thrust. This flight introduces cogently the fourth and final agenda item.

> Although he promised before the king and many others that before a few he would answer concerning his faith and his law, when the said lord was outside the city, he secretly fled and departed.[7]

Through this reference to Jewish law, the author of the Latin report has touched on each of the four agenda items noted at the outset. According to this author, the first three were formally broached in the presence of the king; the fourth and last was intended for discussion in a more restricted setting but was never raised and debated because of the rabbi's flight. One last observation on the closing section of the Latin account. The alleged failure of the famed rabbi clearly implied for the author of this Latin account not a lack of personal ability but rather the ultimate indefensibility of the Jewish position.

My conclusion with respect to the Latin account is that it does not exhibit the weaknesses claimed by Baer. Never intended as a narrative account of the proceedings in Barcelona, the Latin text represents a résumé of the proceedings from the point of view of a committed Christian observer. It was not intended as a narrative depiction of the chain of events, nor was it intended to be as full as the Hebrew report. It was written to serve as an overall statement of the aims and achievements of the Barcelona disputation and does so in cursory but coherent fashion.[8] Neither external considerations of the kind proposed by Loeb nor internal considerations of the kind advanced by Baer can successfully disqualify this Latin record as a reliable source. In coming to this conclusion, I am by no means asserting that it is *the* reliable record of the Barcelona confrontation. I have, to this point, simply examined the case made against the Latin record and found that case wanting.

Indeed, I am uninterested in an attempt to disqualify the Latin account in some decisive and all-embracing fashion. It seems to me a carefully drawn up—albeit brief and fragmentary—statement of the Barcelona disputation. While I see no reason for blanket condemnation of it and wholesale rejection of the information it provides, I suggest that it is surely a one-sided and tendentious presentation of the event. This means two things. In the first place, the fluid event in Barcelona is viewed from a distinctly Christian perspective. The sense that the outcome of the confrontation was a Christian victory is neither right nor wrong; it is simply a reflection of the overall position the author held on issues of Christian-Jewish controversy. I have no difficulty in seeing this as a biased look at the events in question; I find untenable the notion that this report represents some kind of objective statement to which all observers of the debate would have had to agree wholeheartedly. This biased perspective, when recognized and allowed for, in no way obviates responsible utilization of the source. Beyond perspectival bias, there are also signs of what I have earlier designated embellishment and exaggeration. The picture of the distinguished Nahmanides unable to respond to issues that he must surely have anticipated, confused to the point of incoherence, insulted by his coreligionists, and eventually forced to flee ignominiously strains credulity. I find it highly unlikely that a scholar of the stature of Nahmanides, prepared for the new missionizing argumentation that Friar Paul introduced, would have been thoroughly overcome in the manner depicted in the Latin account. I can only see this aspect of the record as highly exaggerated. Once again, however, even exaggeration does not disqualify this source from useful exploitation. My interest lies in mining this account for information shared with its Hebrew counterpart, identifying those areas in which radical disagreement is manifest, and attempting on the basis of the shared and divergent perspectives of the two surviving sources to reconstruct, within the limits possible, the outlines of the historic confrontation in Barcelona.

What, then, of the Hebrew counterpart to this Latin report?[9] The Hebrew account of Nahmanides has been subject to less objection than its Latin counterpart, but it has surely not been immune from criticism. Let us begin our discussion of it with the same question that we asked of the Latin source: What was the purpose that animated its author? Again, we are unfortunately provided with no explicit auctorial statement of goal. In this case, however, the author's purpose is actually easy enough to fathom. Unlike the author of the Latin record, Nahmanides was clearly not writing for a restricted bureaucratic audience; he was writing an account intended for a fairly broad Jewish reading public.[10] This account was intended, minimally, to provide a full statement of the new Christian lines of argumentation, of what Nahmanides perceived to be his successful rebuttal of that argumentation, a sense of what Nahmanides saw as maximal Jewish achievement in Barcelona, and—beyond all that—a statement of the overall inferiority of Christianity and superiority of Judaism.[11]

Appreciation of these goals enables us to understand a number of the characteristics of the Hebrew record. As noted already, the Hebrew account is surely lengthier and fuller than the Latin. Whereas the author of the Latin account was satisfied with a fairly brief résumé of the themes of the disputation and its major results, the Jewish author's public purposes necessitated an extensive recounting of the event. For reasons to be proposed later, for Nahmanides's purposes, the narrative format provided considerable advantage.[12] There has been widespread recognition, although without adequate clarification, of the literary excellence of the Nahmanidean account. It must be noted that literary excellence—like literary mediocrity—tell us nothing with respect to the reliability of the composition. The issue of reliability must be decided on other grounds.

The attack on the reliability of the Nahmanidean account began early, immediately in the wake of its appearance. In 1265, the rabbi of Gerona was hailed before a royal court as a result of the appearance of his opus, and in 1266, the work elicited a papal complaint, emphasizing heavily its mendacity.[13] For Denifle, as we have seen, the combination of papal condemnation with the evidence of direct conflict between the Latin and Hebrew accounts on the last stages of the confrontation—the Latin record's claim of the rabbi's flight and the Hebrew record's claim of dignified leave-taking of the king whose seal was affixed to the Latin source—sufficed to indicate the utter lack of reliability of Nahmanides's narrative. Denifle leveled one important internal criticism as well. He argued that the depiction of the argumentation over the Trinity reported by Nahmanides as part of the synagogue colloquy that took place some days after the close of the formal disputation is simply unthinkable, that expert theologians such as Raymond of Penyafort could not possibly have been silenced in the way depicted by Nahmanides.[14]

I find none of Denifle's objections compelling. The external evidence provided by the papal letter is in no way decisive for the modern nonpartisan historian. For the pope, embodying the views of the circle out of which the Latin document emerged, the encounter was surely a decisive victory for the Christian camp, and the counterportrait of the rabbi could only have been viewed as a lie. Given our assumption of a fluid happening, open to a variety of views, the papal claim does not invalidate the Jewish source. The overt contradiction between the portrait of the fleeing rabbi and the rabbi parting in dignity and grace from the king seems unbridgeable, necessitating a conclusion that one or another of the sources is thoroughly in error. For Denifle, the royal provenance of the Latin document means that the error—the term "lie" would not be inappropriate under the circumstances— must be in the Hebrew source. Yet, even here I would resist the either-or temptation. In his important article cited earlier, Loeb already suggested that this striking discrepancy in the two sources is not as radical as it first appears. Loeb notes that the Latin record claims that, "although he [Rabbi Moses] promised before the king and many others that he would answer concerning his faith and his law [a reference to the fourth agenda item], when the said lord was outside the city, he secretly fled and departed."[15] Loeb suggests the possibility of a genuine misunderstanding, with the rabbi feeling that his responsibilities had been fully discharged and the Christian side convinced that the departure from Barcelona represented

flight.[16] This possibility seems to me reinforced by reference in the
Latin account to the rabbi's alleged extravagant promise to "remain
in Barcelona for that purpose [to debate the issues proposed] not
only for a day or a week or a month, but even for a year."[17] There
may well be reflected here, too, a reasonable divergence of views,
with the Christian side seeing in the rabbi's behavior disgraceful
flight and the rabbi himself convinced of the propriety of his return
to Gerona. Finally, Denifle's objections to the exchange over the
Trinity seem to me to reflect once more the likelihood of exaggeration. I have already suggested that the picture of a great Jewish
scholar silenced and humbled by Christian claims that he certainly
should have anticipated is surely overdrawn. In the same way, the
portrait of outstanding Christian theologians being silenced by
rather simple Jewish claims represents for me the converse, the
Jewish tendency to present things occasionally in embellished
fashion. Such embellishment in no way disqualifies the source in
its totality.[18]

Thus, I find Denifle's objections to the Hebrew account as unconvincing as the Loeb and Baer objections to the Latin record.
Here, too, the result, for me, is far from thorough acceptance of
the Jewish account. I return to the stance of Baer, the only scholar
to offer an alternative to the outright rejection of Denifle, on the
one hand, and the total acceptance of the Hebrew account, on the
other. For Baer, the Hebrew record is, in its own way, a work of
religious propaganda, addressed to the Jewish community of
Catalonia in which Nahmanides played such a leading role.[19] While
this does not mean for Baer, or for me, disqualification of the Hebrew narrative, it does mean that it must be utilized with care.

For me, the divergence between the Hebrew and Latin accounts
flows in part from differing perspectives on the event and in part
from programmatic embellishment, meant to serve the purposes
of the compositions. Thus, the overall sense of victory patent
throughout the Hebrew account, which contrasts markedly with
the Christian perception, seems to me to reflect simply a divergence in point of view that is almost inevitable. What else might
we reasonably anticipate? Such divergence in no sense requires a
decision in favor of one perception or the other. Indeed, to take
sides in that manner means simply to join one of the two conflicting camps.

In addition to perspectival clash, there is also in the Hebrew record evidence of embellishment and exaggeration, observable in a number of features of Nahmanides's engaging narrative. In the first place, the portrait is simply too clear-cut. In each and every interchange, it is the rabbi who has the last and decisive word. Public disputations in any era lack such absolute qualities. There is inevitably a succession of claim and counterclaim, interruption, speaking simultaneously and at cross purposes. All of this is woefully lacking in the Hebrew report; it is simply too neat and tidy to be thoroughly believable as the actual depiction of a flesh-and-blood interchange. Here the material from the later Tortosa disputation provides an interesting alternative. The valuable Hebrew account of that engagement makes no effort to present such a clear-cut picture. It notes frequently that argumentation continued and was protracted. The overt recognition of ongoing debate and discussion makes the Hebrew Tortosa account far more believable, although the same quality surely robs it of some of the impressive certitude of the Nahmanidean narrative.[20]

There is a second aspect of the Hebrew account that seems to me problematic, and that is the inclusion of material directly derogatory of Christianity. Clearly, the entire confrontation was organized and rigidly controlled by the Dominicans, with the collusion of the king of Aragon. Under these circumstances, for the Jewish representative to make public utterances that would be openly offensive to Christianity strains credulity. While I shall deal with this issue more thoroughly in subsequent chapters,[21] let me confine myself here to citing but one instance of an utterance reported by Nahmanides which can hardly have been made in such brazen fashion. In the course of the lengthy speech that Nahmanides attributes to himself at the opening of the second day of the debate, he claims to have made the following important observations:

> The heart of the case and the dispute between Jews and Christians lie with the fact that you attribute to the essence of the divinity something most unpalatable. You, our lord the king, are a Christian son of a Christian man and woman. You have heard all your life priests and Franciscans and Dominicans speaking of the birth of Jesus. They have filled your brain and the marrow of your bones[22] with this doctrine. [This doctrine] has been ingrained in you as a result of this habituation. However, that which you believe—and in-

deed it is the cornerstone of your faith—reason cannot accept and nature does not permit, and the prophets never said such a thing. Even the miraculous cannot be extended to apply to this doctrine, as I shall prove with thorough proofs at the proper place and time. [This unacceptable doctrine is] that the Creator of heaven and earth and everything in it returned and passed into the womb of a certain Jewess and grew in it for seven months and was then born tiny. Subsequently he grew and was then turned over into the hands of his enemies, who judged him to death and killed him. You say that subsequently he lived and returned to his former place. [All this] cannot be borne by the thinking of a Jew or of any person. Vainly and pointlessly you make your claims, for this is the heart of our disagreement.[23]

We shall ask, at a later juncture, why Nahmanides chose to incorporate this important passage in his narrative. His purpose in so doing will tell us much with respect to his overall goal in the composition of his Hebrew account. For the moment, however, let me confine myself to indicating that it is extremely unlikely that the circumstances would have permitted such a blasphemous utterance on the part of the rabbi. Once again, the Tortosa material is valuable. In the Hebrew reports of that confrontation, there is clear evidence of the potential for arousing Christian ire through statements infinitely less abrasive than that made by Nahmanides. The better Hebrew report notes, for example, an explosion of papal wrath over citation of a rabbinic dictum that excoriates those who attempt to reckon the end of days. Seeing such a statement as derogatory to the biblical Daniel, the pope exploded in anger.[24] While one may reasonably argue that the mood in Barcelona was somewhat freer, it was not free to the point that would permit such a brazen public statement by the Jewish protagonist.

This last point leads further. While I argue this matter more fully a bit later, let me note briefly here that the technique of citing rabbinic sources represented a brilliant ploy on the part of the Dominicans. It meant essentially that the issue of Christian truth in the abstract was not under discussion: the Jew was in no position to refute the truths of Christianity. The best that the Jewish spokesman could possibly do was to show that rabbinic sources—and only rabbinic sources—do not bear witness to Christian truth. Were the Jewish protagonist thoroughly successful in so doing, the truth claims of Christianity, as viewed from the Christian perspective, would have been in no way diminished. Tactically—as well as in other ways, as we shall see—this was an inspired innovation. To have developed such a potent new technique and then let it be readily contravened by the Jewish protagonist further strains credulity. Yet this is precisely what Nahmanides claims to have done. He presents a portrait of himself as arguing the superiority of Judaism over Christianity, a possibility that the new argumentation was intended to obviate. I find it hard to believe that the clever minds that adumbrated the new approach would have let it be undone so readily. Rather, I share—with, I hope, greater detail—Baer's sense of a work intended for internal Jewish purposes, a work that involves some distortion of what actually took place. Again, as in the case of the Latin account, this does not lead me to label the Hebrew report either mendacious or unreliable. It simply suggests to me that the narrative must be used with care. As I said above, what is called for is an examination of both sources, a collating of shared information, an identification of points of significant divergence, and an effort to reconstruct, with adequate tentativeness, those aspects of the event that were viewed differently in the two competing camps.

We must now proceed to the events themselves. As we move through this investigation of the events of 1263, we shall at every point remain sensitive to the source problems, indicating regularly whether the proposed reconstruction is based on both sources together, whether one is preferred over the other, or whether conflicting perspectives necessitate tentative depiction of a nuanced reality that was seen in diverse ways by the two camps.

Surely, the first step toward proper understanding of the Barcelona debate is a simple one—recognition that there was no equality in the encounter. The Barcelona "disputation" was not an open intellectual engagement between two equal opponents operating under the same rules; it was in no sense a debate on the relative merits of Christianity and Judaism. This intellectual confrontation involved fundamental inequality, with the two sides operating under widely disparate regulations. Evidence of this fundamental inequality is reflected in (1) the obvious Christian—more specifically, Dominican—initiative in calling the event into being, with corresponding Jewish reluctance to participate; (2) the offensive position accorded to the Christian spokesman and the correspondingly defensive position accorded to the Jewish representative; and

(3) structuring of the engagement in such a way as to obviate any real embarrassment to the Christian side. Let us examine each point in slightly more detail.

Christian initiative in the calling of the Barcelona encounter is indicated unequivocally in both the Latin and Hebrew sources. The Latin account identifies the two critical forces in this Christian initiative:

> Moses the Jew, called "rabbi," was summoned from Gerona by the lord king at the urging of the Dominicans and was present there [at the royal palace in Barcelona] along with many other Jews, who seemed and were reputed among other Jews most learned.[25]

According to this account—and there is no reason to cast any doubt on it—the missionizing confrontation was conceived by the Dominicans and was put into effect through the support of the king of Aragon. This same picture is painted in the Hebrew account. Rabbi Moses ben Nahman opens his report by quoting a talmudic passage that depicts a set of Christian claims and Jewish counterclaims. The point of this talmudic tale is that because these early Christians were supported by the political authorities, their Jewish adversaries were forced to respond to their meaningless claims. According to Nahmanides, his thirteenth-century situation was parallel. He was required to reply to the inanities of Friar Paul, obviously because the friar, like the Christians in the talmudic story, was supported by the political authorities, in this case, the king of Aragon. Indeed, Nahmanides says that "our lord the king ordered me to dispute with Friar Paul in his palace in Barcelona, before himself and his advisors."[26]

The Christian side not only engineered the confrontation but clearly stipulated an offensive role for the Christian protagonist and only a circumscribed defensive posture for the Jewish spokesman. The disparity in roles is reflected sharply in both accounts. The brief Latin record shows the rabbi in a thoroughly defensive position, constrained to reply to a series of Christian thrusts. In the Hebrew account, despite Nahmanides's reporting his remarks at far greater length than those of Friar Paul, it is obvious that every single exchange begins with a text adduced by the friar and a question elicited from that text by the Christian protagonist. At two critical points in the proceedings, Nahmanides portrays himself as seeking the right to speak first. At the beginning of the second day of the disputation, he reports the following exchange between himself and the king:

> I said to our lord the king: "My lord, hear me." He said to me: "Let him speak first, for he is the interrogator."[27]

This identification of Friar Paul as the active presenter of questions and issues is significant. A second and more determined attempt at role reversal was made by the rabbi at the beginning of the fourth and last day of the deliberations. Nahmanides portrays himself as arguing that "justice requires that I pose the questions one day and Friar Paul answer me, since he posed questions which I answered for three days." Just or not, the request was peremptorily rejected by the king: "Nonetheless you must respond to him."[28] The point is clear. These proceedings were not convened as a fair and equal exchange of views on religious truth; they were set in motion by the Christian side as a means of confronting Jews with Christian truth. The Jewish side was rigorously restricted to defending itself against the Christian thrusts that were at the heart of the encounter.

The fullest expression of Christian control of the proceedings is to be found in the careful contrivance of the agenda in such a way as to make any Jewish attack on Christian truth and thus any embarrassment to the Christian initiators of the discussion impossible. As indicated sharply in both the Christian and Jewish sources, Friar Paul set out to prove to the Jews, on the basis of talmudic sources, that Jesus was the promised messiah. Utilization of rabbinic sources constituted a major innovation in the Christian missionizing endeavor, with a variety of advantages. To confine ourselves for the moment to the tactical advantages, it meant that the truth of Christianity was in no sense under investigation. In the words of the Christian report on the disputation, which has not been taken seriously enough but which is in fact highly accurate on this point,

> Deliberation was undertaken with the lord king and with certain Dominicans and Franciscans who were present, not that the faith of the Lord Jesus Christ—which because of its certitude cannot be placed in dispute—be put in the center of attention with the Jews as uncertain, but that the truth of that faith be made manifest in order to destroy the Jews' errors and to shake the confidence of many Jews.[29]

Because the Christian side was accorded total initiative, as we have already seen, the likelihood of any attack on Christian truth would in any case have been minimal. Reliance on rabbinic sources eliminated completely the possibility of an assault on Christianity. The possible eventualities at Barcelona were in theory only two: either Friar Paul would successfully prove from talmudic materials that Jesus was the messiah, in which case Jews should certainly have been brought to conversion, or, alternatively, he would fail in the effort, meaning only that rabbinic materials cannot be utilized for conversionist purposes. In the event of the friar's failure, however, there would be no implications for the truth of Christianity itself. Put in other terms, the structuring of the disputation meant that the Christian side could anticipate either a victory or a meaningless standoff; it could not conceivably suffer a defeat of any kind. Conversely, the Jewish side might, at best, gain a meaningless standoff or, at worst, suffer a serious defeat. Thus, there was more involved than simply the Christian side's enjoyment of an offensive position. The deliberation was structured in a way that promised the possibility of a missionizing success with no danger of any sort of embarrassing defeat.

It might possibly be objected here that this portrait of the structuring of the Barcelona disputation leans too heavily on the Christian account. To this I respond, in the first place, that Nahmanides himself indicates the centrality of rabbinic materials in the proposed debate. To be sure, he effaces considerably the full implications of this reliance on rabbinic materials; nonetheless, he does acknowledge the centrality of this innovative approach. This is one of the points at which the materials from the later Tortosa disputation prove quite helpful. The two Jewish sources from that later encounter both highlight the sense of one-sidedness in structure that we have gleaned from the Latin report on Barcelona. Let us cite the formulation of the better of the two Hebrew sources. The anonymous author of this firsthand account depicts in the following fashion the opening address of the pope to the assembled Jewish sages.

> The pope began and said: "Hear me, you Jews and Christians. I shall declaim before you my words and I shall inform you of the purpose of this gathering which I have effected here." He spoke at length in this address. The essence of his words and their goal was to show the gentiles and the nobles the intention of the disputation—how

and why. The substance of the statement was that it was not his intention in this disputation to prove with respect to the religion of
the Jews and the Christians which one of them is true in his eyes
and in the eyes of every Christian. Rather it was his intention to
show the Jews and to prove to them that, in the Talmud, it is said
explicitly that the messiah has already come. With respect to this he
spoke at length.[30]

The same stance is reflected in the opening moments of the second
session of the Tortosa disputation, the first session in which substantive issues were discussed.

> We returned before him [the pope] on the morrow, which was the
> eighth day of the month of February. There gathered there gentiles
> and Jews in numbers similar to the preceding day. The lord pope
> commanded Master Geronimo that he present his claims and that
> he speak to the issue of the disputation, without digressing into
> sermonics. Rather, he should indicate essentially that this is not a
> disputation, but that [it is] to show that in the Talmud there are
> statements that indicate explicitly that the messiah has already
> come.[31]

Thus, this Jewish testimony concerning the Tortosa disputation
corroborates thoroughly the Christian testimony concerning the
Barcelona disputation, enabling us to emphasize properly the indications to the same effect in the narrative of the Ramban and to
set aside for the moment the Nahmanidean embellishments that
lead in other directions. The picture that emerges is a consistent
one. The encounter was viewed as an effort to utilize Jewish
sources to prove to Jews the Christological teachings embedded
in their own rabbinic tradition. As noted, what could emerge was,
from the Christian perspective, a stunning success or a harmless
standoff or, from the Jewish perspective, either a harmless deflec-
tion of the new thrust or a serious debacle.

Because of the importance of the Maccoby treatment of the
Barcelona disputation, it is worth recalling at this juncture his
summary statement on what he perceived to be the divergent
Christian and Jewish strategies in the debate.

> Despite the unequal conditions of the debate (which were never-
> theless fairer than in any of the other disputations), Nahmanides
> managed to make some far-reaching statements of the Jewish stand-
> point vis-à-vis Christianity. While his opponent, Pablo Christiani,
> sought to confine the discussion to trivial points, so that he could
> catch out Nahmanides in "admissions" the importance and rele-

vance of which he could then exaggerate, Nahmanides continually sought to turn the discussion to matters of real importance, in which the fundamental differences between Judaism and Christianity could be displayed.[32]

While I agree with Maccoby's modernist preference for a debate that would have examined fundamental differences between the two faith systems, that is emphatically what the Dominican organizers of the confrontation were determined to avoid. Not sharing the modernist bias of either Maccoby or Chazan, they were determined to control the engagement in a way that would obviate any real engagement on these underlying issues. Rather, this was to be a one-sided missionizing endeavor, in which Jewish sources were to be adduced in support of Christian truths—and nothing more than that. To suppose that such a major engagement would have been so skillfully engineered and then undone so readily by the Jewish protagonist seems highly unlikely, and I count the Nahmanidean depiction of such direct contrasting of the Jewish and Christian positions as one of the distortions of his account, the purposes of which we shall investigate subsequently.

The carefully organized and controlled confrontation that I have described was in fact a clever extension of the missionizing campaign that had already been launched by Friar Paul Christian. From the early 1240s on, the king of Aragon had supported the new Christian missionizing, and Jews had been regularly compelled to hear Christian sermons, generally delivered in their synagogues.[33] The forced sermon, for all its advantages, had one major and inescapable disadvantage: it was a frontal assault on an essentially passive audience. The sermonizer had no way of assessing the impact of his words on his auditors. As the pace of the missionizing intensified, there developed a desire to test the new proselytizing argumentation. For such a testing, it was necessary to create the circumstances of a controlled give-and-take, and this was the genesis of the Barcelona disputation. For the Dominicans, the confrontation was not a simple intellectual joust; it was a rigidly structured discussion in which their innovative argumentation was advanced, with the Jews forced to respond openly and publicly to the new claims, thus paving the way for identification and rebuttal of Jewish objections. The Barcelona disputation was intended to serve as a major test of the innovative missionizing argumentation advanced by Friar Paul. Either it would be publicly tested, proven, and acknowledged or it would be decisively turned back by compelling Jewish objections or flaws might be exhibited which could then be examined and removed, with the altered and improved argumentation then available for continuing proselytizing.

Let us next identify the major thrusts of the Christian argumentation. As already noted, the key innovation in Friar Paul's argumentation was his utilization of rabbinic texts for the proof of Christian claims. We have cited this innovation in terms of its tactical advances, but now it must be addressed in substantive terms. This new tack represents a fresh wrinkle to an old and generally ineffective line of Christian argumentation. Christians had argued, since the very earliest days of their faith, that divinely revealed prophecies could only be properly understood as foretelling the advent of Jesus and a series of further cornerstones of Christian belief. Jews, of course, had an exegetical tradition of their own, the roots of which predated the development of Christianity. Part of the later unfolding of this Jewish exegetical tradition was played out against the backdrop of Christian contentions. As Christianity grew and spread, Jews could hardly remain oblivious to its claims, and, not surprisingly, they created a set of exegetical views designed to rebut major and well-known Christological assertions. So long as there was little genuine missionizing ardor within European Christendom, the *adversus Judaeos* literature was content to marshal traditional Christian argumentation, with little real concern for its effectiveness in Jewish circles. At the point at which enthusiasm for missionizing among the Jews was truly kindled in Western Christendom, the protagonists of this effort could not remain aloof from the reality that the traditional biblically grounded claims could have no significant impact among Jews long inured to these claims and possessed of a counterexegetical tradition of their own. At this point, the innovative missionizing argumentation of Friar Paul Christian turned in a new direction, claiming to the Jews that their own exegetical traditions, rather than buttressing anti-Christian thinking, actually supported central Christians beliefs. This was the heart and soul of the new missionizing argumentation.

Let us adduce, using both our sources, a simple and straightforward example of Friar Paul's utilization of rabbinic exegesis, involving a biblical pericope long disputed by Christians and Jews. On the first day of the confrontation, according to the Hebrew record, Friar Paul introduced the famous passage in Isaiah that speaks of the Servant of the Lord and suggested its standard Christological interpretation, ending with the question, "Do you believe that this passage speaks of the messiah?" Rabbi Moses's response was predictable.

> According to its true sense, it [this passage] speaks only of the people of Israel in the aggregate, for thus the prophets always designate them—Israel my servant, Jacob my servant.

Friar Paul's response is reported only briefly by Nahmanides, but the point is obvious.

> But I shall show you from the words of their sages that it [the passage] speaks of the messiah.[34]

The Latin account corroborates thoroughly this Christian approach, although disagreeing on the Jewish response.

> It was therefore asked of him whether chapter 53 of Isaiah—"Who could have believed what we have heard"—which according to the Jews begins at the end of chapter 52, where it is said: "Behold my servant shall prosper," speaks of the messiah. Although he consistently claimed that this passage in no way speaks of the messiah, it was proved to him through many authoritative texts in the Talmud which speak of the passion and death of Christ, which they prove through the said chapter, that the aforesaid chapter of Isaiah must be understood as related to Christ, in which the death, passion, burial, and resurrection of Christ is obviously contained. Indeed, forced by authoritative texts, he confessed that this section must be understood and explained as relating to Christ. From this it is clear that the messiah was to suffer.[35]

Thus, both sources agree in their depiction of the Christian approach, which involves introduction of a standard biblical passage, eliciting a predictable Jewish response, with Friar Paul then arguing that the traditional Jewish objections are in fact belied by rabbinic tradition itself. This approach argued that the authoritative literature of the Jews supported Christological lines of exegesis.

A second pattern of utilization of talmudic literature involves rabbinic dicta unrelated to the Bible. Let us again note an example attested in both sources. According to the Hebrew account, on the very first day of the disputation, the friar introduced a well-known talmudic passage, unrelated to biblical exegesis, that suggests the prior advent of the messiah.

> That fellow then said that in the Talmud it is said explicitly that Rabbi Joshua ben Levi asked Elijah when the messiah will come. He [Elijah] answered him [Rabbi Joshua ben Levi]: "Ask the messiah himself." He [Rabbi Joshua] said: "Where is he?" He [Elijah] said: "At the gate of Rome, among the sick." He [Rabbi Joshua] went there and found him.[36]

Reference to the selfsame rabbinic source, albeit in typically sketchier form, is found in the Latin account.

> It was then proved to him clearly, both through authoritative texts of the law and the prophets, as well as through the Talmud,[37] that Christ has truly come, as Christians believe and preach. Since he was unable to respond, vanquished by proper proofs and authoritative texts, he conceded that Christ or the messiah had been born in Bethlehem a thousand years ago and had subsequently appeared in Rome to some.[38]

According to both accounts, Friar Paul argued, in utmost simplicity, that the talmudic story about Rabbi Joshua ben Levi reflects overt rabbinic recognition of the advent of the messiah.

The new approach offered a number of significant advantages. Most important of all was simply its newness. Given the reality of a lengthy history of unsuccessful Christian efforts at missionizing among the Jews through appeals to the Bible, to canons of rationality, and to empirical observation, a new approach held out the promise of achieving a breakthrough unrealized through the prior lines of argumentation. Innovation was prized, to some extent, for its own sake. In addition, Christian confidence in the new approach was generated by growing awareness of Jewish veneration for rabbinic literature. Ironically, this awareness was, in part, created by the mid-thirteenth-century assault on the Talmud. As leadership in the Church became increasingly attuned to the central role the Talmud played in Jewish life, this awareness might well have moved some to experiment with utilization of the Talmud for Christian missionizing purposes.[39] Finally, there was, it seems to me, a significant psychological advantage in the new utilization of rabbinic materials. This appeal to the Talmud had to give some Jews a disturbing sense of the growing intellectual power of the Christian world, now capable of mastering Jewish tradition itself. It surely had to be distressing to mid-thirteenth-century Jews to hear their rabbinic sources, so long their own exclusive preserve, now quoted by the enemy in the name of Christian truth.

What were the issues to which this new use of Jewish sources was to be addressed? While the technique was highly innovative, they were the most traditional imaginable. Let us begin by citing once more the Christian source's formulation of the agenda issues for the disputation.

> Friar Paul proposed to the said rabbi that, with the aid of God, he would prove from writings shared and accepted by the Jews the following contentions, in order: that the messiah, who is called Christ, whom the Jews anticipate, has surely come already; also that the messiah, as prophesied, should be divine and human; also that he suffered and was killed for the salvation of mankind; also that the laws and ceremonials ceased and should have ceased after the advent of the said messiah.[40]

This presentation of issues is more accurately articulated than that of Nahmanides,[41] and the give-and-take recorded in both sources shows that all three of the initial issues specified were in fact addressed. The fourth issue was not debated at Barcelona, although we have ample sense of what was involved.[42]

Friar Paul's essential goal was to prove that Jesus was the messiah promised in biblical revelation. If that assertion could have been proved to the Jews, then they would have had to acknowledge that Christianity, based on belief in Jesus as messiah (and more), was true. The choice of the messianic role of Jesus as the central positive contention to be argued was an intelligent one. The messianic doctrine was one that Jews and Christians shared, and the textual foundation for this shared doctrine was abundant in both biblical and rabbinic literature. This was the simplest issue to argue with Jews, particularly given the proposed new technique of utilizing talmudic materials.

The effort to prove Jesus' messianic role was of course not new to Barcelona; it was the oldest element in Christian argumentation against the Jews. Now, how did Friar Paul, through use of rabbinic literature, hope to mount this argument? By proving the truth of a series of three independent statements that, when combined, afforded unshakable evidence of Jesus as messiah. If he could successfully argue that the messiah had already come, that the messiah was prophetically predicted to be both divine and human, and that the suffering and death of the messiah were likewise prophetically predicted, then only one figure could possibly demonstrate these three major characteristics, and that figure would be Jesus of Nazareth. I have elsewhere designated this tactic "deliberate abstraction."[43] Friar Paul, in arguing that the messiah had already come, did not wish to introduce the historical figure of Jesus. He wished to deal with all three assertions independently and abstractly, only at the end combining the strands into irrefutable proof for the truth of Christianity. This tactic of deliberate abstraction was artificial and problematic. Nahmanides attacked it vigorously, and Friar Raymond Martin abandoned it totally.[44]

Let us look more closely at the three individual assertions. The first is clearly the decisive one. If the messiah has already come, then Jesus must have been the messiah. Nahmanides quotes himself as saying that "there has been no one who has claimed or concerning whom it has been claimed that he is the messiah, except for Jesus."[45] The Latin source quotes Nahmanides in much the same way.

> Then in the palace of the lord king, the said Jew was asked whether the messiah, who is called Christ, has come. He responded with the assertion that he has not come. He added that the messiah and Christ are the same and that, if it could be proved to him that the messiah had come, it could be believed to apply to none other than him, namely Jesus Christ, in whom the Christians believe, since no one else has come who has dared to assume for himself this title nor has there been anyone else who has been believed to be Christ.[46]

In effect, Rabbi Moses would have been willing to concede the truth of Christianity if it could be proved that the messiah had already come. Rabbi Moses continued to argue the centrality of this issue on the last day of the disputation. After being asked by Friar Paul whether the messiah was to be human or divine, Nahmanides says,

> Behold at the outset we specified that we would speak first of the messiah—whether he has come as you say. After that we would speak of whether he is divine. But behold you have not proven that he has come, since I have refuted all the vain claims that you have adduced. Thus I have won my case, since it is your responsibility

to bring the proof, as you have taken upon yourselves. If you do not acknowledge that I have won this case, I accept responsibility to bring definitive proofs on this issue—if you will hear me out. Since it will be clear that your Jesus is not the messiah, there is no point in your claiming, with respect to the messiah yet to come for us, whether he is fully human or something else.[47]

Clearly, here again Nahmanides sees the heart of the issue in the first agenda item: if it could be proven that the messiah has come, then Jesus must be acknowledged as the messiah. Since, according to Nahmanides, prior advent of the messiah had not been proved, then there was no point in discussing the further agenda items.[48]

The other two assertions—that the messiah was predicted to be both divine and human and the messiah was fated to suffer and die—served, from the Christian perspective, a dual purpose. They reinforced the identification of Jesus as the messiah, which would have flowed in any case from the initial assertion of the prior advent of the messiah, and, at the same time, they served to fend off two major traditional Jewish objections to Christianity—the doctrine of Incarnation and the notion of an ignominious death for the messiah.

Let us now examine the specifics of the argumentation as depicted in our two sources. Let us begin with the more extensive of the two, the Hebrew account of Rabbi Moses ben Nahman. This depiction will be organized by session, sources adduced, and issues addressed.

Item	Session	Sources Adduced	Issue Addressed
1.	I	Gen. 49:10 plus T.B. San. 5a	prior advent of the messiah
2.	I	Mid. Eikhah Rabb. 1:57	prior advent of the messiah
3.	I	Isa. 52:13–53:12 plus rabb. exeg.	messiah's suffering and death
4.	I	T.B. San. 98a	prior advent of the messiah
5.	II	Isa. 52:13 plus rabb. exeg.	messiah as divine

Item	Session	Sources Adduced	Issue Addressed
6.	II	Rabb. midrash	messiah's suffering
7.	II	Dan. 9:24 plus standard rabb. chronology	prior advent of the messiah
8.	II	Rabb. midrash	messiah as human
9.	III	Maimonides	messiah as human
10.	IV	Ps. 110:1 plus rabb. exeg.	messiah as divine
11.	IV	Rabb. midrash	messiah as human
12.	IV	Gen. 1:2 plus Gen. Rabb. 2:5	messiah as divine

Schematization of the Christian argumentation in this fashion enables us to highlight easily a number of features of Friar Paul's argumentation, as fairly fully depicted in the Jewish source. The Christian thrusts were equally divided in their appeal to Jewish sources between rabbinic exegesis of biblical verses (6) and freestanding rabbinic dicta (6). Similarly, there is relatively equal distribution in issues addressed, with four sources cited to show the prior advent of the messiah, three to prove that the messiah was intended to be divine, three to show that he was intended to be human, and two to argue that the messiah was intended to suffer and die. It should be noted that the second agenda item, proof that the messiah was intended to be both human and divine, involved an effort on the part of Friar Paul to muster an equal number of texts to illustrate rabbinic perceptions of the divinity of the messiah and his humanity.

As noted, the Latin account is far less detailed than the Hebrew record. Nonetheless, there is a high level of correspondence between the two in their depiction of the Christian argumentation. In the Latin account, there is no narration of thrust and response; there is simply the listing of issues raised by the Christian side and the Jewish reactions. Also the Jewish sources utilized are not so fully identified as in the Hebrew record. Nonetheless, it is possible to chart a schematic depiction of the Latin presentation.

Item	Issue Addressed	Source or Sources Adduced
1.	prior advent of the messiah	unidentified rabbinic sources indicating birth of the messiah in Bethlehem and appearance in Rome
2.	messiah as human	no specification of rabbinic sources
3.	prior advent of the messiah	Gen. 49:10 plus T.B. San. 5a
4.	messiah's suffering and death	Isa. 52:13–53:12 plus rabb. exeg.

What emerges is, on the one hand, thorough agreement between the two sources and, on the other, the far fuller and more detailed nature of the Hebrew account. Thus, with respect to the lines of Christian argumentation, there turns out to be no significant disagreement at all, either with respect to the basic strategy of the Christian case or the issues addressed or even the precise arguments mounted.

Having completed this examination of the Christian case, in which we have encountered no real discrepancies between our conflicting sources, let me close with two further observations. The first involves an important, though unarticulated implication of the Christian case, involving an issue that will become important for our understanding of the aftermath activities. Christian proof of the messianic role of Jesus included *eo ipso* a negative assertion with regard to the Jews and their fate. If in fact Jesus was the promised messiah, then all the messianic predictions had been fulfilled with his coming, leaving the Jews bereft of messianic hopes for the future. In this sense, the positive thrust of the argumentation included a powerfully negative corollary as well. As we shall see, Jewish thinking in the wake of the disputation was highly sensitive to this important implication of the claim that Jesus had already appeared as the promised messiah.

One last point must be made. Let us recall once more the language of the opening paragraph of the Latin report on the Barcelona proceedings. According to this account, Christian truth was not to be "put in the center of attention with the Jews as uncertain." There was to be no give-and-take as to the truth of Christianity itself.[49] Rather, the goal of the disputation was "that the truth of that faith be made manifest in order to destroy the Jews' errors and to shake the confidence of many Jews."[50] We have already seen how the technique of citation of rabbinic sources enabled the Dominicans and Friar Paul to attempt to convince the Jews of Christian truth, without exposing that truth to any sort of questioning in its own right. I would like to emphasize at this juncture the closing words of the aforecited sentence which indicate the intention of shaking the confidence of many Jews. This point should not be minimized in its significance. From the perspective of the ecclesiastical forces that had set the new missionizing campaign and the Barcelona disputation in motion, Jews did not truly have to be convinced of the positive and specific truths of the Christian faith. Rightly or wrongly, these ecclesiastical figures saw conversion as requiring merely the upsetting of ingrained patterns of Jewish belief. Were Jews brought to the point of questioning their received beliefs, so the missionizers were convinced, the result would be acceptance of Christianity. Thus, the thrusts of the Christian camp, which the Jewish spokesman in his account derides, must be seen in terms of the intentions of the Christian side. Its goals were to mount arguments capable of raising Jewish doubts. The engendering of doubt was the key, based on the assumption that a doubting Jew would ineluctably see the truth of Christianity.

Let us now turn our attention to the Jewish side of the disputation. As we have seen, the engagement was forced on the Jews by a combination of Dominican instigation and royal support. The Jews had no choice as to whether to involve themselves or not. They were commanded to participate and had no alternative but to do so. Christian initiative in arranging the confrontation was clearly not greeted by Jewish enthusiasm for the encounter, since, as we have already seen, the agenda was organized in such a way that the Jews had much to lose and nothing whatsoever to gain. The talmudic story quoted by Nahmanides at the opening of his account reflects nicely Jewish reluctance to participate in such a contrived encounter. The Jewish spokesman's reluctance is indicated far more explicitly at the opening of the last day of the convocation. Nahmanides reports his lengthy statement indicating unwillingness to continue and his ultimate agreement—again reluctant—to resume.[51] In the course of this statement, Nahmanides points to a further liability from the Jewish perspective. Not only were the Jews in a no-win situation forced on them by the ecclesiastical and political authorities but they stood in danger as well of offending Christian society in the process of seeking to defend themselves from the Christian assault. The picture is thus a consistent one of both Christian initiative and extreme Jewish reluctance.

The rabbi of Gerona does portray himself as playing a role in the establishment of the agenda for debate, but even this claim seems exaggerated. Rabbi Moses depicts the establishment of the agenda in the following terms:

> I opened and said: "The dispute between Christians and Jews concerns many issues in the customs of the faiths which do not involve essentials of belief. However, I do not wish to dispute in this honored court except over matters which are essential."
>
> They all responded and said: "You have spoken well."
>
> Therefore we agreed to speak first of the matter of the messiah—if he has already come, according to the faith of the Christians, or if he is yet to come, according to the faith of the Jews. Subsequently we shall discuss whether the messiah is actually divine or if he is fully human, born of man and woman. Subsequently we shall discuss whether Jews possess the true law or whether Christians fulfill it.[52]

The portrait shows the Jewish spokesman fully involved at least in establishment of the agenda. Even here, however, the rabbi's claims seem unlikely. Indeed, he portrays himself as arguing subsequently that the issue of the messiah was not in fact at the heart of the Christian-Jewish dispute.[53] The inescapable conclusion is that despite the efforts of Nahmanides to accord himself some level of active involvement, the entire setting, including the requirement to debate, the utilization of rabbinic sources as the point of departure for the Christian argumentation, and the specific points to be proved, was thrust on him.

Given total Christian initiative in convoking the disputation and setting its agenda, we may well wonder who chose the rabbi of Gerona to serve as the Jewish spokesman. Here our two sources present us with some intriguing and irreducible discrepancies. Nahmanides, in his Hebrew narrative, presents himself as the central Jewish figure in the disputation from its inception. In his account, the decisive Christian figure is King James I, and it is the monarch to whom the rabbi's role is recurrently related. According to his own report, Rabbi Moses was commanded directly by the king to debate Friar Paul.[54] At no point do other Jewish leaders make any appearance. Even at the end of his narrative, when he reports on rumors of a forced sermon, on his decision to remain in Barcelona, and on his response to the king, to Friar Raymond, and to Friar Paul, he depicts himself as acting independently, indicating no consultation with or support from the leaders of Barcelona Jewry.[55] While the king surely had the right and authority to designate Rabbi Moses as the Jewish spokesman in the debate, it is somewhat surprising that he would have been singled out to respond to the sermons in the Barcelona synagogue without at least some involvement by the leadership of that community. Overt reference to such involvement is totally lacking in the Nahmanidean account. At the critical junctures in the disputation, it is the king to whom the rabbi relates, and the royal reactions are essential for Nahmanides's claim of success.

The one place where the involvement of other Jews may (or may not) be indicated in the Nahmanidean account is in the rabbi's speech at the opening of the fourth session. There he speaks of a large assemblage, which had urged him not to proceed further. That assemblage may or may not have included the Jews of Barcelona. A bit later in that address he mentions some Christians urging a few of the Jews that he not continue.[56] It is only in these ambiguous passages that any evidence of other Jewish involvement, including possibly objection to Nahmanides, is mentioned. The clear sense that Rabbi Moses himself wished to convey was the direct imposition of royal will on him, with the Jewish community and local Jewish leaders playing no significant role at all.

The depiction of Rabbi Moses's role is somewhat different in the Latin report. According to that report, the king commanded a number of learned Jewish leaders to assemble for the purpose of debating with Friar Paul. The Latin account suggests that these Jewish leaders, not the king, decided to select Rabbi Moses as their spokesman.

Since they [the learned Jews assembled by the king] could not defend their errors, these Jews indicated that the said rabbi [Rabbi

Moses ben Nahman] could sufficiently reply to each and every question which would be placed before them.[57]

Thus, according to this account, it was the Jews themselves who chose Rabbi Moses to represent them. More striking yet is the assertion, later in the Latin account, that the Jews eventually became dissatisfied with the spokesman they themselves had chosen. According to this account, Jews were doubly negative to Nahmanides. Some of them publicly insulted him, and some went so far as to prohibit him from debating further.[58] Clearly, this picture of the relations of Nahmanides with his coreligionists conflicts markedly with that found in Rabbi Moses's own report.

At this juncture, there is no sure way of ascertaining the role of Nahmanides, or more specifically who was responsible for according him a position of centrality. Given the earlier contact between James I and Nahmanides, royal selection of the rabbi of Gerona as the Jewish spokesman is not unthinkable. Such a selection would be in accord with the purposes of the Dominican instigators of the debate. If the new missionizing argumentation was to be given a serious trial run, then a respected and learned Jewish spokesman was imperative. To set up a confrontation with the Jews that involved a lesser figure would achieve nothing of any substance.

Jewish selection of Nahmanides as a spokesman, and even some measure of Jewish dissatisfaction with this representative, is likewise far from inconceivable. There is nothing problematic in the notion that the Christian initiators of the confrontation permitted the Jews themselves to choose the individual or individuals who would best represent them. Again, there was no real missionizing gain in a hollow victory over an incapable Jewish spokesman. Moreover, it would not be surprising had there in fact been dissension among the Jews present at the disputation over the performance of their spokesman. The stakes were fairly high, and the thrust with which the rabbi of Gerona was faced was relatively new. The rabbi's central responsibility was to create a reasoned and reasonable set of responses to the new argumentation. At a much later juncture, in the Tortosa disputation, when the new missionizing argumentation was already quite well known, the beleaguered Jewish spokesmen disagreed vociferously among themselves as to the most effective lines of rebuttal.[59] For their predecessors at Barcelona to disagree similarly among themselves would not be unthinkable. At the same time, it seems highly unlikely that the venerable rabbi of Gerona, whether chosen as spokesman by the king or by his Jewish peers, would have been subjected to the kind of extreme abuse depicted in the Latin account. That depiction of radical disaffection must be counted as one of that account's exaggerations.

It is, to be sure, not difficult to understand why Rabbi Moses might wish to efface recollection of some measure of Jewish dissatisfaction with his performance, if such dissatisfaction—milder than that depicted in the Latin account—did, in fact, surface. The simplest explanation is, of course, personal pride. A distinguished and senior figure in Aragonese Jewry, Rabbi Moses ben Nahman would hardly have welcomed dissent from his tactics and would have been likely to omit references to such dissent in his narrative. There is, in addition, a weightier reason for omitting such material. The overall purpose of Rabbi Moses's narrative was to convince his Jewish readers that the new argumentation was unsuccessful and, more specifically, to indicate the lines of rebuttal that he had developed and that he was suggesting to Jews elsewhere as their appropriate rejoinder. While the specific arguments of Nahmanides are the core of this narrative, its tone also is significant. As I shall argue subsequently, Nahmanides's vilification of Friar Paul was not incidental to his purposes. By continually denigrating his opponent, he was in effect assuring his Jewish readers that the new argumentation could have no real merit. Similarly, for these larger purposes, Nahmanides might have felt it appropriate to eliminate reference to internal dissension within Jewish ranks. Such dissension might have lessened the desired impression, which was absolute certainty on the Jewish side and ignorance and confusion on the Christian side.[60] Again, what I have suggested is hypothetical only; I have simply argued that selection of Nahmanides as the Jewish spokesman by the Jews themselves, dissension among the Jews with respect to his performance, and omission of such dissension from the Nahmanidean report are far from unthinkable.

Nahmanides himself might have urged greater attention to the substance of his argumentation than to some of these organizational details. Let us begin with an understanding of the Jewish spokesman's objectives. This involves, in particular, an awareness of the dual audience he was addressing. First, he was attempting to convince the Dominican organizers of the disputation that the new line of argumentation was pointless. Success in that direction would have constituted the optimal achievement from the Jewish perspective. Even failing such an achievement, however, there was a second audience to be addressed, and that was the community of Jewish auditors at the disputation itself and—yet more important—the community of Jewish readers of the Nahmanidean account. For his Jewish audience, also, Nahmanides had to prove that the new initiative was pointless. This he undoubtedly undertook in his oral presentation at Barcelona and clearly set out to do in his written record. As we shall see, in his written record, he attempted to do even more.

Let us attend to the major lines of rebuttal essayed by Rabbi Moses ben Nahman, again as reflected in the conflicting records. The high level of agreement with respect to the Christian thrusts is replaced by thorough disagreement with regard to the Jewish response. It is the effectiveness of the Jewish response that is the point of contention between Christian and Jewish perceptions of the public debate.

Let us look more closely at the patterns of Jewish response, again beginning with the fuller Hebrew narrative. Nahmanides portrays himself as presenting a number of lines of rebuttal to the Christian claims advanced by Friar Paul. These included (1) arguing repeatedly that Friar Paul misunderstood the material he quoted; (2) claiming that the text adduced does not prove the intended point; (3) attacking the technique of deliberate abstraction, insisting instead on introducing the figure of Jesus to show that the rabbinic sources adduced could not possibly have had reference to him; (4) taking the somewhat controversial position that aggadic statements do not require Jewish adherence, that, in other words, the texts cited by Friar Paul were not, in fact, authoritative; (5) claiming, in the broadest possible way, that the entire approach was senseless, that the notion of rabbinic authorities teaching Christian doctrine was patently absurd. There is, in addition, a sixth line of attack presented by Nahmanides in his own report of the encounter, and that is unremitting vilification of Friar Paul. We may legitimately wonder whether he was actually able to say such things in the public encounter. Whether he did or not, this was clearly one of the messages of his narrative account, written, as we shall soon see, to reinforce Jewish faith in the wake of the public disputation.

Since I have earlier established a schematization of the Christian thrusts, let us utilize the same table for identifying the Jewish responses.

Item	*Jewish Response*
1.	misunderstanding of the text
2.	incompatibility of the text with the historical Jesus
3.	text does not prove the purported point
4.	text does not prove the purported point
5.	misunderstanding of the text
6.	misunderstanding of the text and incompatibility with the historical Jesus
7.	misunderstanding of the text
8.	text does not prove the purported point
9.	text does not prove the purported point
10.	misunderstanding of the text
11.	misunderstanding of the text and incompatibility with the historical Jesus
12.	misunderstanding of the text

Like the prior schematization, this one, too, is enlightening. What is immediately obvious is the appearance in the actual give-and-take of only three of the six lines of rebuttal depicted by Nahmanides in his Hebrew account. The suggestion that aggadic texts are nonbinding was purportedly mentioned at a number of points during the disputation, but the argument is not portrayed as decisive for any specific text. The claim that the entire approach was pointless was voiced at the outset and was embodied prominently by Nahmanides in his report but was not used in response to any of the specific claims. The vilification of Friar Paul is indicated repeatedly but clearly is not advanced as a specific rejoinder to any text. In effect, Nahmanides portrays himself as arguing doggedly over each text, asserting that it was misunderstood by Friar Paul, that it failed to prove the point at hand, or that it could in no way be construed as a reference to the historical Jesus.

Once again let us turn to the alternative account, in an effort to identify its view of the rabbi's responses. Let us utilize our foregoing schematization of the Latin record to identify the lines of response attributed to the Jewish protagonist.

Item	Jewish Response
1.	acknowledgment that the messiah had been born but contention that he had not yet come in his messianic role, that is, that the text does not prove the point
2.	unable to respond
3.	claim of proof that Jews had political authority after Jesus but acknowledgment that this has not been the case for the previous eight hundred fifty years
4.	acknowledgment that the Servant of the Lord passage does relate to the messiah

These specific rebuttals, presented as weak and ineffective, are then succeeded with the following important passage:

> Since he did not wish to confess the truth unless forced by authoritative texts, when he was unable to explain these authoritative texts, he said publicly that he did not believe these authoritative texts which were adduced against him—although found in ancient and authentic books of the Jews—because they were, he claimed, sermons in which their teachers lied for the purpose of exhorting the people.[61]

To be sure, the information provided is recognizable to the reader of the fuller Hebrew narrative and, given the availability of that record, is neither unintelligible nor totally fabricated. In fact, while there is a striking paucity of responses indicated, those that are portrayed are recognizable. Nahmanides himself depicts a line of response that distinguishes between the birth of the messianic figure and his advent as messiah. It was a line of response that he did not show himself utilizing to its fullest extent because the two texts to which it was appropriate offered other lines of rebuttal as well. The notion that Nahmanides had no response to the claim that the messiah was human is misleading but not unintelligible. That is to say, the agenda item promised to prove not that the messiah was human but that he was both divine and human simultaneously. In fact, Nahmanides's own portrait of the messiah is that of a distinctively human figure. Thus, the notion that he accepted such a view, while phrased in misleading fashion, is not inaccurate. The Jewish response to Gen. 49:10, and its interpretation in T.B. Sanhedrin is not really divergent, again except with respect to the tone of the portrayal. From the Nahmanidean perspective, to prove that the exilarchate had been disrupted for the prior eight hundred fifty years would have been sufficient, since even such a date would have served to prove the incompatibility between the messianic figure resulting therefrom and the historical Jesus of Nazareth. The rabbi indicates in his Hebrew record that he had acknowledged publicly that the Servant of the Lord passage was related by some rabbinic authorities to the messiah and then claims that he had proceeded to argue further that such identification in no sense serves Christian truth claims. Finally, it is easy enough to relate the Latin depiction of Nahmanides's rejection of aggadic materials to that of the Hebrew account, allowing once more for significant difference in tone. Thus, the Latin account is not guilty of fabricating its depiction of the rabbi's responses out of whole cloth. It seems highly likely that the author was, in fact, a witness to the disputation and was reporting, from his own particular perspective, the critical give-and-take.

This is not to say, however, that there is really no difference between the two sources in their depiction of the Jewish responses. While the details are readily recognizable, there is an enormous difference in the extent and tone of the reporting. Of the six lines of rebuttal presented in the Hebrew text, only three make their appearance in the Latin account. To be sure, the appearance of vilification of Friar Paul in the Christian source is unthinkable. Less legitimate, however, is omission of the Jewish argument for misunderstanding of key sources and the claim that the approach in its entirety makes no sense at all. Of course, the Christian author was not profoundly interested in the full range of Jewish responses.

Furthermore, even in those rebuttals that are presented, there is sketchiness and omission of themes presented more fully in the Hebrew account. With respect to rabbinic exegesis of the Servant of the Lord passage, for example, according to the Hebrew narrative, Nahmanides acknowledged that the Servant of the Lord pericope is occasionally seen by the rabbis as applicable to the messiah but balanced that acknowledgment with the strenuous argument that even those rabbis who choose to see the Servant of the Lord passage as a reference to the messiah would not agree to the claims associated with the Christian messiah. The Latin account notes the acknowledgment but omits all reference to the continuation of the Nahmanidean contention. The contrast of fullness versus sketchiness that we have noted in this particular passage is characteristic of the broad divergence between the sources in depiction of the Jewish response.

Finally, there is a radical difference in tone between the two texts. To highlight this, let us focus on the last line of Jewish defense adumbrated in the Latin account, the possible rejection of aggadah on the grounds that it represents mere sermonics. While close enough to the Hebrew report to be recognizable, there are a number of salient differences in the depiction of this line of defense in the two records.[62] For the Christian author, it was a statement of reproof against the respected teachers and the authoritative literature of the Jews; for the Jewish author, it was an approach stated respectfully and seen as thoroughly consonant with Jewish tradition itself. For the Latin account, it was a ploy designed to serve as a panacea in the face of the overwhelming Christian argumentation; for the Hebrew account, it was one tactic among many. Indeed, according to the Hebrew text, this approach was never utilized as the decisive rebuttal during the actual give-and-take. Finally, for the Latin source, the suggestion that rabbinic teaching might be rejected was a move of desperation, undertaken by a Jewish spokesman who had been soundly defeated in his effort to rebut the new argumentation; for the Hebrew account, it was one stratagem among many, one in no sense predominant and in no sense desperate. In the Hebrew narrative, this devise is introduced on the first day and reiterated early on the second. It does not take on added significance as the debate unfolds.

What are we to make of these identifiably related yet considerably divergent presentations of the Jewish responses to the new missionizing argumentation? In part, they reflect differing foci of interest. The Jewish author is deeply concerned with portraying in detail the Jewish responses, while the Christian author is far less involved in such a depiction. For the latter, the key is the recurrent assertion of the inability of the Jewish spokesman to respond effectively. A second element in the divergence is surely contrasting assessment of the effectiveness of the Jewish response. For the Jewish author, the Nahmanidean strategies were highly convincing and successful; for the Christian author, they represent ineffectual quibbling, meant to obscure the decisive force of the Christian contentions. Again, it is difficult for the modern historian to intrude too fully into these assessments.

At the same time, while respecting perspectival divergence, it does seem appropriate to note one area in which the Latin report seems to lapse into unwarranted embellishment. The depiction of the rabbi as thoroughly discomfited strikes a discordant note. Just as it strains credulity to think that Nahmanides might have said publicly the blasphemous things that he reports, so, too, is it unthinkable that Nahmanides, chosen to represent the Jews of Catalonia by either the monarch or his coreligionists and well aware of the lines of the new missionizing argumentation, would have been reduced to the kind of silence portrayed in the Latin account. While Christian and Jewish observers may well have disagreed over the effectiveness of the rabbi's responses, it seems highly unlikely that he would have been as inept as depicted in the Latin record.

The key divergence between our two sources lies in the depiction of the lines of Jewish response. Even here one can hardly speak of wholesale lying and fabrication; rather, what has clearly taken place is selective emphasis on aspects of the Jewish response and placing of those responses in one of two conflicting contexts: for the Christian observer, the context is Christian victory and Jewish humiliation; for the Jewish observer, the context is thoroughly successful rebuttal of the new Christian argumentation. As argued in the introduction, there are no grounds for accusations of lying. What has taken place, rather, is divergent perception of a complex and fluid event. Discussion that was vigorous and heated took place over a protracted period. Viewers almost inevitably saw the exchanges from the perspective of their respective camps. From this jointly experienced but differently perceived event emerged, not surprisingly, two accounts that clearly relate to the same set of exchanges but that portray them in strikingly divergent fashion. I have made an effort, in the process of analyzing this divergence, to point in a number of directions in which the two sources are in agreement with respect to the Jewish rebuttals, to identify key areas of disagreement, and to suggest points at which each of the two accounts clearly moved beyond the bounds of reasonability. Beyond all this remains an area in which medieval observers could reasonably disagree and for which the same would ultimately be true for modern readers as well.

Having analyzed the organization and content of the disputation, we should turn our attention at this point to its concluding stages, more specifically, to the unsuccessful attempt to suspend the proceedings at the beginning of the fourth day and to their actual suspension at the close of that session. The first of these two—the abortive effort to suspend the proceedings—affords us yet another example of two divergent portraits that are, in fact, quite close to one another, distinguished only by their assessment of the overall significance of the details on which they more or less agree. According to the fuller account of Nahmanides, at the beginning of the fourth day of the debate, he made a concerted effort to have the proceedings halted.

> I said to the king: "I do not wish to debate further."
>
> The king said: "Why?"
>
> I said: "Behold, there is a great crowd here.[63] All of them have discouraged me and entreated me in this regard. For they are very fearful of these people, the Dominicans, who cast terror everywhere. Indeed, the leading and most respected priests sent me [messages], saying that I not continue. Likewise, many notables from your own household, my lord the king, have told me that I do harm by speaking publicly against their faith. Likewise, Friar Peter of Genoa, leader of the Franciscans, told me that this is not good. Likewise, from the quarters of the city,[64] [they] told some of the Jews that I must not continue."
>
> Indeed, thus it was. However, when they [the Christians cited by Nahmanides] perceived the will of the king, they all vacillated and said that I should do so [i.e., continue]. There was lengthy conversation among them on this. Eventually I said that I would debate.[65]

Let us contrast the briefer Latin account.

> Moreover, since he was unable to respond and was often publicly confused and since both Jews and Christians insulted him, he persistently claimed before all that he would in no way respond, since the Jews prohibited him and Christians, namely Friar P. of Genoa

and certain upstanding men of the city, had sent him messages advising that he in no way respond. Concerning this lie, he was publicly refuted by the said Friar P. and by these upstanding men. Whence it is clear that he tried to escape the disputation by lies.[66]

The details are strikingly similar—purported warnings on the part of both Christian and Jews against continuation, specific mention of the role of Friar Peter of Genoa, recanting or denial on the part of those who had allegedly given the warnings. What separates the two accounts is clearly assessment. For the Hebrew, the warnings were real and sincerely given, recanted under pressure; for the Latin, they were fanciful, the result again of Jewish desperation.

What, however, was the basis for these warnings, whether real, as claimed in the Hebrew account, or fabricated, as claimed in the Latin record? The Latin account does not dignify what it sees as fabrications by specification. Nahmanides, however, does indicate the concerns that caused a number of observers to suggest suspension of the proceedings. The key element in this concern is clearly fear of the impact of the rabbi's "speaking publicly against their [the Christians'] faith." What precisely might this mean? I have argued that the debate was limited to proofs from rabbinic literature which the Jewish spokesman had the right to combat; I have further suggested (and will argue more fully later) that the reported Nahmanidean assaults on Christian doctrine are embellishments and could not have been delivered as reported. Nonetheless, there is ample material in the more limited agenda imposed by the Dominican organizers of the debate to arouse public Christian animosity. Since, for example, the first agenda item proposed to show from Jewish sources that the messiah has already come and since it was Nahmanides's task to show that Jewish sources do not indicate prior advent of the messiah, the resultant popular perception would simply be Jewish denial of the coming of the messiah, a public stance that might very well arouse broad animosity. To put the matter more clearly, the arrangement of the agenda was a clever and sophisticated move on the part of the Dominicans to spare any embarrassment to the Christian side. The perspective reflected in this manipulation of the agenda is sophisticated and scholarly. For a broader audience, insensitive to these subtleties, the overall impression remains one of offensive Jewish intransigence. It is, in all likelihood, this popular perception that underlay the advice that the proceedings be suspended.

There is an interesting reference in the Nahmanidean account to the terror cast by the Dominicans. This does not seem to be the basis for the request for suspension. It does, rather, seem to be the reason that the suggestion was made to Nahmanides and not directly to the Dominican instigators of the confrontation. What Nahmanides seems to be saying is that, frightened by popular reactions, responsible Christian leaders, who were fearful of approaching the Dominicans directly, urged Nahmanides himself to refuse to continue. Both sources agree that the rabbi's request was, for the moment anyway, denied.

The divergent depictions of the actual conclusion of the confrontation seem at first blush far sharper. For the Hebrew account, the debate concluded on a note of dignity that was as close as the Jewish protagonist might come to victory. In fact, there is external corroboration of a sort for the Jewish spokesman/author's claim. A document of 1265 indicates royal borrowing from the Jew, Isaac of Barcelona, a portion of which was used to pay the sum of 300 *sueldos* to the rabbi of Gerona.[67] This would seem to substantiate the rabbi's contention of a dignified leave-taking from the king. In contrast, the Latin record has the rabbi slipping away during the monarch's absence. This account as well would seem to have external support, to wit, the affixing of the royal seal to the document that records this supposed flight. Who better than the king himself would know of the real note on which the disputation ended? Here, more subtly than in the case of the abortive effort to suspend the proceedings early on the fourth day, we may once again find ourselves confronted with reasonably diverging perspectives, rather than gross falsehood. As I have already noted, given the suggestion that the rabbi had allegedly promised to remain in Barcelona for even a year if necessary and had committed himself to a private continuation of the discussion, aimed at elucidating the fourth agenda item, the issue of the postmessianic status of Jewish law, each side may have viewed the rabbi's leave-taking in its own way. Given the rabbi's own statement on the last day of the formal disputation that the case for the prior advent of the messiah had not yet been made and that there was therefore no point in discussing the further agenda items, he may have felt with yet fuller justification that it would be pointless to discuss the status of Jewish law subsequent to the coming of the messiah when a convincing case for that advent had not yet been made.

Having confronted once more the divergence in our sources, let us again probe in greater depth the underlying realities reflected in both. Both sources agree that the public format was abandoned at some juncture. The Latin source is hazy on the details; the Hebrew account tells us that the suspension took place at the close of the fourth day of the proceedings. If the details afforded in the Hebrew report are accurate—and there is no reason to suspect these superficial details—then the request for suspension made at the opening of the fourth session was not altogether useless. While that session itself was not canceled, the argument advanced would seem to have had the desired impact. Both accounts agree that the public disputation was brought to a close, the Latin claiming that there was agreement to discuss the fourth agenda item in closed session and the Hebrew discerning in the royal action a pure and simple ending to the engagement. The Latin account's reference to a change of venue from public to private discussion would seem to indicate that the anxiety voiced by the rabbi over the impact of the debate on public opinion was in fact decisive. Concerned over the danger of such an impact, the king decided to end the public spectacle. The monarch's protective stance toward his Jews, which we have noted already and will see more fully in chapter 3, is very much in evidence.

What, in fact, have we gleaned from this lengthy analysis? First, a series of aspects of the Barcelona disputation have emerged with considerable clarity from these discordant sources: the engagement was initiated and controlled by the Christian camp, in particular, the Dominican missionizers; the Christian side was accorded an aggressive missionizing position, with the Jewish camp limited to responding to the Christian thrusts; the new stratagem of proving Christian truth from rabbinic sources further skewed the encounter away from an equal debate over religious principles into a missionizing effort in which only one side could emerge victorious, for nothing that the Jews might say could disprove Christian truth; finally, the basic agenda of items to be proved is broadly identifiable from both sources. All this has emerged reasonably from the two divergent sources. Beyond this area of agreement, there are areas of understandable disagreement: each camp saw its protagonist as victorious; more precisely, there is radical disagreement with respect to the success of the Jewish protagonist in deflecting the new Christian thrusts. From the Christian perspective, Rabbi Moses ben Nahman was ultimately incapable of warding off the new thrusts; from the Jewish perspective, he achieved brilliant success in his rebuttal. Finally, there are areas where each of the reports seems to go too far, to offer information or assessment that strains credulity. For the Latin account, this is particularly noticeable in the portrait of the ineptness of the rabbi, a portrait that cannot be decisively disproved but that seems much overdrawn. For the Jewish narrative, there seems to be considerable exaggeration in the depiction of the range and vigor of the rabbi's refutation. Nahmanides portrays himself making public pronouncements that are scarcely credible. In the process of undertaking this extensive analysis, we have—I hope—both reconstructed as faithfully as possible the Barcelona confrontation and, at the same time, honed the skills needed for working with radically divergent source materials.

3

The Aftermath of the Disputation:
Broad Perspectives

Our investigation of the disputation itself has shown that the two
extant sources are poles apart in their evaluation of the outcome
of the historic Barcelona encounter. While careful analysis has enabled us to identify elements of agreement in these divergent depictions and to suggest aspects of the portrayals that are clearly
exaggerated, there is no way to bridge the ultimate gap in assessment and surely no point in a modern nonpartisan observer's
attempting to award the victor's palm to one or the other side.
Declarations of victory and defeat were ultimately meaningful only
within the rival medieval camps. They were assertions meant for
internal consumption and were merely extensions of the larger disagreement, the disagreement over ultimate religious truth, with
Christians convinced of the truth of their religious heritage and
Jews of the truth of theirs. While enormously important for internal purposes, declarations of victory and defeat—like assertions of
religious truth—can have no real place within the common ground
of nonpartisan scholarship.[1]

   This is not to say, however, that the modern scholar must simply refrain from any assessment of events such as the Barcelona
disputation. There remains an area of assessment well within the
competence of impartial modern observers and indeed obligatory
for them. It is surely possible to probe beyond the broad declarations of outcome in a search for the subsequent behavioral implications of the event under study. That is to say, patterns of behavior
in the wake of an event such as the Barcelona disputation will reveal, from a different perspective, how it was viewed by the Christian and Jewish camps. Such patterns of behavior may belie the
public declarations of success and failure or they may strongly cor-
roborate them. By corroboration, I do not mean that they will provide proof that either the Christians or Jews won the debate; I

mean, rather, that they will indicate that the Christian or Jewish camp genuinely believed that it had emerged victorious. We must proceed to examine the post-1263 behaviors of the Christians and Jews of Catalonia to probe further the outcome of the engagement, as perceived in both groups.

Let us begin by projecting theoretically the potential outcomes from the perspectives of both sides. From the Christian vantage point, the hoped-for outcomes were the following:

1. a total Christian victory, with the Jews obviously convinced of the claims advanced by the Christian spokesman and convert-ing in numbers as a result. While this might have been seen as a theoretical possibility, it could hardly have been held forth as a realistic likelihood. The history of Jewish intransigence was too long and too well known to have allowed for real hopes of such dramatic results.

2. a considerable Christian victory, with the Jews not sufficiently convinced of the new Christian contentions to convert but yet incapable, in Dominican eyes, of sustaining an effective rebuttal to the new arguments. In this case, the Christian side would have been reinforced in its sense of the effectiveness of the new claims and would have surely redoubled its efforts to confront larger and larger numbers of Jews with these claims.

From the Jewish perspective, the hoped-for results were the following:

3. a total Jewish victory, meaning the uncovering of a fatal flaw in the new argumentation, acknowledged by the Dominicans, who would therefore abandon completely the new line of ar-gumentation. For the Jews, this would mean maximal achieve-ment, although it would not relieve them of all missionizing pressures; from the Dominican perspective, such an outcome, while disappointing, would at least have the virtue of ending any investment in a line of missionizing that would have ulti-mately proven worthless in any case. Better to know sooner rather than later.

4. a considerable Jewish victory, with the Dominicans not neces-sarily convinced of the failure of the new missionizing argumen-tation but with the Jews firm in their conviction that it had been

nullified. In this instance, the Jewish leadership would have been comforted in its sense that no real losses could be anticipated from the innovative efforts.

While these were the optimal goals from the perspectives of the Christian and Jewish sides, there was yet one more scenario, involving divergent assessments of the outcome of the encounter:

5. a Christian sense of considerable victory, leading to a commitment to repair shortcomings in the argumentation that might have been revealed and to press on with the missionizing endeavor, coupled with a Jewish sense of considerable victory, with a sure sense that the potential threat of the new missionizing argumentation had been blunted and a commitment to communicating the weaknesses of the argumentation and effective lines of rebuttal to fellow-Jews who might soon be exposed to the same thrusts.

We have already seen that both camps proclaimed victory. That the pattern of postdisputation activity might indicate a genuine conviction of success in each camp would not be shocking.

Unfortunately, materials that would enable us to track systematically postdisputation activities in each camp are not extensive. Nonetheless, I shall try to extract as much insight as possible from the minimal materials at our disposal.

Let us begin with the follow-up missionizing visit to the synagogue of Barcelona, well known from Nahmanides's absorbing account of it.[2] Interestingly, there is no reference to this missionizing visit in the Latin account or in any other Christian source. This missionizing visit was surely related to the public disputation, for it involved many of the key figures from the Christian camp, including the king, Friar Paul, and Friar Raymond of Penyafort. At the same time, it does not represent in any sense a continuation of the disputation itself. What is particularly striking is the absence of the new missionizing argumentation rooted in the utilization of Jewish sources. According to the Nahmanidean account, there were two missionizing sermons, one by King James and the other by Friar Raymond. Neither preacher was in a position to utilize the new approach of Friar Paul, and it seems highly likely that neither did. According to Rabbi Moses's extremely brief report, the king "preached extensively, saying that Jesus was the messiah."[3] While this was the central theme of the disputation, the key to the debate was the advancing of proof based on Jewish sources. Nahmanides offers no hint that the king continued that approach, nor is it much of a likelihood. Presentation of Friar Paul's argumentation required some level of expertise in rabbinic literature, which King James obviously lacked. While the rebuttal that Nahmanides attributes to himself (the brilliance of which we shall note)[4] tells us nothing of the precise argumentation advanced by the king, we are probably quite safe in assuming a traditional missionizing argument, in all likelihood based on standard biblical verses. Friar Raymond's sermon is presented in similarly sparse detail: "Subsequently Friar Raymond of Penyafort arose and preached on the matter of the Trinity. He said that it involves Wisdom, Will, and Power."[5] Here even the subject represents a departure from the disputation itself. The Jewish response portrayed by Nahmanides indicates clearly that the style of argumentation was traditional, involving philosophic-theological considerations but not the new-style argumentation based on Jewish sources. Thus, the public disputation may well have moved the Dominicans and the king to make their visit, but the visit shows none of the special signs of the new missionizing of Friar Paul.

The traditional quality of the argumentation used in the synagogue in no way represents repudiation of the new missionizing tack tested in the public disputation; it simply reflects a public follow-up to the disputation involving speakers incapable of presenting the new missionizing line. By contrast, the important legislation of late August 1263 shows direct continuation of the new argumentation, unabated Dominican support for Friar Paul and his new approach, and ongoing—albeit complex—royal support for this enterprise.

The registers of King James record three royal orders concerning further missionizing among the Jews. The first edict, dated August 26, is an order directed to a variety of royal officials.[6] This order is in no sense innovative. It is, in effect, a repetition of a much earlier decree, issued by the king in 1242. The enactment contains four provisions, three having to do with converts and one with preaching toward conversion. The three items regarding converts specify that there must be no interference with those wishing to convert, that they must be safeguarded in their property rights, and that they must be protected from any calumny on the part of their former coreligionists. Given the enactment of precisely these measures two decades earlier, it hardly seems warranted to see in these stipulations evidence of actual conversion stemming from the confrontation of July 1263. Again, had such conversions been effected, it is difficult to imagine that they would not have been triumphantly announced in the Latin protocol. What reenactment of these measures seems to reflect is ongoing commitment to missionizing, with specification of safeguards for those to be attracted to the faith.

The item regarding conversionary preaching indicates royal support for Dominican preaching among Jews and Muslims, who are to be forced by royal officials to present themselves for sermonizing. The only additional note in the 1263 document is specification of the possibility of fines for those Jews or Muslims unwilling to comply. To be sure, this legislation need not be seen as a direct outgrowth of the Barcelona disputation, since its antecedents go back twenty years and there is no specific mention of Friar Paul and the innovative missionizing argumentation. As in the case of the follow-up preaching in the synagogue of Barcelona, the best that we can say is that the Barcelona confrontation certainly shows no signs of dampening missionizing ardor and that, to the contrary, the debate seems to have strengthened the Dominican commitment to active and aggressive preaching.

The order dated August 29 introduces us fully into the ambience of the new missionizing personnel and argumentation.[7] This order is addressed directly to the Jews of Aragon, with no reference to the parallel circumstances of the Muslim population. The closing lines order royal officials to see to execution of the order imposed directly on the Jews. In this document, Friar Paul plays the central role of preacher among the king's Jews, and there is explicit reference to his new technique of proving Christian truth from Jewish sources. From this document, there can be no doubt as to ongoing Dominican support for the missionizing efforts of Friar Paul. This ongoing support indicates that the claims embodied in the Latin report in fact represent fairly accurately a Dominican sense of considerable achievement, reflected in the desire to pursue intensively the new argumentation. Such commitment on the part of the

Dominicans belies any notion of real recognition of the rabbi's triumph masked by mendacious depiction of a Christian victory. The Christian sense of achievement seems real, and Friar Paul was supported by both the Dominicans and the king in proceeding further in his missionizing efforts. It is worth noting that the king was sufficiently committed to the enterprise to pay the expenses involved. While the royal order specifies that the Jews must defray the friar's expenses, their costs were to be deducted eventually from the sums owed the royal treasury. Again, we are presented with the picture of a monarch genuinely devoted to the missionizing cause and willing to bear the costs of the preaching endeavor— within limits.

The third document in the series, that dated August 30, represents a significant and fascinating shift in royal stance.[8] This order is directed once more to royal officialdom, and it adds two important qualifications to the prior support for forced sermonizing among the Jews. The first, although important, turns out to be of lesser significance. It specifies that Jews are not to be forced out of their own quarter to hear missionizing sermons. A protection of considerable significance for the Jews of Aragon, it is far overshadowed by the second qualification, which in effect removes the element of force from the forced sermons. The point is made twice. The royal officials are first told that they must not force Jews outside the Jewish quarters for the purpose of hearing conversionist sermons; rather, "if any brother of the Preaching Brethren wishes to enter their Jewish quarter or their synagogues and there to preach to them, they must hear him, *if they wish* [italics mine]." This same point is reiterated by saying that Jews may not be forced outside the Jewish quarter for the purpose of hearing conversionist sermons, "nor [may they be caused] forcibly to hear in any location such a sermon."[9] I see no reason to interpret this royal shift as a repudiation of Friar Paul and his new missionizing argumentation. What has clearly happened, rather, is effective Jewish lobbying with the king to eliminate the burden of forced sermons. Once again, we see King James the Conqueror walking a fine line between support of ecclesiastical initiatives and concern for his important Jewish population. More important, we are left with a sense of an Aragonese Jewry that was far from depleted in its resources. It seems obvious that this shift in policy could only have been effected through intensive Jewish lobbying. We are entitled to conclude that the Jews had been successful both in suspending the danger-laden public confrontation and in stripping the preaching campaign of its all-important royal support. The shift represents a major achievement for the yet powerful Jewry of Aragon.

That this shift cannot be viewed as repudiation of Friar Paul and his new missionizing argumentation is clear, first of all, from the general nature of the change. There is no rebuke here to Friar Paul and his specific line of argumentation; the change has to do with the broader issue of exercise of royal force on behalf of missionizing interests. More important are the signs of continued activity by Friar Paul all through the decade subsequent to the Barcelona confrontation, continued support by the Dominican Order, and ongoing entrée into the important courts of western Europe. I have detailed this continued activity elsewhere, and there is no need to repeat that description here.[10] Important to our purposes is, again, the sense that the Latin account's portrait of Christian victory is in no way belied by the events that followed the end of the public debate.

There is, to be sure, one important sign of a measure of discomfort with Friar Paul's achievement, and that is the intensive effort invested in perfection of his new missionizing argumentation. As I have argued extensively elsewhere, the *Pugio Fidei* clearly represents a refinement of the missionizing argumentation innovated by Friar Paul.[11] To the extent that the need for refinement reflects dissatisfaction with Friar Paul's early efforts, then we may speak of a measure of repudiation. However, the investment in perfection of the new argumentation reveals much more satisfaction than dissatisfaction. Such an investment would have been unthinkable had Friar Paul been decisively shown up in the public debate. The readiness to invest considerable resources in the *Pugio Fidei* indicates much more support than disenchantment. The failures of Friar Paul were simply the normal shortcomings of most innovative systems, which often require considerable refinement before reaching their mature state. Indeed, we are justified in concluding that the Barcelona disputation achieved what we might designate a level of restrained success for the Christian side. While not breaking through Jewish defenses in a decisive way, the encounter provided enough evidence to its Dominican initiators to suggest that the new line of argumentation was promising and that further refinements would result in a highly effective vehicle for carrying the Christian message into the Jewish community. While the Latin report clearly overstates the level of discomfort on the Jewish side, it is not mendacious in conveying a sense of considerable Christian satisfaction.[12]

We have focused thus far on the results of the debate from the perspective of the Christian camp. Unfortunately, there is less material available for tracking the results in the Jewish camp. Again, we may begin by eliminating the extreme possibilities. Jewish leadership could surely be pleased that no significant movement of conversion developed during or after the disputation itself. However, it also had to be quite clear to these Jewish leaders that the new missionizing ardor had not been dampened and that the new missionizing argumentation had not been discredited. For all the vigor of Nahmanides's narrative report, at no point does he suggest either Dominican or royal disenchantment with Friar Paul. Given the continuation of the missionizing endeavor, Jewish efforts had to proceed in two major directions. The first was the exercise of political power to ward off the forced missionizing campaign. As we have seen, this effort was remarkably successful. The second effort lay in the intellectual-spiritual sphere and involved informing Jews of the effective lines of rebuttal developed by Rabbi Moses ben Nahman and convincing these Jews of their efficacy. It was for these purposes that Nahmanides composed his narrative report on the event. This report is so important and the techniques utilized in composing it so complex that it warrants a chapter in its own right. For the moment, let us simply observe that, just as the satisfaction articulated by the Christian camp is reflected in its subsequent activities, so too the satisfaction proclaimed by Nahmanides in his remarkable account is mirrored in the patterns of postdisputation activity in the Jewish community. There are no signs that the public postures represented a face-saving lie on either side.

The disputation was essentially a missionizing endeavor, and the critical postdisputation activities in both camps involved, above all, further proselytizing and further protective efforts against such proselytizing. Such an important and complex event as the Barcelona disputation inevitably, however, set in motion a series of related activities as well. The most important of these concerned allegations of offensiveness in rabbinic materials. Indeed, initial ecclesiastical awareness of rabbinic Judaism had sparked, back in the late 1230s and early 1240s, profound Church concern over the alleged offensiveness of talmudic teachings, serious investigation of the charges, and—in royal France at least—condemnation of the Talmud.[13] Scholars have taken a number of positions with respect to the relationship of condemnation of the Talmud, on the one hand, and exploitation of the Talmud for missionizing purposes, on the other. For some, such approaches are mutually exclusive, while for others they represent stages in ecclesiastical grappling with the realities of the Jews' rabbinic heritage. In fact, neither approach is correct. There is no inherent contradiction between condemnation of talmudic materials and exploitation of rabbinic teachings, nor need the two tendencies represent distinct phases in the Church's developing awareness of postbiblical Judaism.[14] The common denominator binding the two approaches is rabbinic material itself. Such material is, for the Church, religiously meaningless. It has no value for the Christian community, since it reflects the development of Judaism away from its original and true course. Stances toward this material could vary widely. On the one hand, given the growing inclination to control more rigorously patterns of thought in Christian society, ecclesiastical leadership—in particular, the Dominican Order—was constantly concerned with the possibility of offensive materials in the rabbinic corpus. On the other hand, the developing commitment to missionizing brought to the fore the conviction that this rabbinic corpus might serve a useful purpose in the proselytizing effort. Utilization of talmudic materials for missionizing purposes does not signify reverence for the rabbinic corpus and repudiation of the danger of offensiveness. It merely reflects a sense that, minimally, this religiously meaningless corpus contains material that might be exploited or that, maximally, this religiously meaningless corpus contains nuggets of insights that Jews might be brought to acknowledge. Even this latter, more positive formulation in no way results in an overall view of the rabbinic corpus as true or above reproach. That talmudic literature might, at one and the same time, contain occasional insight and reprehensible matter is by no means excluded by the missionizing argumentation. Thus, the fact that the public confrontation might entail in its wake a reopening of prior charges of offensive-ness is not surprising. Lengthy public discussion of talmudic ma-terials was likely to eventuate in airing of some materials that might raise once more the specter of offensiveness.

Once again, the royal registers provide us with interesting and valuable evidence of this ancillary result of the public confron-tation. The first document, dated August 28, is quite specific in its condemnation of one of the books of Maimonides's *Mishneh-Torah*.[15] This book, designated *Soffrim* but clearly *Sefer Shofetim*, was to be collected from the Jews and burned, on the grounds that it contained blasphemies against Jesus. In the Nahmanidean narra-tive, there is an interesting report on the discussion of Maimonides that inter alia gives us a better sense of the way in which the ancil-lary allegation of blasphemy might develop.[16] The passage begins with Friar Paul calling for Maimonides's *Sefer Shofetim* in order to prove from this highly respected Jewish sage the Jewish view that the messiah would die in normal human fashion, thereby proving, as it were, the human aspect of the messianic duality.[17] Nahman-ides, in a rebuke to Friar Paul's lack of learning, noted that the passage sought was not to be found in the said book of Mai-monides but acknowledged, as he had recurrently, the Jewish view of a human messiah, a view that he regularly espoused. He fur-ther reports that the book was brought to Friar Paul, and, as Nahmanides had indicated, the friar could not find the passage he sought. Once again, as he so often claims to have done, Nahman-ides pressed the issue further.

> I took the book from his hand and I said: "Listen to the words of the book which he has brought. I read to them from the beginning of the chapter: 'The king messiah will in the future arise for Israel, will rebuild the Temple, and will gather the dispersed of Israel.'"[18]

After describing an amusing interchange between one of the ob-servers and the king, Nahmanides depicts himself as having pro-ceeded to present in greater detail these key characteristics of the messiah—gathering the dispersed of Israel, rebuilding the Temple, and ruling over all the nations. He then claims to have stated pub-licly that Jesus did none of these. He portrays himself as conclud-ing with biblical predictions of the downfall of Israel's enemies, which he applied to Islam and Christendom. I have already raised questions as to the historicity of these claimed frontal assaults on

Christianity. Nonetheless, the purported exchange, whatever its precise contours might have been, does indicate nicely the way in which texts introduced into discussion might have been further elaborated, in the process bringing into Christian consciousness allegedly offensive materials. In one way or another, the passage in Maimonides's *Sefer Shofetim* which speaks of both Jesus and Muhammad as simply precursors for the true messiah came to Christian attention through the public discussion and eventuated in the royal order of burning.[19]

A day later, a more wide-ranging order was promulgated, an order that dealt not with one particular Jewish book but with the entire spectrum of rabbinic literature. This order was again a result of the concern with blasphemy, in this instance against both Jesus and Mary.[20] To obviate such blasphemy, a rather elaborate system of self-censorship was to be instituted. Jews were to investigate their own books and were, in addition, to have offensive passages pointed out to them by a commission consisting of Friar Paul, Friar Raymond of Penyafort, and Friar Arnold of Segarra (Friar Paul is clearly the key figure here). Such offensive passages were to be extirpated within a three-month period, never to be reinstated. With the conclusion of the three-month period, discovery of such offensive materials would result in the burning of the books and the imposition of a heavy fine.

Since there is a considerable body of information available on the prior assault on rabbinic literature, it is valuable to examine this new effort from a slightly broader perspective. It is interesting to note, first of all, the limited concern voiced here. The issue is blasphemy only, not the wide-ranging attack on rabbinic literature revealed in the data from the 1240s in northern France.[21] In both the command to burn *Sefer Shofetim* and the edict to censor the rest of rabbinic literature, the focus of Christian attention is on blasphemy, specifically, blasphemy against Jesus and Mary. Second, it is interesting to note the imposition of responsibility on the Jewish community itself. Whereas, in the northern European attack on the Talmud, rabbinic literature was confiscated and dealt with directly by the ecclesiastical authorities, it is clearly a milder stance to allow the books to remain in Jewish hands and to place responsibility for censorship on the Jews themselves. The involvement of Friar Paul and his associates is limited to bringing offending passages to the attention of the Jewish authorities; they are not put in a position of direct control. Finally, as I have shown elsewhere, the corrective steps to be taken where the offensiveness of rabbinic literature was established were in some dispute during the early outbreak of concern over this literature. What emerged in the late 1240s was an internal quarrel in Church circles over whether the proper procedure was destruction of the offending literature in its entirety or removal of only the offending passages. In effect, the central authorities of the papal court took the milder position, while the ecclesiastical authorities of northern France took the harsher stance.[22] King James in his edict of August 29 clearly espoused the milder view, permitting not only censorship but indeed self-censorship. To be sure, one book, Maimonides's *Sefer Shofetim*, was to be destroyed immediately, and Jewish books in which offending materials were not exorcised were eventually to share the same fate.

In early 1264, the Jews made a successful appeal with respect to the foregoing arrangements.[23] What they secured was clarification of the process. Rather than bearing essential responsibility for self-censorship, in the wake of which they might be fined heavily and punished by burning of their books, it was specified that the Jews would have offending materials pointed out to them, would have an opportunity to respond to the allegations, and only then might be held responsible for failure to take the necessary steps. The amelioration for the Jews was considerable. Whereas previously, direct Jewish responsibility for self-censorship might eventuate rather easily in subsequent charges, fines, and burnings, the new procedure meant that all allegations against Jewish books would have to be processed by a five-man commission, with the right of appeal. Only then would the threat of fine and burning take effect. Clearly, under these new arrangements, the likelihood of fines and burning of books was much reduced.

Ecclesiastical dissatisfaction with these arrangements is not surprising and is, in fact, reflected in papal letters of 1267 addressed to the episcopal leadership of Aragon and to King James himself.[24] While the precise details of an alternative system are not spelled out, the general emphasis is on the responsibility of the Jews to present all of their literature to a commission of Dominican and Franciscan friars, under the leadership once more of Friar Paul.

This commission would make the essential distinction between licit and illicit Hebrew writings. Again, the details are not spelled out, but the clear thrust is toward greater ecclesiastical control of the process. There is, however, no evidence that this more rigorously controlled system was put into effect.

Thus, the proceedings in Barcelona eventuated, not surprisingly, in more than missionizing effort and Jewish response. Along the way, rabbinic texts were discussed extensively, and, on occasion, objectionable material—from the Christian perspective—was uncovered. By now we are fully accustomed to the main lines of the royal response. On the one hand, the king of Aragon was sensitive to his duty as a Christian monarch and took steps to deal with the problem. On the other, he remained sensitive to the needs and desires of his Jewish subjects, framing his regulations in a manner that provided considerable protection and amelioration for these Jewish subjects and their books. Once again, I would argue that there is more involved here than royal goodwill. The overall sense that we have been gleaning is one of a Jewish community still very much in command of significant resources and still capable of lobbying effectively with its monarch.

The last—and related—element in the activities that followed in the wake of the disputation involved the Jewish protagonist, Rabbi Moses ben Nahman. The rabbi was called on to walk a fine line in his public presentation. Too forthright a presentation would bring down on him the wrath of the Christian authorities of both church and state; too weak a presentation would endanger the spiritual well-being of his fellow-Jews. Precisely how assertively to present his case was surely one of the major decisions facing the Jewish spokesman. To be sure, the latitude afforded him in this decision was severely limited both by the setting (he was speaking in the presence of both the ecclesiastical and secular leaders of Aragonese society) and by the clever ground rules imposed on the discussion (he was, in effect, limited to replying to Christian thrusts based on talmudic literature). There was yet a second juncture at which Nahmanides faced a decision as to the level of assertiveness, and that was when he committed himself to penning his narrative record of the encounter. I have suggested already that the Nahmanidean narrative is far from a stenographic account of the proceedings and that it includes both an understandable tendency to see

events from a Jewish perspective and some inclination toward embellishment. What we must now investigate with some care is the
nature of the subsequent attack on Nahmanides himself, attempting to discern accurately the focus of this attack.

This attack is known to us from two documents, one from the
royal register and one emanating from the papal chancery. The
royal document, dated April 12, 1265, depicts proceedings against
the rabbi of Gerona.[25] In these proceedings, complaints lodged by
Friar Paul, Friar Raymond of Penyafort, and Friar Arnold of Segarra were heard by an ecclesiastical tribunal. After the complaints
were heard, the king consulted with his ecclesiastical tribunal and
decided on a punishment of two years of exile for the rabbi and
burning of his book on the disputation. This punishment was unacceptable to the original complainants, and the king announced
in his letter that any future proceedings would only take place in
royal presence. In effect, all punishment was, for the time being,
suspended. The lengthy papal letter of Clement IV includes, inter
alia, reference to the proceedings against the Nahmanidean narrative, fulminating bitterly against the lack of proper punishment for
this insult to the Christian faith.[26]

Unfortunately, the picture that emerges from these two documents is not as detailed as it might have been. There are a number
of points that must be reconstructed painstakingly and with a
measure of uncertainty. The first issue is the timing of the Dominican complaint. Nowhere is this specified, although it is a matter
of some importance. The broad sense is that the royal document
of 1265 reflects accusations and proceedings that had been initiated
sometime early that year. It seems unlikely that the issue had
dragged on for a lengthy period before eliciting this royal statement. This sense of a complaint lodged sometime (approximately
a year and a half) after the event seems to be corroborated from
the prior sources. There is no reference to such a complaint in the
Latin protocol, in the spate of documents that were promulgated
in late August 1263, or in the Nahmanidean narrative itself. Both
the royal document and the papal letter highlight the Nahmanidean narrative, and it seems reasonable to conclude that the
appearance of this written report and its wide dissemination, emphasized in the papal missive, gave rise to discomfort in Dominican circles and to the attack on the rabbi of Gerona.

The dating of the complaint is an important point that leads us into the crucial issue, which is the precise nature of the complaint. Here the two documents diverge somewhat. The royal edict specifies that the Dominicans "asserted that he [the rabbi] had said certain things in defamation of our Lord and of the entire Catholic faith, and that he had made of them a book, of which he gave a copy to the bishop of Gerona."[27] Nahmanides is portrayed as claiming, in his defense, that he had been accorded the right of free speech by the king and Friar Raymond of Penyafort and that the book he had composed had been written at the request of the bishop of Gerona. The emphasis in the papal letter is somewhat different. There the focus is exclusively on the mendacious book composed by Nahmanides and widely disseminated. What are we to make of this inconsistency? In the first place, the importance of dating the complaint is now obvious. My proposal that the complaint was set in motion by appearance of the Nahmanidean narrative suggests that the issue was, in all likelihood, that written account. To substantiate this conclusion, we must examine more thoroughly the other alternative, that the complaint was lodged against Nahmanides's oral presentation at Barcelona. To do so, we must examine with some care an opening exchange reported by Nahmanides himself, identify instances of defamatory statements included by Nahmanides in his narrative, and attempt to envision more fully the realities of the confrontation.

At the very beginning of his narrative, Nahmanides depicts— colorfully as always—the opening stages of the disputation. After indicating that he was ordered by the king to dispute with Friar Paul, he claims conditional acceptance of the royal order.

Our lord the king commanded me to debate with Friar Paul in his palace, in his presence and that of his advisors, in Barcelona.

I responded and said: "I shall do according to the dictate of my lord the king, if you give me permission to speak as I will. I request in this regard the permission of the king and the permission of Friar Raymond of Penyafort and is associates who are here."

Friar Raymond of Penyafort replied: "So long as you do not speak deprecatingly."

I said to them: "I do not wish to run afoul of your laws in this matter. But I must speak freely with respect to the debate, just as you speak freely. I have the good sense to speak properly with respect to the debate, as you have said, but it must be according to my will."

They all gave me permission to speak freely.[28]

What is reflected here? The rabbi demands the right to speak freely; Friar Raymond imposes the condition that such free speech not include deprecation of Christianity; the rabbi acknowledges the existence of Christian "laws in this matter," which must surely refer to his awareness of the danger of blasphemy; the rabbi assures his "good sense to speak properly" but insists that his speaking must be "according to my will." Again a charming depiction but one that is ultimately problematic, for there is no real middle ground between observing the rules against blasphemy, of which the rabbi was clearly aware, and speaking freely, at least as reflected in the Nahmanidean narrative.

Let us identify in detail those statements reported in the written narrative which would have been clearly perceived as objectionable from the Christian perspective had Nahmanides uttered them publicly as he claims to have done. They include the following:[29]

1. a section of Nahmanides's lengthy speech at the opening of the second day of the proceedings, in which the rabbi reacts to Friar Paul's interpretation of the annulment of Adam's sin in messianic times as a reference to salvation from hell. The rabbi responds contemptuously that this interpretation reminds him of the folk proverb that "he who wishes to lie should distance his witnesses," that is, that the Christian doctrine is clearly untrue but cannot be rebutted because it establishes circumstances that cannot be checked;[30]
2. again in the same lengthy speech, the rabbi's scathing indictment of the Christian doctrine of Incarnation, which was quoted directly in the previous chapter;[31]
3. still in that same address, Rabbi Moses's full statement denying Jesus' fulfillment of messianic predictions and, in the process, attacking Christianity for its bellicosity and moral laxity;[32]
4. Nahmanides's rebuttal of the first Christian thrust of the second day of the proceedings, which was based on rabbinic commentary to Is. 52:13. In the course of his rebuttal, the rabbi extols

the future achievements of the messiah who will exceed all other great figures of Jewish history. According to the rabbi, "he will come and order the pope and all the kings of the nations in the name of God: 'Send forth my people that they might worship me.' He will perform many great signs and wonders among them and will in no way fear them. He will remain in their city of Rome until he destroys it."[33]

5. the closing item in the brief depiction of the exchanges on Maimonides during the third day of the proceedings, noted above, in which Nahmanides explains the punishments to be delivered on Israel's enemies as set forth in Deut. 30:7 as a direct reference to Christendom and to the world of Islam.[34]

Quite clearly, the rabbi's notion of speaking freely and the friar's insistence on nonoffensiveness clash dramatically in these five statements. They exhibit absolute freedom of speech, not any limitation based on offensiveness or any reflection of the rabbi's "good sense to speak properly." In the clash between the dangers associated with public blasphemy and the rabbinic right of freedom of speech, I can only conclude that the latter must surely have given way before the former. Again, the entire debate was structured in such a way as to obviate any frontal assaults on Christianity, further reducing the likelihood of such public utterances.

Now let us pursue the matter a step further. If Nahmanides had said such things publicly, what might have been the response? To posit that Friar Raymond of Penyafort, the other ecclesiastical leaders present, and the king of Aragon would have permitted such statements to be made publicly, would have let the matter lie for a year and a half, and then would have proceeded to prosecute the rabbi for uttering statements through which they had sat silently simply makes no sense. The same king who prohibited Nahmanides from taking the initiative in posing questions, instead of merely responding to Christian thrusts, would surely have stepped in—indeed, would have been forced to step in—to impose limits and sanctions on a rabbi making such direct assaults on the Christian faith.[35] It seems likely that latitude of speech was, in fact, discussed at the outset, for Nahmanides is cited in the royal document of 1265 as making reference to recognition of his rights.[36] Whatever rights might have been granted him, however, could

surely not have included the freedom to make the kinds of statements we have noted. Even if the offending statements were
milder than those depicted in the Nahmanidean narrative, the notion of subsequent prosecution for statements of whatever kind
made in the presence of distinguished ecclesiastical and political
leaders and only subsequently found offensive is similarly problematic. The existence of a written Christian account of the proceedings, penned not long after their completion, adds further
weight to the argument that Nahmanides could not have uttered
the blasphemies he himself reports. It is unthinkable that the Latin
account I have cited so frequently could have been written without
highlighting such blasphemies, had they actually been uttered. We
recall that in this Latin account, Nahmanides is upbraided for his
stance on rabbinic teachings. Had he made the statements that he
attributes to himself about Christianity, they could surely not have
been passed over in silence by the author of the Christian account
of the disputation.

Thus, it seems to me that the only way in which the subsequent
efforts at prosecution of Nahmanides can be understood is to follow the lead of the papal document and see the heart of the
problem in the publication of the rabbi's report. It is, I suggest, the
written account and the written report of statements allegedly
made in the public forum that occasioned an immediate—rather
than a delayed—outcry by the Dominicans. Suggesting the written
report as the cause of the judicial prosecution of Nahmanides removes all the serious problems we have encountered. The embellishments introduced by Nahmanides—the important purposes of
which we shall discuss in chapter 4—were the source of clerical
agitation.

One more problem emerges from the royal document with respect to this issue, and that is the Nahmanidean claim that his narrative was written at the expressed request of the bishop of
Gerona. While it is not at all clear what the bishop of Gerona might
want with a Jewish report on the Barcelona proceedings, such a
request cannot be ruled out. That the Hebrew narrative we possess
is the report made for the bishop or a Hebrew translation of that
report is most unlikely. Careful examination of the Nahmanidean
narrative, which we shall undertake in chapter 4, reveals it to be
a brilliantly crafted work, clearly meant for a Jewish audience. That

this was the document written for the bishop of Gerona, however friendly he might have been to the rabbi, is untenable. It seems to me likely that a report for the bishop was written by the rabbi, but it could not have been the narrative that we now possess.

Let me make a summary statement. The rabbi was, I suggest, much constrained in his public pronouncements, which, in fact, aroused no ire in either ecclesiastical or political circles. The onset of concern coincided with his publication of a written record of the Barcelona proceedings. While the rabbi may have composed a report for the bishop of Gerona, the Hebrew version that we now possess was composed for the needs of the Jewish community, as he saw those needs, and was forthright and outspoken. It was this version, which clerics like Friar Paul could read along with the Jews, that set in motion the cycle of prosecution that is reflected in both the royal and papal documentation. This leaves us with the further question of why the rabbi of Gerona was willing to write such an outspoken and defamatory report, although surely fully aware of the likelihood that it would be read by Christian hebraists like Friar Paul, as indeed it was. The only answer I can supply is that Nahmanides was deeply convinced of the need for such a work and retained some confidence in the capacity of Jewish leverage to protect him, as it eventually did. Whatever the difficulty in understanding his composition of such a potentially dangerous narrative, the problem remains confined to his own decision making. The notion that he might have delivered some of these scathing indictments publicly raises problems that go beyond the rabbi himself. As I have argued, more problematic than the rabbi's outspokenness would be the silence of his clerical and secular listeners, a silence that can simply not be reasonably posited. Writing attacks that might have placed him in jeopardy is not easy to understand; such a step can at least be comprehended as flowing from the rabbi's sense of the urgency of the matter.

Our final question, which I shall not be able to answer, concerns the relation of this prosecution to the eventual emigration of Nahmanides from Aragon and his journey to the Holy Land. While it is generally agreed that Dominican prosecution of the aged rabbi brought about his leaving for the Land of Israel, Baer already noted that there was no necessary connection between the two.[37] Such a connection is entirely feasible, but our present documentation does not substantiate it. As we have already seen, the royal document ends on a note of protection for the rabbi. His punishment of two years of exile had been refused by the Dominican plaintiffs. The king ended his letter by emphasizing that all future proceedings must involve him, thereby affording the rabbi excellent protection. There is no evidence of any direct impact to the papal complaint. So far as we know, given the present state of documentation, no further action was taken. This means that the rabbi's decision for emigration could have been the result of the discomfort occasioned by the Dominican efforts or, alternatively, of spiritual factors that had nothing to do with his involvement in the Barcelona debate. Unfortunately, the meager personal materials penned by Nahmanides in the course of his settlement in the Holy Land afford no assistance in clarifying this matter.[38] For the moment, anyway, the reasons behind this important decision must remain obscure.

A closing word is in order. Both sides clearly saw the outcome of the disputation as favorable to their interests. Both the Christians and the Jews involved pursued their efforts assiduously, based on a positive assessment of what had been achieved in the public confrontation. Almost inevitably, the public engagement raised in its wake other issues as well, in particular, a renewal of the charge of blasphemy against rabbinic literature. Less inevitably, the publication by Nahmanides of his written Hebrew account of the proceedings gave rise to a clamor among the Dominicans and eventuated in putting the rabbi on trial as well. In all three cases—Dominican pursuit of the missionizing effort, Dominican efforts at censoring rabbinic literature, and Dominican prosecution of Rabbi Moses ben Nahman—the king of Aragon found himself caught between the demands of the friars and the pressures generated by his Jewish subjects. Surprisingly, the Jews did fairly well, eliciting from the monarch significant safeguards against the renewed forced preaching, protection against excessive interference with their talmudic texts, and even a measure of safety for the aged rabbi of Gerona. The Jewish community is revealed as a potent political force, still capable of marshaling considerable leverage and clout. While I have mentioned along the way the Nahmanidean narrative as part of the aftermath of the public disputation, it is so significant that it warrants separate discussion.

4

The Narrative Account of
Rabbi Moses ben Nahman

The Barcelona disputation, as we have seen, was initiated, organized, and controlled by the Christian side, more particularly, by key figures in the Dominican Order. Likewise, in the wake of the disputation, it was the Christian side that had the power to set in motion a series of subsequent activities. Our comments thus far on the Jewish side of the postdisputation activities have been minimal, confined to indications of lack of conversion among the Jews of Catalonia and reflections of successful Jewish lobbying in the royal court. It is now time to discuss in greater detail the most important of the Jewish activities undertaken in the wake of the public debate, namely, the writing of the narrative record of the encounter by the Jewish protagonist, Rabbi Moses ben Nahman of Gerona. We must examine the purposes, strategies, and achievements of the rabbi of Gerona in penning his narrative. As was true in the disputation itself, the Jewish side had at its disposal limited resources. Once again, for the Jews, it was the intelligent marshaling of minimal resources, particularly resources of the mind, that would spell the difference between successful resistance to aggressive Christian pressures and weakened responses that might jeopardize the material and physical health of Catalonian—and, more broadly, Iberian—Jewry.

During the confrontation, it fell to the rabbi of Gerona to take the lead in fending off the thrusts of the new Christian missionizing. As we have already seen, this involved two distinctly different efforts: to discourage the Christian side from continuing its innovative assault and to reassure the Jewish side that the new assault was of no consequence. In the first effort, Rabbi Moses was surely not successful. While he did effectively reveal shortcomings in the new argumentation, he in no way derailed the missionizing endeavor. We have already examined evidence for the continuation of the new missionizing, along with a series of further activities. In contrast, both the Christian and the Jewish records suggest that the rabbi was quite successful in reassuring his fellow-Jews during the Barcelona discussion, for neither suggests any conversion whatsoever during the course of the confrontation.

With the close of the disputation, the rabbi's responsibilities did not come to an end. He was left with the burden of providing his fellow-Jews with requisite guidance for continued rejection of the new Christian missionizing. Rabbi Moses might have chosen any one of a number of literary formats in which to couch this ongoing guidance. For reasons I shall seek to lay bare, he selected the format of a narrative record, opting to illuminate his coreligionists through an extensive running report on the disputation. Through the medium of this narrative account, he was able to depict at length the new Christian claims and reasonable Jewish rebuttals. As we shall see, the narrative format allowed him to do much more. His account is, I shall argue, a literary tour de force, a masterpiece of Jewish polemical literature.[1]

Rabbi Moses ben Nahman surely did not undertake his account of the Barcelona disputation out of a concern for simply providing an objective record of the event. There was little such concern in evidence during the Middle Ages. More often than not, medieval accounts of contemporary events were occasioned by a sense of the importance of the events and the implicit message they bore.[2] On occasion, this led to narration that was highly stereotyped and fanciful, with the message introduced directly and pointedly;[3] on occasion, medieval chroniclers attempted to be more or less accurate in reportage, leaving the events to speak for themselves.[4]

In the case of Nahmanides's account of the Barcelona disputation, the situation is a bit unusual. The event itself involved none of the standard features that normally produced exciting and dynamic medieval Jewish narrative—violent persecution, remarkable heroism, divine intervention.[5] Why then did the rabbi of Gerona elect to inform his coreligionists of the Barcelona encounter through the medium of an unusual narrative? The narrative format offered Nahmanides three advantages, each of which was considerable. In the first place, the narrative format enhanced the readability of his account. Involved in the Barcelona disputation were claims and counterclaims that held some intrinsic interest for many Jewish readers but that remained, nonetheless, relatively abstract and theoretical. A topical presentation of these claims and counterclaims would have had some appeal to Jewish readers; a lively depiction of the give-and-take of the public encounter promised far greater attraction to those whom Rabbi Moses sought to instruct. The Nahmanidean tale was intended to appeal to a broader audience than a drier catalog of Christian contentions and Jewish rebuttals could have. Second, the narrative format was particularly well adapted for highlighting the thrust and parry of the encounter. Since the key was Christian assertion and Jewish response, the narrative format lent itself smoothly and comfortably to providing both the details of the interchanges and some feeling for the movement back and forth. Finally, and perhaps most significantly, the narrative format provided a setting of drama and resolution; it afforded the possibility of transforming an intellectual encounter into a compelling event, replete with suspense, tension, and—most important—resolution. Through the format of the tale well told, the Jewish reader who might not follow every nuance of the argumentation would know at the end that his side emerged victorious. In constructing a work of public edification, this was a considerable advantage. Nahmanides's message of intellectual victory would take on concrete, human dimensions.

Contemporary stances toward medieval narrative run a wide range. On one extreme, modern historians have often treated medieval narrative accounts as thoroughly factual depictions of the events portrayed. Thus, for example, recent biographies of Rabbi Moses ben Nahman regularly devote a full chapter to the Barcelona confrontation, utilizing Nahmanides's report as a stenographic account of the proceedings.[6] At the other extreme, contemporary researchers, particularly literary theorists, have raised the most profound questions concerning the underlying epistemological and aesthetic assumptions that govern and control the writing of history by both premoderns and moderns.[7] The stance of this analysis lies somewhere between these two extremes. On the one hand, I reject the approach that takes the Nahmanidean account as a stenographic report.[8] Even a cursory look at the text indicates that it cannot be viewed as a thorough account of the confrontation. The narrative is far too short for that; the reportage on the

Christian thrusts is far too restricted; the unfolding of events is far too neat. The Nahmanidean narrative is clearly a carefully crafted record aimed at creating a certain set of impressions in the minds of its readers.[9] On the other hand, while I am concerned with the crafting of the account by Rabbi Moses, I have not been moved to attempt an investigation of the fundamental epistemological and aesthetic assumptions of the thirteenth-century author. While these assumptions could surely be gleaned from careful study, such has not been my concern. I begin with the assertion that this valuable and highly popular account is a literary masterpiece, an inspired piece of narration that is carefully contrived to arouse interest, to convince readers of the veracity of the author's depiction of the event, to provide the projected Jewish audience with a clear sense of the new missionizing thrusts and, more important, of persuasive lines of rebuttal, and, in a more general way, to assure Jewish readers of the fundamental errors of Christianity and the undeniable truths of Jewish tradition. The purpose of this investigation is to identify the techniques through which the interest of the reader is aroused, the confidence of the reader is won, and the Jewish convictions of the reader are reinforced. We shall have to question, at a later point, the extent to which narrative shaping was effected at the expense of objective reportage.

The first goal of Rabbi Moses ben Nahman was surely to win the attention of his readers, and this he did brilliantly.[10] In part, Nahmanides simply capitalized on the unusual circumstances of the Barcelona confrontation. As we have seen, the disputation took place in the presence of a galaxy of notables, and Nahmanides was careful to portray these unusual circumstances, both for their intrinsic color and for the tension they generated. In his depiction of the proceedings on the second and fourth days of the encounter, Rabbi Moses includes a full description of the large and varied audience assembled for the occasion.[11] The setting alone made for considerable drama and audience interest. When placed side by side with the usual polemical dialogue texts, the narrative advantage enjoyed by Nahmanides is clear.[12] Even Judah ha-Levi's fictionalized narrative of a discussion held with the king of the Khazars lacks the inherent drama and powerful attraction of the Nahmanidean account.[13] The only medieval Hebrew narrative that can compare with Rabbi Moses's for the éclat of the setting is the account of Rabbi Yehiel's defense of the Talmud before a distinguished Paris audience in 1240. It must be noted that the narrative skill of the author of this latter report did not match that of Nahmanides.[14]

Nahmanides did far more, however, than simply capitalize on the inherent splendor and drama of the Barcelona circumstances. He augmented the tension through the details of his narration. The entire account is flavored by the sense of the Jewish spokesman caught, as it were, between the Scylla of offending his distinguished Christian audience through excessive assertiveness and aggressiveness and the Charybdis of failing to defend the Jewish position with sufficient verve, thereby leading to serious spiritual damage to his community. The threat of offensive behavior is highlighted early on and maintained throughout. The convocation was a splendid one which carried with it considerable danger. The reader is drawn into the account through the tension generated by the potential for disaster. We have already analyzed in some detail Nahmanides's report of his demand for freedom of expression, the limitation imposed by Friar Raymond of Penyafort, and Nahmanides's response. What this interchange does is suggest to the reader immediately some of the dangers associated with the debate.[15] The ominousness of the circumstances is reinforced by Nahmanides's report of the opening exchanges of the fourth day of the encounter, which we have already noted. On that day, Nahmanides purportedly sought to bring a halt to the proceedings, claiming to the king that he had been advised by a number of Christian observers that the proceedings were fraught with danger for the Jews, that, in effect, the rabbi was doing harm by speaking out in public in opposition to the Christian faith.[16] All of this surrounds the debate with an air of imminent danger. Indeed, the circumstances were most threatening. There was more than a little chance of seriously offending a public gathering of distinguished Christian lay and clerical leaders.[17] There was, to be sure, a second danger as well—one not explicitly noted by Nahmanides but implicit throughout. That was the danger of inadequate rebuttal of the new Christian thrust, resulting in a dangerous setback for the community Rabbi Moses represented. The twin dangers and the need for a carefully balanced posture give the Nahmanidean report its dramatic tension. The Ramban as author conveys this sense of dilemma superbly to his readers, thereby augmenting the excitement of his narrative and its audience appeal.

The air of drama and suspense that characterizes the narrative in its entirety is continued into the individual exchanges as well. Long before Rabbi Moses of Gerona, Jews, Christians, and Muslims had discovered the literary advantages in conveying polemical argumentation in dialogue format. This format held out a number of advantages, one of which was the simple pleasure of an intellectual joust. Abstract and theoretical issues were enlivened with some of the excitement of an athletic contest: "he thrust; then I parried; he followed up; then I broke through." The liveliness of such exchanges made dialogue the preferred literary genre for popularly oriented polemical materials. Nahmanides was surely well aware of this tradition, but he brought the utilization of the dialogue format for dramatic purposes to unusual heights. Particularly striking are the lengthy exchanges, in which thrust and parry are extensive.

Let us note a few instances of this effective narrative technique. The very first exchange catches the reader up into the excitement of the intellectual joust.[18] Friar Paul begins by citing Gen. 49:10, one of the verses cited most commonly in Christian-Jewish polemical debate. He suggests in a straightforward manner that the verse speaks of Jewish political authority conferred on Judah until the messiah comes. Since such political authority is no longer in evidence, the obvious inference is that the messiah has surely come. One can almost imagine the Jewish reader relaxing, out of a sense that Friar Paul represents no new challenge at all.[19] Nahmanides provides his readers with a traditional Jewish response to this time-worn Christian challenge, arguing that the verse does not simplistically confer political authority on the tribe of Judah until the coming of the messiah. Rather, it indicates that Judah will be the sole legitimate political authority until the coming of the messiah, although that political authority will not necessarily be exercised in unbroken fashion. Indeed, Nahmanides argues, historical evidence indicates clearly a series of suspensions of political authority in earlier periods. Thus, the present suspension of political authority in no way proves that the messiah has already come. This comforting give-and-take is disrupted by Friar Paul's introduction of rabbinic materials that, he claims, prove that Jewish political authority had in fact never been suspended in earlier times. Rabbinic exegesis of Gen. 49:10 indicates that the rabbis understood the authority of the exilarchs and the patriarchs to flow from the Davidic promise. Thus, Nahmanides's claim of prior suspensions is incorrect, and the present-day lack of Jewish political authority—including that of the exilarchs and the patriarchs—indicates incontestably that the messiah has already come. At this point, it becomes necessary for Nahmanides to take a new tack in rebutting Friar Paul. What I wish to emphasize here is the dramatic quality of the narrative—seemingly traditional Christian thrust, traditional Jewish reply, introduction of rabbinic material that undoes the traditional Jewish gambit, and the need for a new defensive tack by the Jewish spokesman. In his account, Rabbi Moses has provided a considerable measure of drama and excitement by emphasizing the series of claims and counterclaims.

Let us note one more striking instance of the same narrative technique.[20] On the last day of the proceedings, after the lengthy discussion of whether to continue or to suspend the proceedings, Friar Paul, arguing for the divinity of the messiah, introduced yet another verse long cited in Christian-Jewish argumentation, Ps. 110:1: "The Lord said to my lord, 'Sit at my right hand, while I make your enemies your footstool.'" Friar Paul draws from this verse a double conclusion:

> Who is it that King David would address as "my lord," except for the divinity? And how could a human being sit at the right hand of God?[21]

To heighten the dramatic quality of the discussion, the king is made to interject a comment, based on his own personal experience.

> He asks well. For if the messiah were totally human, actually from the seed of David, David would not address him as "my lord." If I had a son or grandson from my seed, even were he to rule over the entire world, I would not address him as "my lord." Rather, I would wish that he address me as "my lord" and that he kiss my hand.[22]

Rabbi Moses depicts himself as turning scornfully on Friar Paul.

> Are you the wise Jew who discovered this insight and apostasized as a result? And are you the one who told the king to gather before you the sages of the Jews so that you could debate with them over these insights that you discovered? Have we not heard this

claim heretofore? Indeed, there is neither a priest nor an infant who does not pose this difficulty to the Jews. This question is most antiquated![23]

According to Nahmanides, the king insisted that he respond, nonetheless, which he did—in highly traditional fashion. The heart of Nahmanides's response lay in arguing that, while written by David, this psalm was composed for the Levites, and the reference to "my lord" was meant to be uttered by them and to refer to King David. Again, at precisely this juncture, Friar Paul introduces his rabbinic text, which, he claims, indicates that the rabbis understood "my lord" to refer unequivocally to the messiah. Once again, rather than simply introducing the reader straightaway to the rabbinic source, Nahmanides takes the circuitous course of thrust and parry, in the process augmenting the drama and interest of his narrative. In this instance, he goes so far as to castigate Friar Paul for introducing an antiquated argument, a charge that he himself undoes by depicting the innovative turn that the friar's case took in fairly short order. The reader has once more been given a sense of give-and-take that enhances considerably the excitement of the narrative.

For the purposes of dramatic enhancement, Nahmanides often extends the give-and-take by introducing additional participants in the discussion. Let us note briefly a telling example. In the first interchange, based on Gen. 49:10 and its rabbinic interpretation, Nahmanides builds an extensive case for understanding the verse as implying legitimate royal rights accorded to the tribe of Judah, without necessitating unbroken political power actually exercised by a member of the tribe of Judah.[24] At the conclusion of his full statement of this view, he has a third figure enter the fray.

> Then Friar Peter of Genoa responded: "This is correct. For Scripture says only that it [political authority] would not be annulled totally. However, it would be possible to have an interruption to it [i.e., to the exercise of political power by the tribe of Judah], i.e., *vacare* in Latin."
>
> I said to the king: "Behold Friar Peter has decided the matter according to my view."
>
> Friar Peter said: "I have not decided the matter. For the seventy years of Babylonia [Babylonian exile] constitute a small time. There were still many who recalled the First Temple, as is written in the book of Ezra. This [such a brief time span] may be called interrup-

tion, which is *vacare* in Latin. However, now when you have remained for a thousand years or more [without political authority],
it is complete abrogation."
I said: "Now you have retracted. There is no abrogation in the case
of something that will be renewed, and there is no distinction in the
words of the prophet [i.e., Jacob] between many [years] and few
[years]."[25]

What has happened here is that the drama of the narrative has
been embellished by the introduction of yet another figure, a technique that is utilized recurrently throughout the account.

Thus, the first goal of Nahmanides in the construction of his
narrative was admirably achieved. He was successful in fashioning
an account that was and remains most appealing to the reader.
This was achieved by highlighting the inherent splendor and the
concomitant dangers of the encounter and, yet more important, by
emphasizing the tension and drama of the encounter in its totality and in the individual exchanges. The net result is an account
that, first of all, rivets the reader's attention. At the same time, by
resolving the individual exchanges and the total confrontation in
a manner satisfactory to the Jewish side, Nahmanides begins,
through the medium of his tale, to reassure his Jewish readers of
the victory of their spokesman and hence of the underlying truth
of their religious vision.[26]

In order that the author's case be properly received and his reassurance be properly assimilated, it was, of course, important that
the reader, in addition to being attracted to the account, be convinced of its veracity. The techniques adopted by Nahmanides for
assuring his audience of the facticity of his report are varied, in
some instances obvious and in other instances rather subtle. The
most obvious is the first-person auctorial stance. From the opening words of the account—"Our lord the king commanded me"—
through the closing—"I left him [the king] with great affection"—
the central figure, Nahmanides, speaks directly to the reader of his
own personal experiences. There is the overwhelming sense of a
powerful and clearheaded personality who is the transmitter of the
information provided in this record. To buttress the sense of reliability derived from the first-person depiction, the author provides
an explicit statement, at the close of his account of the four days
of debate, of its utter veracity.

This is the matter of the disputations in their entirety [a reference
to the four encounters]. I have changed nothing consciously with
regard to them.[27]

While the notion of changing nothing consciously can, on reflection, surely not mean that the record is stenographic—four days
of debate could certainly not be condensed into the Nahmanidean
account—what the author is telling us is that he has reproduced
the essentials faithfully and that his narrative is to be trusted. In
addition, the length of the report and its copious detail are meant
to assure the reader of its trustworthiness, and indeed they do
successfully convey such a sense. While not a stenographic report,
the Nahmanidean account is sufficiently long and detailed to be
convincing.

Less obvious is the impact of the narrative format itself. I have
suggested above that Nahmanides chose the narrative style in
order, first of all, to attract the interest of his readers, which he
achieved brilliantly. Beyond that, the narrative format operated
subtly to reinforce the sense of verisimilitude that he earnestly
sought. Narration implies the removal of an interposed inter-
mediary. While a résumé or an analysis of such a public event
would serve to highlight the persona of the author of the résumé
or analysis, narration suggests, by contrast, a simple report of
the event, stripped of all interpretation. An interesting sentence in
the Loeb study of the Barcelona encounter alerts us to the impression of verisimilitude that the narrative format produces: "A
moins d'avoir un sténographe ou un phonographe à sa disposi-
tion, il était impossible de faire un rapport plus exact."[28] In late-
twentieth-century parlance, we might amend that to read: in the
absence of a videorecorder, it would be impossible to produce a
more exact depiction. Indeed, in many ways, for the pre-phono-
graph and pre-videorecorder age, the narrative (and by extension,
the realistic novel) was the most precise recording instrument
available. Contemporary literary analysis warns us of the misleading qualities of videorecordings, still photographs, audiorecord-
ings, purportedly realistic novels, and first-person narrations.
Nonetheless, Nahmanides's choice of the narrative format—indeed, the first-person narrative format—won for his account a high
degree of verisimilitude.[29]

The credibility of the Nahmanidean narrative was profoundly enhanced by its scrupulous avoidance of stock figures and ex machina devices. The tone of the tale is realistic throughout. The fact that the king is not depicted in broad folkloristic strokes, despite a long Jewish tradition of such depictions, alerts the reader to the seriousness of purpose in the work. Perhaps more important, the ambiguity of the king's posture—as depicted by Nahmanides—is even more useful. The determination of the king to support the Dominican effort is patent throughout; at the same time, the author claims the king's unremitting friendship as well. This ambiguity suggests an author who was above rearranging his account for the sake of consistency, an author who was committed to telling the truth, even though it pointed to his honored monarch as staunchly supportive of the deleterious new missionizing program. Perhaps most striking is the author's portrait of himself. While there is, to be sure, nothing negative in this portrait, Nahmanides does acknowledge the limitations that continually impinged on him: he was constrained to debate, he was forced to work within a constricting set of rules, he was supported only in limited fashion by the monarch whom he honored and on whom he in many ways depended. The openness with which the difficulties of his position are acknowledged serves to reinforce the reader's sense of the veracity of the account. There is no simple way out of the difficult position into which the Jews had been forced; no unrealistic device is introduced to extricate the Jews from their problematic situation or to overturn their difficult circumstances. All of this "realism" greatly enhances the sense that Nahmanides clearly wished to create of a detailed, responsible, and trustworthy account of the proceedings at Barcelona.

The subtlest of the techniques employed to reinforce the sense of verisimilitude is the adoption of an unusual and highly effective language style. Study of the various language styles adopted in the divergent genres of medieval Hebrew literature is yet in its infancy.[30] It is useful, therefore, to gain some sense of the issue by turning to a different period of Hebrew writing in which such analysis is already more fully developed. In his important study of the emergence of the modern Hebrew novel, the critic Robert Alter devotes considerable attention to the language problem involved in creating the illusion of realism and to the linguistic techniques employed by a variety of late-nineteenth- and early-twentieth-century writers of Hebrew fiction. Alter's emphasis on the relation of the illusion of verisimilitude to the language style utilized (or in some instances created) alerts us to the unusual qualities of the Hebrew style employed by Nahmanides in his narrative—unusual with respect to the rest of the corpus of his own writing and to parallel writings by other medieval Jewish authors.[31]

My preliminary remarks on Nahmanides have emphasized, in accord with the general consensus, the multifaceted nature of his creativity.[32] To this broad observation we might now add that in the diverse genres in which he created, the Ramban utilized a language style appropriate to the genre. Talmudic novellae, halakhic treatises, biblical commentary, homiletic exhortations, wide-ranging epistles, poetry—for all these diverse formats, Nahmanides used the appropriate Hebrew idiom. For the creation of his Barcelona narrative, he wrote in yet a different style, one characterized by simplicity, directness, and lack of embellishment. The sentences of his Hebrew account are relatively short and to the point. The vocabulary is fairly limited and straightforward. While the author is a master of the Hebrew lexicon, he clearly chooses to limit the range of his vocabulary to reinforce the sense of direct and down-to-earth depiction. The most common temptation of medieval Hebrew writing—the introduction of bombastic rhetoric, designed to highlight the author's knowledge and skills—is rigorously eschewed. The result is a style that is spare and straightforward, a style that strongly enhances the drive to create a sense of reliable and unmediated storytelling.[33] We might indicate in passing that Septimus's argument, noted earlier, for the Andalusian impact on Nahmanides is reinforced by the diversity of language styles just noted and by the facility of Nahmanides in moving from style to style. Language facility was, after all, one of the highly prized achievements of Andalusian Jewish culture.[34]

Indeed, when compared with the narrative style utilized by a number of major medieval Jewish narrators, Nahmanides's direct and convincing style stands out. When we turn, for example, to the near-contemporary Hebrew account of the Paris condemnation of the Talmud, we are immediately struck by the difference in language style. The high-blown rhetoric of this Paris narrative alerts the reader instantly to the intrusion of the author and to the strong possibility of significant exaggeration in the account. Through the rhetorical flourishes, the author intrudes himself, and, in the process, the sense of verisimilitude is diminished. Even the northern European crusade narratives, which do succeed in creating a significant sense of realism, do not achieve the directness of style of the Ramban. In these works, there is a high style that, on the one hand, provides a sense of the heroism involved and the cosmic significance of the events depicted and, on the other hand, alerts the reader once again to the element of contrivance in the account.[35] Nahmanides set for himself no goal of creating a mood of extraordinary heroism and cosmic significance. This allowed him a plainness of diction that much reinforces the sense of unmediated narration. The Hebrew record closest to the Hebrew style of Nahmanides is the often-cited Hebrew depiction of the Tortosa disputation, which shows a simplicity parallel to that noted in the Nahmanidean account. All in all, the achievement of Nahmanides in fashioning an idiom appropriate to his purpose of enhancing a sense of reliable narration is impressive. On every level, his narrative commends itself to the reader as straightforward and unmediated, a thoroughly trustworthy account of the events it purports to depict.

Having analyzed Nahmanides's techniques for winning reader interest and trust, we are now in a position to investigate more fully his higher purposes, that is to say, his portrayal of the new missionizing argumentation and its refutation and his more general effort at reassuring his Jewish readers of the eternal validity of their faith. We have examined previously the heart of the innovative missionizing case presented by Friar Paul and the essential objections mounted by Rabbi Moses of Gerona. There is no need here to repeat that analysis. It must be emphasized, however, that a crucial element in the composition of the Nahmanidean account was the elaboration, within an appealing narrative framework, of the Christian thrusts and the Jewish rebuttals. It was perfectly obvious that the new missionizing argumentation had not been derailed. In view of the continuation of these efforts, Nahmanides bore the heavy responsibility—indeed, a direct continuation of his prior responsibility—of delineating with care the Christian case and the proper Jewish response. This he did extremely well.

Yet the narrative framework allowed him to do more than simply present the Christian case and the Jewish reaction in an interesting format. It further permitted him to reinforce the abstract message of the rightness of the Jewish case in more tangible and more human terms. This was achieved through the appealing interplay of the three major personalities that dominate the proceedings—the friar, the rabbi, and the king—leading to resolution of the underlying uncertainty and tension through a purported denouement. The interplay of personalities subtly reinforces the overt message of failed Christian argumentation and successful Jewish rebuttal. The three central characters play out a drama that, on a second level, drives home the core of the Nahmanidean message of a misguided Christianity and a divinely oriented Judaism. Three personalities dominate the Nahmanidean narrative, and the portrayal of each bears a crucial message.

The first of the major figures is Friar Paul.[36] The one-time Jew, now Dominican friar, is portrayed in strikingly nebulous and depersonalized terms. We are told nothing whatsoever of his life as a Jew, of his conversion, or of his personal qualities. He is not portrayed as vengeful or vicious.[37] Description is limited to his activities at the disputation, and even there the description is fairly circumscribed. He is given no extensive speech that reveals him as a person. Friar Paul of the Nahmanidean narrative is the instigator of the Barcelona disputation and the Christian spokesman in that encounter. The speeches attributed to him are brief, pale, and to the point. He is a shadowy figure, whose central characteristics are his superficiality and his limited knowledge.

The major assertion of the rabbi with respect to his rival is the insistence that he fails to understand the true meaning of the material on which he has based his new missionizing argumentation. Thus, for example, in the very first exchange, which involved rabbinic interpretation of Gen. 49:10,[38] the rabbi attacks the friar's utilization of the rabbinic material in the following terms:

> I shall show you that it was not the intention of the rabbis, of blessed memory, to interpret this verse except as reference to actual kingship. However, you fail to comprehend law and halakhah, comprehending only a bit of the aggadot in which you have trained yourself.[39]

On the second day of the disputation, when Friar Paul introduced the difficult Dan. 9:24, Rabbi Moses again highlights the friar's allegedly broad incompetence, by challenging him to explain this difficult verse.

> Explain this passage in its entirety, according to your view, and I shall provide a rejoinder. For you will be unable to explain it under any circumstances. But you are not embarrassed to speak of that which you know not.[40]

Let us cite one last example. On the final day of the encounter, indeed, in the last substantive exchange of the dispute, Friar Paul cited a midrash that explicated the words in Gen. 1:2, "and the spirit of God swept over the water," as referring to the spirit of the messiah. For Friar Paul, this homiletic explication served as an indication that the rabbis recognized the divinity of the messiah. Rabbi Moses begins his rejoinder with the following:

> Woe for one who knows nothing and considers himself wise and knowledgeable. Behold, there they [the rabbis] further said: "'And the spirit of God swept over the water'—this is the spirit of the first man." Now, did they [the rabbis] say that he [Adam] is divine? One who knows not what is above and what lies below in books distorts the words of the living God.[41]

Dramatically, Friar Paul serves essentially as the counterpart to his Jewish rival—ill-informed as opposed to knowledgeable, insensitive to textual nuance as opposed to strikingly perceptive, slow-witted as opposed to rapier quick in thought and expression. This portrayal of the Christian protagonist bears in and of itself a powerful message. Without even attending to the content of the reported give-and-take (which was surely not to be neglected), the Jewish reader was supposed to sense immediately that there could be no real truth in a set of arguments adumbrated by an opponent of such little ability. The narrative itself, in this case, the role of the friar within that narrative, serves to reinforce powerfully the central message of the composition.

Clearly, the major figure—indeed, the dominant figure—in the narrative is Rabbi Moses ben Nahman himself. While there may be an element of self-aggrandizement in according himself such centrality in the narrative he composed, it is arguable that such a figure was crucial for the larger purposes of the composition. The rabbi of the Nahmanidean account is, first of all, far and away the most interesting, attractive, and impressive figure in the dramatic tale. His wisdom and wit are clearly intended to attract Jewish readers and to win their sympathy. To be sure, there is, in the depiction of the Jewish protagonist, a more serious goal as well. If the ultimate purpose of the narrative was to reassure a threatened Jewry, then a central Jewish character who is composed, knowledgeable, witty, utterly unflappable, and intellectually invincible is crucial. The reassurance that was the ultimate goal of the composition might be abstractly achieved through the marshaling of arguments. The entire thrust of this analysis has been to argue that Nahmanides chose to reinforce his intellectual message through the medium of the well-told tale. In his tale, the dangerous traps laid by the Dominicans were circumvented by the prescient Jewish hero. For the purposes of such a narrative, the knowledgeable and clever Jewish hero figure was indispensable.

There are a number of key elements in Nahmanides the author's depiction of Nahmanides the disputant. The first salient characteristic is the rabbi's broad command of the sources and the issues raised by his opponent. At no point is he at a loss for familiarity with the relevant texts or for accurate understanding of these texts, whether biblical or rabbinic. Indeed, he shows himself fully familiar with essentials of Christian doctrine as well.[42] The core of his great strength lies in the range of his knowledge and the power of his intellect. Contrasted with the alleged intellectual weakness of his rival, the rabbi's towering ability provides immediate reassurance to the Jewish readers of the narrative. The case presented by such a mind could surely not be amiss. More profoundly, such a mind would never espouse that case were it not a faithful reflection of the truth.

There is, however, a good deal more. Knowledge and intellect, while indispensable to the circumstances of the Barcelona disputation and to the requisite postdisputation reassurance, are not necessarily interesting and appealing traits. The hero figure that the Ramban makes of himself is much more than simply an intellectual giant. Perhaps most appealing and intriguing is the sense of a man who lives brilliantly by his wits. The rabbi of Nahmanides's account is almost a folk hero in the cleverness of his rejoinders, in his capacity to rebuff the Christian thrusts without appearing unduly offensive. He is a master of the implication, a genius at extricating himself from difficult circumstances. For a community of readers who, like the rabbi, were continually mired in circumstances that limited their actions, he is a model of more than simply right thinking; he is also a model of the requisite ability to live by one's wits, to circumvent the machinations of a powerful set of enemies and opponents through sheer inventiveness.

Let us note one instance of Nahmanides's portrayal of his own cleverness. Early in the first day of deliberation, Friar Paul adduced the famous midrash that speaks of the birth of the messiah on precisely the day of the destruction of the Second Temple. The rapid-fire exchanges that take place demonstrate the rabbi's capacity for quick thinking.

> I said: "In truth I do not believe that the messiah was born on the day of the destruction [of the Second Temple]. This aggadah—either it is not true or it bears another explication having to do with the mysteries of the sages. However, I shall accept it in its simple sense, as you have proposed, for it serves as a proof for me. Behold it says that, on the day of the destruction, after the Temple was destroyed, on that very day the messiah was born. Therefore Jesus is not the messiah, as you claim, for he was born and killed prior to the destruction. His birth was approximately two hundred years prior to the destruction in truth. Even according to your calculations, [he was born] seventy-three years [prior to the destruction]."
>
> Then that man was silent.
>
> Master William, the royal judge, responded: "The disputation does not now concern Jesus. The question is whether the messiah has come or not. You say that he has not come, and this book of yours says that he has come."[43]

While Nahmanides presents this as an unanticipated thrust from an unexpected quarter, he portrays himself as responding instantaneously and cleverly.

> You choose, as is your custom, to respond deviously in judgment.[44] In any case I shall answer you. The sages did not say that he came, rather they said that he was born. For on the day that Moses our teacher, peace unto him, was born, he did not come and he did not serve as a redeemer. Rather, when he came to Pharaoh at the command of the Holy One, blessed be he, and said to him: "Thus says the Lord, 'Send forth my people etc.'"—at that point he came. Likewise the messiah, when he will come to the pope and will say to him at the command of God: "Send forth my people"—then he will have come.[45]

There is more than one kind of cleverness reflected here. In the first place, Nahmanides depicts himself as responding quickly and adroitly to Friar Paul, facing a new challenge from an unexpected quarter, and responding with alacrity to that challenge as well. In fact, the rabbi did much more than simply deflect the Dominican thrust. In addition, he pronounced a series of key Jewish doctrines, in the process twitting his Christian auditors.[46] The sense here is of the rabbi outwitting regularly his politically and numerically more powerful foes.

While the entire Hebrew narrative abounds in such portrayals of the Jewish protagonist, let us note just one more, perhaps the most brilliant of the rabbi's ploys. As noted already, a week after the conclusion of the disputation, a large Christian delegation, led by King James and Friar Raymond of Penyafort, visited the synagogue of Barcelona, with both the king and the friar delivering missionizing addresses, seemingly of a most traditional type. Nahmanides remained in Barcelona to reply to these proselytizing sermons. Here he faced a new challenge. While he had, so he claims, thoroughly refuted the Dominican Friar Paul Christian, showing the shallowness of his arguments at every turn, how might he rebut the king without being disrespectful? The techniques that he had used with Friar Paul could now no longer be invoked. The royal preacher had to be treated with utmost tact, yet at the same time his claims had to be blunted. Every Jewish reader could understand the deep dilemma of the rabbi. The tactic he used was exceedingly clever, acknowledging fully the majesty of the king, yet stressing at the same time the limitations of this majesty in a manner calculated to give no offense. This is the way Nahmanides depicts his response to the royal sermon that had argued for Jesus as messiah.

> The words of our lord the king are in my eyes noble, superior, and revered, for they proceed from the mouth of a noble man, a superior man, and a revered leader—indeed there is none like him in the world. However, I cannot praise these words as correct. For I have obvious proofs and counterclaims as clear as the sun that truth is not as he says. It is, however, not appropriate to disagree with him. One thing only shall I say. I am most surprised at him. For the words that he speaks in our ears—that we should believe in Jesus as the messiah—Jesus himself was the one who brought this claim to our ancestors. He was the one who attempted to convey it to them. In his very presence they repudiated him thoroughly and firmly. Now, he was the one who knew and was able to prove his claims more than the king, according to your view that he was divine.[47]

The riposte is exceedingly clever in that it gives no umbrage to the king. To see the king's glory as exceeded by that of Jesus implies not an iota of disrespect. In this way, the rabbi is able to disagree, to present traditional Jewish objections in a manner calculated to give no offense and to provoke no anger. What is of interest here is not the content of the answer as much as the sense of the rabbi as extraordinarily talented in clever repartee. Once more, the image of the weak but clever combatant, the contestant who wins the palm through shrewdness, is reinforced. The portrait of the rabbi is meant, as emphasized throughout, to attract the interest of the reader, to reinforce the sense of danger and drama, and—most important—to reassure the Jewish audience that the Jewish case must be correct and that perspicacity always wins out in the end.

There is one more facet to the rabbi that should be noted, and that is his capacity for quiet irony and mockery. There is a thread of wittiness that runs throughout the report, with Nahmanides depicting himself as gently mocking his Christian adversaries. Let us note but one example, involving the closing comments of the first day of the encounter. As noted, one of the claims raised by Friar Paul at this time was that rabbinic sources acknowledged that the messiah has already come. Rabbi Moses portrays himself as taking a number of tacks, showing the incompatibility between these sources and the historical Jesus, on the one hand, and arguing that, on the other, the birth of the messiah—or even his physical presence—in no way signifies his appearance in a messianic role. At the close of the day's discussion, the king himself intervened.

> Then our lord the king responded: "If he [the messiah] was born on the day of the destruction of the Temple, from which more than a thousand years have elapsed, and he has not yet come, then how can he yet come. For it is not in the nature of man to live for a thousand years."
>
> I said to him: "The conditions were that I would not dispute with you and that you would not intervene in the disputation. However, there were already among the early humans Adam and Methusaleh [who lived] close to a thousand years, and Elijah and Enoch more than that. For life [lies in the hands] of God."
>
> He said: "And where is he today?"
>
> I said: "That is not a requirement of the disputation, and I shall not answer you. Perhaps you might find him at the gates of Toledo, if you send there one of your couriers." I said this in mockery.[48]

The occasional mockery and irony is intended as a complement to the more central image of cleverness.

The positive portrait of the rabbi—knowledgeable, clever, witty—is capped by the claim that these characteristics won him the full respect of the central Christian figure in the drama, the king of Aragon. This respect is accorded the rabbi throughout the narrative, although it does not undo the requirements of the debating format. The king's respectful stance culminates in the recognition accorded at the close of the disputation and, a second time, after the royal visit to the synagogue of Barcelona. This respect is a reflection of the rabbi's stature. He is so distinguished and his accomplishments are so obvious that even a moderately objective Christian must recognize his ability and his achievement.[49] The significance of this recognition leads us to a consideration of the last of the three central figures in the Nahmanidean account, King James I of Aragon, and his role in the narrative.[50]

The king of the Ramban's account is, as I have already suggested, surely not a stereotyped buffoonlike figure. He is regal, intelligent in an earthy way, a committed Christian, supportive of the Dominicans in their missionizing endeavor, yet at the same time continuously friendly—within the limits imposed by the debate—to the rabbi. The regal qualities of the king are emphasized throughout. He convenes the disputation in its entirety, begins and ends each session, speaks in a manner that reflects his own sense of royal majesty (as we have noted in his brief intervention on the last day of the proceedings), and is constantly addressed by Nahmanides in terms of the utmost respect. This respect is reflected in the narration of the encounter and in the speeches that Nahmanides has himself uttering before the king. The monarch of the Hebrew narrative is a man of extreme dignity and stature; these characteristics make him so important to the message that the narrative is intended to convey.

As we have seen, the Ramban's portrayal of the king balances his unflagging support for the Dominicans with his purportedly warm and ongoing friendship for the Jewish protagonist. Nahmanides clearly portrays the king as a devoted Christian, as supportive of the Dominican missionizing endeavor, and as committed to the essential ground rules of the disputation. Time after time, Nahmanides depicts himself as appealing to the king for one or another sort of redress, and regularly the king is portrayed as utterly supportive of Friar Paul and the rules. All this is depicted by the rabbi without significant animus. Royal support for the Dominican cause is balanced by Nahmanides's claim of the monarch's ongoing friendship for him. This combination provides, first of all, a sense of verisimilitude, as already indicated. The author has clearly eschewed oversimplification: the king is neither clearcut foe nor friend. The ambiguity in royal position lends an air of authenticity to the account. More important, it puts the monarch in a unique position to serve as a sort of external arbiter to the encounter.

As I have emphasized throughout this study, there was no formal external arbiter to the debate. Indeed, the encounter was not really a debate. Since it was not a case of Christianity versus Judaism, there was no need to pronounce one or the other victorious, which would have meant nothing in any case. Since this was a missionizing endeavor, success meant missionizing either at the moment or projected for the future. An external arbiter or an external pronouncement in these circumstances was pointless. Either Jews would convert—now or in the fairly near future—or they would not. However, from Nahmanides's point of view, there was enormous value in the creation of a noble Christian figure who would go as far as a Christian figure could possibly go. That is the function of the king in the dramatic interplay of personalities. Committed to support of the missionizing encounter and surely a deeply believing Christian, the king is portrayed nonetheless as fair-minded and decent, the most that might be expected among opposition ranks. When this king eventually congratulates Nahmanides for defending an incorrect cause in the best possible manner, he is, in effect, putting a stamp of approval on the Jewish case. The importance of the royal image so carefully cultivated by Nahmanides is revealed in this comment. The rabbi has created for his narrative one dignified, decent, and semiobjective character who is in a position to make some kind of evaluative judgment. That positive judgment—the most positive imaginable, since the monarch was surely not going to espouse the Jewish cause[51]—serves to crown the interplay of personalities with a sense of positive outcome for the Jewish side and the Jewish cause.

Earlier, I emphasized the creation of suspense and tension as a Nahmanidean technique for winning audience interest. Now we can appreciate his higher purpose. Just as the interplay of characters reinforces the core message of Jewish truth, so, too, does the rise and fall of tension. This is a story with an ending—from the Jewish perspective, a happy ending. The encounter began, as we recall, with a Christian warning that highlighted the dangers of the Jewish position. The third session was held privately, reflecting in all likelihood some of the tension generated by the public spectacle. At the opening of the fourth session, the rabbi appealed for a halt to the proceedings, because of the dangers associated with it. Given this buildup of tension, the close of the fourth session and its immediate aftermath serve as a remarkably positive outcome to the threatening circumstances. The rabbi depicts the aftermath of this final session in the following terms:

> Afterwards on that very day I stood before our lord the king, and he said: "Let the debate be suspended. For I have never seen a man whose cause is wrong argue it so well as you have done."[52]

All the dangers inherent in the Barcelona disputation had dissipated. The rabbi had emerged unscathed, defending his faith vigorously and successfully without eliciting the wrath of his Christian auditors.

To be sure, Nahmanides immediately plunges the reader back into the maelstrom with his very next sentence. There is no time for the reader to savor the fruits of the rabbi's victory.

> I heard in the court that it was the intention of the king and the Dominicans to come to the synagogue on the Sabbath. I tarried in the city for eight days.[53]

Once again the drama is in full force, this time with the tension far less protracted. Nahmanides depicts himself as again responding cleverly, tellingly, and inoffensively. The denouement has the king giving the rabbi a handsome gift and sending him homeward with warm wishes.[54] Thus, the entire account is pervaded with a sense of ongoing suspense and drama, capped by a double resolution. When it is over, the reader can breathe a comfortable sigh of relief: all the potential for catastrophe of various kinds had been successfully averted. The story has come to a happy close.[55] More important than the sigh of emotional relief is the reinforcement of intellectual and spiritual conclusions. In addition to presenting his Jewish readers with a detailed rebuttal of the new Christian argumentation, Nahmanides's telling of the tale is aimed at convincing the audience that a danger had existed and had been averted. The incident eventuated, according to Nahmanides the narrator, in a happy outcome: the new thrusts were blunted; readers should be left with no lingering questions, only with a sense of emotional and intellectual wellbeing. Polemical arguments and narrative structure are meant to mutually reinforce each other and do so quite successfully.

The provision of a sense of resolution for the confrontation in its entirety is paralleled by the creation of an impression of complete resolution for each and every exchange. In every case, the rabbi is given the last word, and in a number of instances, the friar is depicted as thoroughly discomfited. While modern researchers have, in effect, accepted the rabbi's portrayal, serious reflection suggests that we have here yet another instance of narrative manipulation aimed at reinforcing a sense of thorough elimination of the new Christian threat. Polemical confrontations are never so neat as suggested by Nahmanides. They tend to involve endless haggling, with all sides striving for the last word. Thorough superiority of the kind described by Rabbi Moses is only a figment of the imagination of one or another of the participants. Indeed, to appeal once more to the parallel material from Tortosa, there the Hebrew letters give a sure sense of the realistic tendency to bog down in endless and unresolved debate. Nahmanides's claim of straightforward resolution of each and every exchange, while highly questionable as accurate reportage, serves a significant purpose—the assurance offered to his Jewish readers that the new missionizing thrust had been nullified. On both the broad level of the entire debate and the specific level of individual exchanges, the picture is the same—dangerous tensions and threats admirably and thoroughly resolved.

Nahmanides spun out an engrossing tale, did so in a way that convinced his readers of the veracity of his account, and used his report as a vehicle for informing his Jewish readers of the new missionizing argumentation and its shortcomings. While this was a considerable achievement, he attempted one more goal, in many ways the most significant of all. Nahmanides, in his written account, goes far beyond familiarizing his Jewish readers with the new missionizing argumentation and rebutting it; he proceeds to argue in fundamental fashion the errors of Christianity and the truth of Judaism. To be sure, this lay beyond the purview of the missionizing encounter engineered by the Dominicans, and it may well be that Nahmanides is not entirely reliable in his reportage on this front.[56] At this point, let us merely note that he utilizes his narrative to adumbrate basic criticisms of Christianity and to make a concerted case for the eternal truth of the Jewish religious vision.

Rabbi Moses indicates at the very outset his intention to raise the broader issue of the relative truth of Christianity and Judaism. As I have noted previously, there is a striking discordance between the versions of the agenda reported in the Latin account and the Hebrew narrative. The Latin account identifies the agenda in the following terms:

> Friar Paul proposed to the said rabbi that, with the aid of God, he would prove from the writings shared and accepted by the Jews the following contentions, in order: that the messiah, who is called Christ, whom the Jews anticipate, has surely come already; also, that the messiah, as prophesied, should be divine and human; also, that he suffered and was killed for the salvation of mankind; also, that the laws and ceremonials ceased and should have ceased after the advent of the said messiah.[57]

Nahmanides's presentation of the items for debate is strikingly different:

> We agreed to speak first about the messiah—whether he has already come as the Christians believe or if he is yet to come as the Jews believe. Subsequently, we shall discuss whether the messiah is fully divine or fully human, born of man and woman. Afterward, we shall discuss whether the Jews observe the true law or whether the Christians do.[58]

I have for some time now argued that the Christian report is the accurate one, in its emphasis on the proving of Christian truth from Jewish sources.[59] The question that must be raised is the reason for Nahmanides's distortion. The answer, I believe, lies in the rabbi's determination to make his narrative the occasion for a broad refutation of Christianity and affirmation of Judaism. His skewed presentation of the agenda suggests to the Jewish reader from the outset that the underlying issue is ultimate religious truth, whether it resides in the Christian vision or in the Jewish vision. While this was surely not the issue in the carefully manipulated encounter in Barcelona, the rabbi of Gerona made his report on that encounter the occasion for raising the broader issues that Friar Paul and the Dominicans had gone to such pains to eliminate.

The rabbi's broad statement on religious truth includes both negative thrusts against Christianity and positive affirmations of Judaism. I have earlier identified five passages that are overtly disrespectful of Christianity.[60] Now, a closer look at the substance of the Nahmanidean attack is in order. Let us focus on the lengthy speech that Rabbi Moses attributes to himself at the opening of the second day of the proceedings.[61] A multitude of important issues are addressed, with the author subtly interweaving a variety of themes. The engagement begins quietly with the Jewish spokesman requesting that the king hear him out: "My lord, hear me." The request is ostensibly rejected by the monarch: "Let him [Friar Paul] speak first, since he is the claimant." Nahmanides quickly circumvents the rules by requesting the right to clarify his position. From this point on, if we are to believe his narrative, he controlled the discussion, introducing a number of issues that the ground rules had been designed to obviate. Only after this series of clever interpolations by the rabbi had been completed are the rules reintroduced, with the friar crying out, "This is his habitual practice, making lengthy statements. I have the right to pose the questions." According to Nahmanides, the friar's cry was heeded by the king, who ordered, "Be silent, for he is the poser of questions!" To be sure, this was an instance of too little too late; according to the Hebrew narrative, the clever rabbi had once more outwitted his antagonist and said everything that he had wished to say.

In the course of this lengthy set of statements, the rabbi levels a series of devastating attacks on the Christian faith. Two of them involve the issue of the advent of the messiah. In both cases, Nahmanides portrays himself as moving far beyond the argument that rabbinic texts cannot be utilized to prove that the messiah has already come; he depicts himself as proving in a general way that the messiah of Scriptures has surely not come. Such a frontal assault on Christianity was not supposed to happen, and perhaps it did not. In any case, Nahmanides portrays himself as advancing these claims; in the process, he makes an important statement to his Jewish readers: beyond the vacuous new missionizing argumentation, the very foundations of Christianity are fatally flawed.

The first of Nahmanides's purported claims is the milder of the two. He begins circuitously (again, there is the sense of the clever manipulator) by returning to the issue of the whereabouts of the putative messiah who had been born at the time of the destruction of the Second Temple. While he had previously dismissed the notion of the whereabouts of this messiah by bantering with the king about his possible location in Toledo, on the second day, he suggested more seriously that the messiah was sequestered in earthly paradise until the time of his appearance, since he was free of Adam's sin. This supposedly led the rabbi to ask the friar a related question: "Do you acknowledge my statement that the sin of Adam will be annulled at the time of the messiah?" To this question, which Nahmanides was never supposed to be in a position to pose, the king and Friar Paul responded,

> Yes. But not in the way that you think. For the matter involves the fact that all were consigned to hell because of that punishment [the punishment for Adam's sin]. But in the days of the messiah Jesus, [this punishment] was annulled, for he removed them from there.[62]

Having elicited this statement improperly, the rabbi proceeded to attack this key Christian stance on a variety of grounds. In the first place, he claims that all the biblically specified punishments for Adam's sin are clearly still in place. What Christianity has done, according to the Ramban, is to substitute for the biblically specified punishments a noncanonical punishment that had the virtue of not being directly observable. Thus, Christians argued that the punishment of hell had been annulled by Jesus, but, in fact, proof of such an assertion was impossible to provide.

> All that can be seen and felt [all the tangible punishments] were not atoned for in the time of your messiah. Rather hell, which is not specified with respect to it [to the punishment for the sin of Adam], you claim was atoned for, since no one can refute you. Send one of you and let him come and report![63]

Nahmanides manages, through his account, to remind his Jewish readers of this old Jewish objection. In fact, he adds a second traditional Jewish criticism, that is, that the punishment visited on Adam's descendants had to be physical, related to their physical relation to him. In the view of Nahmanides, it was unthinkable that God might have punished Adam's descendants spiritually for his sin.[64] The point of all this is that there is, according to Nahmanides, simply no proof available for the advent of the messiah from the traditional Christian case that claimed the suspension of divinely ordained punishments with the coming of Jesus.

As noted, this is the milder of the two contentions. The harsher comes after the Ramban has once more maneuvered his opponent into posing a broad question. When Friar Paul unwittingly asks him whether he believes that the messiah has already come, the rabbi replies decisively,

> No! Rather, I believe and know that he has not come. There was never any person who said and about whom it was said that he was the messiah except for Jesus,[65] and it is impossible for me to believe in his messianic role.

Nahmanides specifies a series of scriptural reasons Jesus cannot be acknowledged as messiah. The specifics are valuable both for their technical quality and for the broader critique of Christian society involved.

> The prophet says concerning the messiah: "He shall rule from sea to sea, from the river to the ends of the earth."[66] But he [Jesus] exercised no rule. Rather, during his lifetime he was pursued by his enemies and hid from them. Eventually, he fell into their hands and was unable to save himself. How then could he save all of Israel? Furthermore, after his death he exercised no rule, for the authority of Rome does not proceed from him. Rather, prior to believing in him, the city of Rome ruled most of the world. After they entered his faith, they lost much authority. Now the adherents of Muhammad exercise greater rule than they [the Christians] do.

> Similarly, the prophet says that, at the time of the messiah, "no longer will they need to teach one another and say to one another, 'Heed the Lord'; for all of them shall heed me."[67] He further says: "For the land shall be filled with devotion to the Lord as water covers the sea."[68] He further says: "They shall beat their swords [into plowshares and their spears into pruning hooks]; nation shall not take up sword against nation; they shall never again know war."[69] Now, from the days of Jesus till now all the earth is full of violence and plunder. Indeed, the Christians spill blood more than the rest of the nations. They are also lustful. How difficult it would be for you, my lord the king, and for these nobles of yours if they could no longer learn war.

The prophet further said concerning the messiah: "He shall strike down a land with the rod of his mouth."[70] They [the rabbis] explained in the book of aggadah which is in the hand of Friar Paul: "They say to the messiah: 'A certain state has rebelled against you.' He says: 'Let the locust come and destroy it.' They say to him: 'A certain territory has rebelled against you.' He says: 'Let the insects come and annihilate it.'"[71] This did not happen with Jesus. Indeed, you his servants require armed horses, and, on occasion, even that does not suffice.[72]

Again, all this was not supposed to happen—and perhaps did not. In any case, the written report of Nahmanides bears a powerful message—in fact, a double message—to his Jewish readers. On the simplest level, the Ramban argues that the new missionizing argument from rabbinic literature is not only erroneous in its own right but that it obscures the more fundamental issue, that Jesus did not fill biblical predictions associated with the messiah. There is, of course, nothing at all new in this assertion or in the proof texts that Nahmanides cites. He is obviously anxious, however, to remind Jews exposed to the new argumentation that well-known Jewish objections are still in force and should not be forgotten. In responding to the innovative argumentation, Jews should not lose sight of these securely grounded anti-Christian contentions.

There is yet another level to this argumentation, again by no means innovative. The arguments that Jesus failed to fulfill messianic predictions lay bare as well fundamental flaws in the society that was spawned by the new faith. Nahmanides focuses on two such flaws. The first is, despite seeming evidence to the contrary, the basic weakness of Christian society. According to Nahmanides, political weakness is a hallmark of Christianity from its very birth. Rather than the dominant figure the messiah was supposed to be, Jesus was weak and ineffectual. The power exercised by Christianity was hardly its own; it was the result of its control of the Roman Empire, an empire that was ultimately weakened by Christian accession to authority. By the mid-thirteenth century, according to the Ramban, Christendom was clearly inferior politically and militarily to the world of Islam. There is a second and yet harsher indictment of Christianity, and that is its degraded moral state. The Christian world is a world of violence and lustfulness, according to the rabbi, a world that hardly reflects the exalted biblical imagery associated with the coming of the promised messiah. While the simple argument is that the messiah cannot have come, the deeper message to Nahmanides's Jewish readers is a reminder that the religious vision on which this flawed world ultimately rests cannot be true.

The thrust in all of these critiques of Christianity is refutation of the central Christian contention advanced at Barcelona, that the messiah has already come. Let us note only one more critique, one that addresses altogether different issues. This attack, too, is delivered as part of the rabbi's purported opening address on the second day of the confrontation. At approximately the midpoint of this address (which should never have been permitted according to the basic rules of the encounter), after the rabbi had mounted his argument that Christian proof from the alleged annulment of punishment in the wake of the advent of Jesus was pointless, Friar Paul is depicted as attempting to wrest back control of the proceedings. He is portrayed by Nahmanides as saying, "I shall bring a further proof that the time of the messiah has already come." This leads Nahmanides to undertake yet another lengthy statement, which begins:

> My lord the king, listen to me a bit. Judgment, truth, and right between us does not reside fundamentally [in the issue of] the messiah. For you are more important to me than the messiah. You are a king and he is a king. You are a gentile king and he is a Jewish king, for the messiah is nothing more than a flesh-and-blood king like you.[73]

Having stated that the issue of the messiah is truly secondary, the rabbi portrays himself as attacking directly the central Christian doctrine of Incarnation as utterly unreasonable.[74] He details some of the key features of this doctrine: "[This unacceptable belief is] that the Creator of heaven and earth returned into the womb of a certain Jewess and grew in it for seven months and was then born tiny. Subsequently, he grew and was then turned over into the hands of his enemies, who judged him to death and killed him. You say that subsequently he lived and returned to his former place." He then concludes that all these notions "cannot be borne by the thinking of a Jew or of any person."

Once again, it must be emphasized that this kind of attack on Christianity was not supposed to take place and, likewise, that there is nothing new in this Jewish assault. What is important here is Nahmanides's insistence—to at least his Jewish readers—that the essential irrationality of Christianity cannot be overlooked. Once more, the rabbi sets out to remind his Jewish readers of the fundamental flaws in the opposing faith. The new missionizing attack is interesting and important, and Nahmanides felt compelled by both external and internal pressures to rebut these new contentions. He sought constantly, however, to put it in its proper context and to remind his Jewish readers of what he perceived as the fatal weaknesses of the Christian faith, in its reading of Scriptures, in its essential irrationality, and in its degraded standards of behavior. All these lines of Jewish rejection are standard for the Middle Ages. They were not supposed to be permitted an airing at Barcelona, and perhaps they were not. In any case, the rabbi who had represented the Jewish cause in the confrontation made every effort, in his narration of the proceedings, to keep these classic objections in the forefront of the consciousness of his Jewish readers.

There is one more dimension to the Nahmanidean narrative which remains to be explored. The attack on the fundamentals of Christianity was not enough. While negating the Christian faith, the Ramban also devoted himself to assuring his Jewish readers of the veracity of their own traditions and beliefs. To be sure, the positive depiction of Judaism was in many ways a corollary of the negative thrusts at Christianity. In the passages just now cited, for example, the implications are obvious. While Christianity misreads the prophetic record in its assertions concerning the messiah, the Jewish reading of revelation is scrupulously accurate. While Christianity is founded on a belief that is unacceptable—indeed, obnoxious—to reason, Judaism contains no such belief or beliefs and is rigorously reasonable. While Christianity is steeped in violence and lust, the Jews are decent and abstinent in their behavior. Once again, all these claims are standard for Jewish polemicists of the Middle Ages. Rabbi Moses ben Nahman was anxious to reinforce these traditional notions and artfully wove them throughout his carefully constructed account of the Barcelona proceedings.

One issue in particular deserves special attention. As we noted earlier, the Christian claim that the messiah has already come, in the person of Jesus of Nazareth, implied that the Jews were thereby left without hope for their own future. If Jesus was the promised redeemer, then the redemption that he embodied— whatever might be its precise details—was clearly no longer a redemption of the Jews. This notion is implied throughout the Christian argumentation at Barcelona. It was buttressed at a number of points, again in standard manner, by reference to the extraordinarily long exile the Jews had suffered. Thus, it will be recalled, the opening Christian thrust involved the traditional verse, Gen. 49:10, with Friar Paul mounting the argument that the annulment of Jewish political power indicated that the messiah must have already arrived. Rabbi Moses countered with the traditional Jewish claim that the verse spoke of the right to power, not the actuality of unbroken Jewish political authority. At this juncture, as we earlier noted, the drama of the narrative was heightened by the introduction of another figure, Friar Peter of Genoa, who agreed with the rabbi's explication of the verb *la-sur* as implying the possibility of temporary suspension. When the rabbi then announced that the friar favored his position, the friar demurred, noting and highlighting the great length of the present Jewish exile.[75] Thus, throughout the account and underlying the technical thrusts of the Christian case, there was an undercurrent of emphasis on the degradation of present Jewish circumstances and the utter lack of hope for the future.

Nahmanides was particularly sensitive to this set of issues and went to great length to reassure his fellow-Jews throughout his narrative that the lengthy exile was meaningful in its own terms and that Jewish hopes for future redemption were firmly grounded, reasonable, and correct. In the statement just cited, Nahmanides claims that the issue of the messiah is not at all the key to the Christian-Jewish religious rift. He suggests, rather, that the basis for the divergence lies in the irrationality of the Christian doctrine of Incarnation. Along the way, the rabbi downgrades the messianic issue by claiming that the king is, in fact, more important to him than the messiah. This introduces a curious digression that, while unrelated to the argument at hand, is of considerable significance in understanding Nahmanides's reassurance to his fellow-Jews.

> When I serve my Creator under your jurisdiction in exile and in suffering and subjugation and in the obloquy of the nations, who revile me endlessly, then my reward will be rich, for I make an offering to God of my body. For this I shall merit the life of the world to come more and more. However, when there will be a Jewish king of my faith ruling all the nations, and when I shall be forced to observe the law of the Jews, then my reward will not be so extensive.[76]

While this notion is not well developed by Nahmanides, the point is clear enough. Rather than evidence of divine abandonment, the lengthy exile serves as an occasion of divine testing and thereby an opportunity for Jews to win for themselves great rewards. The situation is quite the opposite of hopelessness. The Jews are placed in their difficult circumstances as a way of providing an opportunity to accumulate the richest of future rewards.[77]

Beyond the present circumstances of exile, the eye of the Jewish narrator of the Barcelona disputation is constantly fixed on the future, on that moment of redemption that he sees as both inevitable and relatively proximate. Throughout the account, the Christian claims for a past messianic redemption are countered by Jewish insistence on the redemption that lies ahead, a redemption that would begin with messianic confrontation with the authority of Christianity itself. Repeatedly, the Ramban portrays himself as speaking forthrightly of a future messianic encounter with the pope patterned after the Mosaic encounter with Pharaoh. Let us note the first such interpolation. The second of the rabbinic sources adduced by Friar Paul involved the juxtaposition of the destruction of the Second Temple and the coming of the messiah. Rabbi Moses indicated his personal rejection of this particular source, at least in its literal sense. He agreed to accept this teaching, however, because he found it useful to his case, since it precluded introduction of Jesus as the messiah accepted by the rabbis. Once more, an additional figure is introduced to enliven the proceedings and, in the process, to indicate once more the inability of the central Christian spokesman, Friar Paul. This intervention led the rabbi to make an important distinction between "coming," that is, functioning in a messianic role, and the physical act of birth. The messiah may have been born on the day of the destruction of the Second Temple, but he has not yet, according to Rabbi Moses, begun his messianic functioning. Nahmanides illustrated this distinction first with the personage of Moses, who began to function as a redeemer of Israel only at the point when he confronted Pharaoh. He then continues:

> Likewise the messiah, when he will come to the pope and will say to him at the command of God: "Send forth my people"—then he will have come. But to this day he has not come and he is not at all the messiah. For King David, on the day he was born, was not the king or the anointed one. Rather, when Samuel anointed him, he

became the anointed one. On the day when Elijah anoints the messiah at the command of God, he shall be called messiah. When he
subsequently comes to the pope to redeem us, then he will be designated as the redeemer who has come.[78]

There is more. In addition to reassuring his readers of a redemption yet to come, the Ramban also indicates that the victory of the
Jews will have, as its corollary, the downfall of Christendom.
While Nahmanides early on indicates the sensitivity of this issue
and suggests that he refrained from speaking publicly about it, in
fact he attributes to himself two major public statements on the
matter. What is key for us at this juncture is to note his emphasis
on this theme throughout his narrative report. To illustrate the
kind of assurance that he offered to his Jewish readers, let us attend briefly to the first occasion on which the matter is raised. In
the lengthy sparring that supposedly preceded the actual deliberations of the second day, the rabbi portrays himself as returning
to the issue of the messiah's prior birth, to his elucidation of a general stand on the issue of aggadah, to his qualified acceptance of
the rabbinic source that speaks of the birth of the messiah on the
day of the destruction of the Second Temple, and to the obvious
discrepancy between such a messiah and the historical Jesus. The
rabbi then raises the issue of the lengthy lifetime thus implied for
the messiah and to the place of his sojourn during this lengthy
period, concluding that this messiah—accepting provisionally the
reality of his earlier birth—would have spent the intervening centuries in earthly paradise. This leads the king to ask, on the basis
of the previous day's discussion, "Did you not say in that aggadah
that he is in Rome?" This leads Nahmanides to reply in the following manner:

> I did not say that his setting was in Rome, but that he was seen in
> Rome on a particular day, for Elijah said to that sage that he would
> find him there on that day. He was seen there and appeared there
> for a reason mentioned in the aggadot, but I do not wish to re-
> late it [the reason for messianic appearance in Rome] in the pres-
> ence of many people such as these [a reference to the large crowd
> assembled].

Nahmanides follows this report of his reply to the king with an
explanatory note to his Jewish readers:

The matter which I did not wish to relay to them concerns that which is said in the aggadah that the messiah will tarry in Rome until he destroys it, as we find with Moses our teacher, of blessed memory, who was raised in the house of Pharaoh until he was requited of him and drowned all his [Pharaoh's] people in the sea. The same is said of Hiram, king of Tyre: "So I made a fire issue from you, and it has devoured you."[79] This is the same as Isaiah said: "There calves graze, there they lie down and consume its boughs."[80] In *Pirkei Hekhalot* it says: "Until a person will say to his friend: 'Take Rome and all its contents for a penny.' And the friend will say: 'It's unappealing to me.'"[81] All this I said to the king between the two of us.[82]

Whether or not Nahmanides did explicate this matter to the king, inclusion of the issue in his report serves the critical purpose of reminding his Jewish readers that the future redemption of the Jews will include, as a corollary to salvation of the Jews, visitation on their enemies—preeminently Rome, that is, Christendom—of thorough destruction.

There is yet one more remarkable twist to Nahmanides's effort to reassure his fellow-Jews of the inevitability of their salvation, and that involves his inclusion in his narrative of a specific reckoning for the messianic advent. This remarkable departure from both the rules of the disputation and from the normal procedures of medieval Jewish thinking comes during the discussion of proofs for Jesus' messianic role drawn from the Book of Daniel. The discussion, as described by Nahmanides, is one of the most rambling and convoluted—perhaps *the* most rambling and convoluted—in the entire debate and must be described in some detail.

According to Nahmanides, Friar Paul opened this segment of the discussion with a fairly straightforward argument drawn from Dan. 9:24: "Seventy weeks have been decreed for your people and your holy city until the measure of transgression is filled and that of sin complete, until iniquity is expiated and eternal righteousness ushered in, until prophetic vision is ratified and the Holy of Holies anointed." Friar Paul suggests that the 70 weeks are to be understood as a reference to years, that is, a period of 490 years. He then combines this understanding of the verse with traditional Jewish chronology to suggest that the 70 weeks equal the period from the destruction of the First Temple to the destruction of the Second Temple, proving the messianic role of Jesus.

Seventy weeks refers to years, meaning the 420 years that the Second Temple stood, along with the 70 years of Babylonian exile. The "Holy of Holies" means Jesus.[83]

The style is standard for Friar Paul—a combination of biblical verse and rabbinic tradition, and the conclusion is parallel to his earlier argument drawn from the rabbinic tradition which links the coming of the messiah with the destruction of the Second Temple.

Rabbi Moses's rejoinder is easily predictable. As he had done in response to the introduction of the rabbinic aggadah that links the coming of the messiah with the destruction of the Second Temple, he argues that Friar Paul's exegesis of Daniel is pointless: it in no way advances the Christian case.

Did not Jesus precede this time by more than 30 weeks [i.e., more than 2 centuries] according to our reckoning, which is the truth attested by his intimates and his associates who were his contemporaries? But, even according to your reckoning, he preceded [this time] by more than 10 weeks [i.e., 70 years].[84]

Friar Paul's reply is presented cryptically in Rabbi Moses's narrative. Taking up the chronological problem indicated by the rabbi, Friar Paul continued with the next verse in the Book of Daniel. The key for Friar Paul was obviously the reference to seven weeks, that is, 49 years. He argued that these 49 years permit squaring the Christian dating of Jesus with the broad prediction contained in Dan. 9:24. That is to say, he argued that Daniel's prediction foretold the coming of the messiah 49 years prior to the elapsing of 490 years from the destruction of the First Temple. Friar Paul's exegesis probably involved reading the verse in something like the following manner: "You must know and understand: From the issuance of the word to restore and build Jerusalem"—after the destruction of the Second Temple—"until the [time of the] anointed leader is seven weeks." In other words, Jesus' mission would predate the destruction of the Second Temple by approximately 50 years. While the result is not a flawless chronology, this reading of Daniel does weaken the force of Rabbi Moses's initial objection.

This problematic reading of Dan. 9:25 elicits Nahmanides's scorn. He argues in some detail the proper chronological order of Dan. 9:25, insisting that the verse begins with the destruction of the First Temple and works forward. According to Rabbi

Moses, the anointed leader mentioned in the verse is Zerubbabel, a suggestion that is challenged by Friar Paul on linguistic grounds and then buttressed by the rabbi through citation of a number of verses.[85]

At this point, Rabbi Moses might well have chosen to halt this particular discussion. He had, after all, more or less blunted Friar Paul's claim based on Dan. 9:24–25. Yet he portrays himself as continuing with unsolicited observations on messianic prediction in that critical biblical source. The statement bears citation:

> I proclaim before our lord the king and all the gentiles that there is in this pericope and in all of the words of Daniel no [indication of] the appointed end to the coming of the messiah, except at the close of the book. For it is indicated explicitly in the Bible, with respect to this pericope and to others, that he prayed constantly that he might know the [appointed] end. Finally, they told him the [appointed] end in the verse that reads: "From the time the regular offering is abolished and an appalling abomination is set up, it will be 1,290 days."[86] Now I shall explain before the gentiles the meaning of this verse, even though it might offend the Jews who are here. It says that, from the time that the regular offering is abolished until the abomination that removed it is made desolate, that is to say, the Roman people who destroyed the [Second] Temple, will be 1,290 years. For the days mentioned here are years.[87]

This is a remarkable statement. It is utterly uncalled for in the context of the disputation; indeed, it again goes far beyond the boundaries established for interchange. Moreover, it is a most unusual departure from normal rabbinic reticence to calculate the precise advent of the messiah. What has happened here, once more, is an effort on the part of Nahmanides to reassure his coreligionists of the inevitability of their future redemption. This extreme step serves as the most potent indication of all that the coming of the messiah lies in the future and that it is an inevitability, so inevitable, in fact, that its date can be specified with precision. This messianic calculation is the crowning element in the Nahmanidean effort at reassurance.[88]

Having analyzed Nahmanides's narrative as a successful literary composition aimed at attracting its Jewish readers, convincing them of its verisimilitude, providing them with requisite information on the new missionizing and its rebuttal, and, beyond all this, assuring these Jewish readers of the veracity of Judaism and the nullity of Christianity, we must return to an issue that was raised in our analysis of the event itself, namely, the reliability of the Nahmanidean account. In the light of our careful study of the literary techniques of the Ramban, we might rephrase our question in the following manner: Has the rabbi, in the process of artfully constructing his narrative, ultimately done violence to the event depicted? Has he altered the flow of the disputation, as it actually unfolded, to serve his complex purposes? More precisely, has our investigation of the literary techniques employed by Nahmanides put us in a better position to identify points at which his account is likely to embody markedly a special perspective and points at which we are justified in suggesting considerable exaggeration or even distortion on his part?

I believe that our analysis enables us to point more sharply than before to both tendencies in the Nahmanidean account. In the first place, much of what we have discussed highlights our sense of a powerfully expressed perspective. The key finding that augments this sense is the suggestion that Nahmanides reinforced his set of arguments through the vehicle of the narrative framework, proposing to his Jewish readers that the correctness of the Jewish argumentation was acutely embodied in the interplay of personalities and in the creation and resolution of tensions. This desire to embody rightness and wrongness in the narrative flow itself resulted inevitably in the creation of an account that represents the Jewish perspective of correctness and success.

This perspectival imposition on the narrative is reflected, first of all, in the disproportionate reporting of Christian and Jewish argumentation, that is to say, the minimal reportage of the friar's thrusts coupled with the extensive recapitulation of the rabbi's rebuttals. It is highly unlikely that the friar would have made such brief presentations, leaving the field open to the rabbi for his lengthy addresses.[89] Indeed, the entire portrait of Friar Paul reflects a strong point of view and may involve considerable distortion. While I have attempted to explain the advantages that accrued from the creation of the friar's image, it is difficult to imagine that the kind of dolt depicted by Nahmanides could have won the confidence of the leadership of the Dominican Order, of the royal court of Aragon, and subsequently of the royal court of France.

Perhaps most significant of all is the total narrative framework of the work. Rabbi Moses composed a dramatic and suspenseful tale of the wise and witty sage challenged by the new missionizing but skillfully rebutting every Christian thrust, with his knowledge and skill eventually recognized by his monarch, a perceptive and fair-minded Christian observer of the confrontation. In framing his narrative in this fashion, Nahmanides conveys, above all else, the sense of a victory, a one-time danger successfully averted. As we have seen, both the individual exchanges and the narrative in its totality have been organized in such a way as to convey a sense of closure. Every exchange ends on a note of convincing Jewish rebuttal. The encounter in its totality ends with the Christian but fair-minded king acknowledging the excellence of the rabbi's efforts. This is the ultimate message and, at the same time, the ultimate imposition of a Jewish perspective on the narrative. Indeed, here we are in all likelihood passing into the realm of exaggeration. For, after all, the new missionizing was not nullified by the author's very capable efforts; the Dominicans and Friar Paul himself were very much committed to its continuation. Jews had to face up, over an extended period of time, to the challenges of this novel assault on their faith. In some senses, the impact of that assault was to be felt for centuries to come. The effort to convey a sense of finality and failure to the new missionizing thrust represents a brilliant stroke on the part of Nahmanides. While this sense of finality and failure was a distortion of the reality, it was the most effective vehicle of all for denigrating the impact of the new proselytizing effort.

Yet more problematic is the inclusion of material in the rabbi's speeches that was most inappropriate to the setting. While the rabbi was unlikely to have criticized Christian doctrine in the direct manner that he attributes to himself, it has been the argument of this chapter that the narrative account served as a perfect vehicle for reminding Jewish readers of long-standing Jewish objections to Christianity and of firmly grounded Jewish counterconvictions. In adding this material, the author transformed his account of the controlled encounter at Barcelona into an absorbing and convincing statement of the truth of his tradition. Our sense of auctorial purpose strengthens, it seems to me, the doubts expressed earlier as to the historicity of this material. Again, it is hardly likely that the Christian instigators and managers of the Barcelona disputation would have allowed the rules of the encounter to be so blatantly contravened. Friar Paul Christian may have been as thoroughly incompetent as Nahmanides suggests, although that in itself seems questionable. Even were Friar Paul as incompetent as Rabbi Moses claims, however, it seems most unlikely that the royal and Dominican observers would have permitted such repeated breaches of the ground rules established for the confrontation. These rules are made abundantly clear in both the Latin and the Hebrew reports. The disputation was to involve Christian efforts to prove the truth of Christianity from rabbinic sources. As a result, the truth of Christianity itself was never to come into question. This was, as noted already, an exceedingly clever ploy. To have created such a clever technique and then to have permitted regular and gross breaching of the established regulations strains credulity. To put the matter even more strongly, that the major leaders of the Spanish church and state would have sat by silently while the rabbi publicly denounced Christianity and spoke directly of its imminent demise is unthinkable. I have examined in some detail the later (mid-1265) prosecution of the rabbi of Gerona and have concluded that this prosecution stemmed from what he wrote in his Hebrew report, rather than from what he said in the public forum.[90] This conclusion much strengthens the sense that what Nahmanides said and what he wrote were somewhat different. In the public arena, he was drastically limited by both the normal constraints imposed on the Jewish minority in a Christian society and by the clever manipulation of the agenda by its Dominican framers. In his written narrative, it was possible for Nahmanides to utilize the broad framework provided by the public debate to provide for his fellow-Jews a statement of Jewish truth that went far beyond what the constrained circumstances of the public debate allowed.

Did the Nahmanidean narrative achieve its purposes? On the deepest level, we can never know. Given my assertion that the ultimate purpose of the composition was to preserve Jews in their faith, we have no way of telling how many Jews were or were not reinforced in their beliefs by this skillful account. On a somewhat more modest level, we can note that the work was very widely disseminated and that it was read by Jews as reflecting a total and thorough Jewish victory at Barcelona. The Nahmanidean narrative was and remains an extremely popular work. There is evidence of its being read and utilized by northern French Jews at the end of the 1260s, of its circulation into Majorca in the 1280s, of knowledge of the rabbi's case during the stressful Tortosa disputation of the early fifteenth century.[91] Both the papal document of 1266 and the Christian text that depicts the Majorca disputation note in particular the wide diffusion of the Nahmanidean narrative.[92] This narrative has come down to us in a large number of manuscripts, again reflecting its considerable popularity.[93] Although generally unremarked, it is worth noting that the Nahmanidean narrative/polemical piece is perhaps the most widely translated of either medieval Hebrew narratives or polemical writings. Translations have been made into Latin, Catalan, French, German, and English—the latter no less than four separate times.[94] This unusual level of attention alerts us once more to the author's success in fashioning an account with enormous appeal.

A major modern student of medieval Jewish intellectual and spiritual life, Isadore Twersky, has noted somewhat lamentingly the lasting appeal of the Barcelona disputation and Nahmanides's account of it. At the close of his introductory essay to the important volume of Nahmanides studies that he edited, Twersky makes the following observation:

> Somewhat symptomatic of the state of scholarship—its foci, priorities, imbalances—is the remarkable statement of Simon Dubnow that Nahmanides's "report on the disputation of Barcelona has historic and religious value and will certainly live longer than his big books in the field of halakah. . . ." Only one who has never studied the *Milḥamot* and *Ḥiddushim* closely, who has not savored the delicacy and dynamism, insight and ingenuity of their expositions—and who implicitly dismissed them as so much arid subtlety—could make such a tendentious statement. It is interesting to note that the disputation has, as far as I am able to see, continued to receive more attention in recent research than any other aspect of Ramban's creativity and historic legacy.[95]

It seems to me that Nahmanides himself would certainly share Twersky's discomfort with the negativism of the Dubnow statement and with the neglect of his halakhic works noted by Twersky. At the same time, I am not at all certain that he would have been uncomfortable with the positive emphasis on his narrative. If the foregoing analysis is correct, then Nahmanides intended this narrative to be a widely read popular statement, both of the Barcelona debate and—much more broadly—of the fundamental supremacy of the Jewish faith. The subsequent success of this popularly oriented statement would have been, it seems to me, the occasion of much delight to an author who lavished such skill on the creation of an appealing and convincing narrative.

Indeed, not only did Nahmanides manage to compose an account that won him large numbers of readers but he was also successful in convincing most of those readers of his total triumph, a goal that was, as we have seen, central to his effort. Thus, in the Christian source that depicts the Majorca encounter of the later 1280s, the Jews are presented as glorying in the successful defense of Judaism by Rabbi Moses ben Nahman, in the face of a large and distinguished gathering of Christian scholars and notables at Barcelona in 1263.[96] This Christian source suggests that the larger goal of Rabbi Moses had indeed been achieved, that, beyond providing guidance in the face of the new missionizing thrust, through his narrative the rabbi had conveyed to his Jewish readers a sense of overall Jewish victory over the Christian foe. As I have already suggested, the Nahmanidean narrative has had considerable impact on modern scholarship as well. The veracity of the account has been implicitly accepted by almost all readers, and the resultant picture is precisely that which the thirteenth-century Jewish author intended: the wise and witty Jewish sage, caught in extremely difficult circumstances created by the material power of Christendom and the concomitant weakness of the Jewish position, winning the day through a combination of the truth of his case and the adroitness of his argumentation.[97]

In considerable measure, it is true that the foregoing analysis has served to diminish the stature of Rabbi Moses ben Nahman as a disputant. I have attempted an analysis that undoes his excessive claims to stunning success. While not proceeding to the opposite extreme of arguing for his failure, I have attempted a balanced account that raises serious questions about aspects of his depiction. At the same time, I suggest that our findings reveal a somewhat unexpected facet of this complex and creative figure. I have, in effect, argued that while the portrait of Nahmanides the debater may be somewhat exaggerated, the skills of Nahmanides the narrator and polemicist are outstanding. Indeed, one may legitimately see his report on the Barcelona confrontation as, at one and the same time, a remarkably successful narration and an unusually effective polemical tract, surely to be ranked among the most accomplished and appealing works of medieval Jewish narrative and polemics. The precise dimensions of Nahmanides's disputational achievement are somewhat unclear; his literary abilities shine forth from every paragraph of his opus.

5

The Issue of Rabbinic Aggadah

Having analyzed Nahmanides's narrative and having praised his complex achievement, I must now point to a striking problem that has emerged out of this narrative—the Ramban's views on rabbinic aggadah. As we shall see, this issue is hardly a central theme in the narrative, but Rabbi Moses's brief remarks have given rise to a considerable literature and to polarized points of view. For some, beginning with the Latin report of the disputation, Nahmanides's statements on aggadah represent a sign of his desperation in the face of the new argumentation; for others, his statements were insincere, simply a ploy designed to derail the new argumentation; for still others, his statements were thoroughly honest and fully in keeping with views stated elsewhere in his literary corpus. This polarization is not as striking as the broader divergence with which this entire study began. It is, nonetheless, of considerable interest and mounts yet another intriguing challenge. Some of the findings reached thus far may be of assistance in clarifying this vexing issue.

Let us begin by noting some of the major views expressed with regard to the Nahmanidean stand at Barcelona. The Latin account affords a reasonable starting point. The author is of course reacting to what he heard during the disputation rather than to what Nahmanides wrote in his subsequent narrative.[1]

> Since he [Rabbi Moses] did not wish to confess the truth unless forced by authoritative texts, when he was unable to explain these authoritative texts, he said publicly that he did not believe these authoritative texts which were adduced against him—although found in ancient and authentic books of the Jews—because they were, he claimed, sermons in which their teachers often lied for the purpose of exhorting the people. As a result, he reproved both the teachers and the scriptures of the Jews.[2]

Once again, the Latin account is not that far from the Hebrew report, which shall be cited shortly. What differs is the tone given to the Nahmanidean statement. In the eyes of the Christian author, this stand on Jewish "authoritative texts" was repugnant, an index of the desperate straits in which the rabbi found himself. While the negative perspective of the Latin report is almost predictable, voices within the Jewish world have over the ages found Nahmanides's stance enunciated at Barcelona, as reported by Rabbi Moses himself, problematic. A striking instance is afforded by Don Isaac Abravanel. In his *Yeshuᶜot Meshiḥo*, devoted to explication of the messianic teachings of rabbinic literature, Abravanel begins with methodological observations, indicating three unacceptable approaches to these rabbinic aggadot. These include (1) a negatively polemical approach, that is to say, rebutting Christological interpretation without offering a positive Jewish exegesis of the rabbinic materials; (2) negation of the authority of these aggadic sources; (3) interpretation of these aggadot in mystical fashion.[3] In his discussion of the second of these rejected alternatives, Abravanel indicates a highly sophisticated set of claims (six) that are advanced as part of the broad negation of the authority of aggadic materials. Interestingly, the only specific figure that he cites for such negation is Nahmanides. He notes that "when he [Friar Paul] questioned him [Nahmanides] concerning a specific aggadah which will be indicated subsequently, the rabbi replied: 'I do not believe in this aggadah.' Many sages have been drawn after him in this direction."[4] As we shall see shortly, this is a perfectly accurate quotation from the Nahmanidean narrative. For Abravanel, the approach espoused by Rabbi Moses was unacceptable.

A number of modern scholars have similarly seen the Nahmanidean stance as problematic, not in the normative sense as perceived by Abravanel but historically difficult to reconcile with what we know of the rabbi of Gerona and his views.[5] Two important modern scholars have seen the Nahmanidean stance on rabbinic aggadah as more than inconsistent; for them, the statements of Rabbi Moses ben Nahman are, in fact, the key to understanding the outcome of the entire disputation. For Martin A. Cohen, the Ramban's negation of the authority of aggadah was—precisely as claimed in the Latin account—a ploy of desperation. After arguing that the mystical circles of which Nahmanides was an integral part leaned heavily on a literalist understanding of the aggadah, Cohen comes to the following conclusion with respect to the rabbi's public pronouncement:

> It is, therefore [given Nahmanides's commitment to a literalist understanding of aggadah], astonishing that at the beginning of the second day's debate Nahmanides categorically denied the importance of the 'Aggadah in Judaism. Instead, he stressed the opinion held by the rationalists that the 'Aggadah was not binding, that its narratives were merely homilies, or *sermones*, as the vernacular knew them, and that they could be rejected at will. This *volte-face* of Nahmanides has mystified scholars who could not deny his belief in the 'Aggadah. It can best be explained as a move of desperation to undermine the foundation of Paul's entire argument, now that the attempt to do so by equating Jesus with the Messiah had failed.[6]

For Cohen, the desperation of this ploy serves as a prelude to the decisive defeat Nahmanides suffered in the public disputation, a defeat that for Cohen was, in considerable measure, foreordained and that must be explained in terms other than intellectual and spiritual.[7]

A second important recent scholar who sees the Nahmanidean stance on aggadah as critical is Jeremy Cohen, in *The Friars and the Jews*. There Cohen argues that forcing the rabbi to deny the authority of the aggadah was, in fact, the ultimate goal and achievement of Friar Paul. Cohen notes that the fourth agenda item—the effort to show "that the laws and ceremonials ceased and should have ceased after the advent of the said messiah"—was ostensibly not broached at the Barcelona encounter. Cohen argues that "one finds it hard to believe that a skilled debater like Pablo would have neglected to mention this most crucial issue [the fourth agenda item] throughout the four days of the discussion."[8] According to Cohen, Friar Paul did introduce the fourth—and for Cohen, the crucial—item on the agenda into the discussion, but he did so in most subtle fashion.

> Forcing his opponent to deny, however reasonably, the authority of talmudic *aggadot* might have sufficed perfectly for the friar. He thereby made the point that contemporary Jewish observance, that which Nahmanides exemplified, represented a break with classical Judaism.[9]

In this sense, the Nahmanidean stance on aggadah affords, again, the key to understanding the fundamental dynamics of the Barcelona encounter.

To be sure, not all observers have shared this sense of the significance of the Nahmanidean stance on rabbinic aggadah; indeed, some even question whether the statement represents any sort of departure from the broad belief system of the Ramban. This issue was treated by Saul Liebermann in the closing pages of his essay, *Shkiin*. Liebermann argues that the position espoused by Nahmanides was a perfectly reasonable one, citing evidence from a variety of sources, particularly the Jerusalem Talmud and geonic literature, to indicate that there was nothing untoward in the Ramban's negation of the authority of rabbinic aggadot.[10]

Septimus, whose study of Nahmanides has been cited recurrently, made a significant contribution to clarification of this issue as well. The point of departure for Septimus's discussion of Nahmanides's attitude to the aggadah is his effort to locate him on the Jewish cultural map of the late thirteenth century. For Septimus, the vexing issue of the Nahmanidean stance toward aggadic teachings offers a valuable perspective for comprehending the Ramban's stance toward the various cultural streams impinging on him. Let me cite the heart of Septimus's question and answer:

> But did Nahmanides also share Ibn Ezra's sense of freedom from aggadic authority? Did he agree with the French anti-Maimunists for whom it was self-evident that any denial of the authority of aggadah was tantamount to heresy, or was there some glimmer of conviction behind his statement at Barcelona? I would venture to say that anyone who reads Nahmanides' commentary will find ample evidence that he did not accept the absolute authority of all aggadah.[11]

Septimus moves far beyond this broad conclusion to make a perceptive and persuasive distinction between Nahmanides's utilization of the term *aggadah* and his utilization of the term *divrei rabbotenu*, a distinction to which we shall return.

Marvin Fox has recently devoted an entire essay to the issue of Nahmanides's view of aggadah, and thus he must be cited as reflecting by far the fullest consideration of the matter.[12] Fox points in three important directions in arguing that the Ramban's position was in no sense one of desperation and that it was, in fact, consonant with both traditional thinking in general and with Nahmanides's own thinking in particular. These three directions involve the nature of aggadah, broad traditional stances toward aggadah, and evidence from elsewhere in the Nahmanidean corpus of the rabbi's personal view of the matter. With respect to the first of these directions, the nature of aggadah itself, Fox points to the vast and heterogeneous corpus of materials that constitute the realm of aggadah, arguing that "anyone who approaches this body of rabbinic exegesis and elaboration will have no choice but to pick and choose. Otherwise he will find himself in the unenviable position of having to affirm simultaneously views that are opposed and even contradictory. Ramban was merely reflecting a long-established teaching of the sages concerning the status and nature of aggadah within the system of Jewish faith."[13] In addition to arguing that the nature of aggadah necessitates choice, Fox marshals impressive evidence of pre-Nahmanidean authorities who recognize latitude in reaction to aggadic materials.[14] He further buttresses his case by arguing that, rather than an aberration forced on Nahmanides by the pressures of the public debate, a selective stance toward aggadah is in evidence in the Ramban's commentary on the Torah.[15] From all this evidence, Fox concludes that "there is no ground for the view that Nahmanides was dissembling when he announced at the disputation in Barcelona that we are not obligated to believe in all rabbinic aggadot."[16]

I believe that my foregoing analysis of the Barcelona confrontation and the Ramban's narrative account of it affords us further perspectives for discussing the issue of the Nahmanidean view of aggadic teachings. What is common both to those who see the famous Nahmanidean statements as problematic and to those who see them as thoroughly reasonable is a failure to discuss the issue in the contexts of the disputation itself and the Nahmanidean narrative report. A closer look at both contexts may prove rewarding.

I have already quoted the Latin report's characterization of the Nahmanidean stance on rabbinic texts. Let us look more closely at this statement and, equally important, its placement in the Latin account. At no point is aggadah or midrash mentioned explicitly in the Latin record. Reference is made simply to "authoritative texts." However, the depiction of Nahmanides claiming that these texts were "sermons in which their teachers often lied for the purpose of exhorting the people," particularly when combined with the Nahmanidean account, can leave no doubt that both the Latin record and the Hebrew narrative refer to the same aggadic corpus. We might note the Latin report's characterization of Rabbi Moses as identifying these aggadic statements as sermons, which Nahmanides portrays himself as doing. To label these sermons "lies for the purpose of exhorting the people" clearly represents a distortion of the rabbi's stance. Whatever he might have said, Nahmanides would certainly never have expressed himself in such a manner.[17] This distortion of the rabbi's words represents a pejorative rendering of his stance, reinforced by the claim that such rejection of rabbinic statements constituted reproof of the sages and the authoritative literature of the Jews.[18] The placement of this depiction is significant as well. As noted in chapter 2, the Latin account, contra Baer, is fairly well organized. I identified five elements in this account, with the last three involving an attack on the rabbi, a depiction of some of the major lines of exchange, and a portrayal of the general discomfiting of the Jewish spokesman. Nahmanides's alleged rejection of authoritative texts is the first item in this last section. That is to say, the author of the Latin account did see this as a recurrent ploy utilized by the rabbi. This author, however, does not suggest that this was the ploy of last resort. This was, according to the Christian observer, a device to which Nahmanides resorted frequently; it was not, however, some sort of device of last resort.

Having examined the Christian view of Nahmanides's purported rejection of rabbinic aggadot, let us now turn our attention to Nahmanides's own portrayal of this matter. To be sure, our attitude toward his narrative must maintain the complexity that has already been established. While in no sense divorcing this narrative from the reality it depicts, I have noted recurrently that the Ramban utilized the medium of his narrative to afford guidance to his fellow-Jews. I have suggested that, as was the case with the Latin record as well, aspects of the Nahmanidean narrative represent a perspectival distortion of the event. Again, like the Latin analytic résumé, at certain junctions, Nahmanides does more than simply depict from his own Jewish perspective: he exaggerates and embellishes. We must obviously be leery of taking the Nahmanidean evidence at face value on the important issue of negation of the authority of rabbinic aggadot. With this warning in mind, we may proceed to examine the Hebrew narrative for evidence of such negation.

The first important point to note is the extremely limited role that this negation plays in the context of the entire narrative. It appears just three times. Each must be specified. The first time that the rabbi rejects an aggadic statement comes during the proceedings of the very first day, in response to the second rabbinic text adduced by Friar Paul. After Friar Paul details the midrashic tale that links the birth of the messiah to the destruction of the Second Temple, the following exchange is purported to have taken place:

> I [Nahmanides] responded: "I do not believe in this story at all, but it is a proof for my view."
>
> He [Friar Paul] then cried out: "Behold, he denies their books."
>
> I said: "Truly, I do not believe that the messiah was born on the day of the destruction of the [Second] Temple. Thus, the story is not true or else it has another meaning drawn from the secrets of the sages. However, I shall accept it at its simple meaning as you claim, for it is a proof for my case." [19]

The second instance in which denial of an aggadah is depicted as part of the disputational give-and-take comes on the third day of the proceedings, in an exchange over an important passage in Maimonides. Friar Paul advanced this passage, which speaks of the death of the messiah and succession of his son, to show that the rabbis believed in a human messianic figure. To this Nahmanides replies,

> It is the opinion of the books of aggadah that he [the messiah] was born on the day of the destruction [of the Second Temple] and will live forever. But it is the opinion of the straightforward exegetes [*ba'alei ha-peshat*] that he will be born close to the appointed time for redemption, that he will live many years, that he will die in honor, and that he will bequeath his crown to his son. [20]

Here, obviously, rejection of an aggadic statement is not a tactic used in countering one of the friar's thrusts. In fact, Nahmanides accepts the friar's statement that the rabbis believed in a human messianic figure. This, for him, was not the equivalent of accepting the Christian notion of a messianic figure both human and divine. It was the second of these two characteristics that Nahmanides denied. [21] In a sense, rejection of an aggadic view is an irrelevance here. Clearly, Nahmanides introduces the possibility as a way of clarifying once more his earlier statement, made on the first day of the encounter.

The third, most important, and most problematic reference

to rejection of rabbinic aggadot appears at the beginning of the lengthy statement that Nahmanides attributes to himself at the opening of the second session of the disputation.

> Friar Paul asked me if the messiah of whom the prophets spoke has already come, and I said that he has not come. He then brought a book of aggadah in which it is said that, on the day that the Temple was destroyed, on that very day he was born. I said that I do not believe in this, but that it is proof for my view. Now I shall explain to you why I said that I do not believe in this. Know that we have three categories of books. The first is the Bible, and all of us believe in it fully. The second is called Talmud, and it is a commentary to the commandments of the Torah. For in the Torah there are six hundred thirteen commandments, and there is not one that is not explained in the Talmud. We believe in it with respect to explanation of the commandments. We further have a third book, which is called Midrash, that is to say sermons. [This is] akin to the bishop standing and giving a sermon and one of the auditors finding it favorable and writing it down. This book—he who believes in it, well and good; but he who does not believe in it does no harm. We have sages who wrote that the messiah will not be born until a time close to the end, when he will come to take us out of exile. Therefore, I do not believe in this book when it says that he was born on the day of the destruction. We further call this book Aggadah, that is to say, stories, meaning that they are only things that people tell one another.[22]

This is a somewhat problematic statement, which we shall have to examine with some care.

In considering the full complement of these references to the negation of the authority of rabbinic aggadot, let me reemphasize the very restrained role that such rejection plays in the Nahmanidean narrative. According to Nahmanides, he mentioned the possibility only twice during the actual give-and-take, with both instances involving one and the same aggadah, the aggadah that speaks of the birth of the messiah on the day of the destruction of the Second Temple. In neither instance did rejection of the aggadah play any role whatsoever in the rabbi's rebuttal of Friar Paul. In the first case, his personal rejection of the aggadah was suspended, out of willingness to rebut Friar Paul on the basis of the rabbinic teaching to which he was personally opposed. In the second, rejection of the same aggadah was introduced gratuitously, to clarify his views with respect to this issue. In not one of the twelve exchanges that were outlined in chapter 2 did rejection of an aggadic text advanced by Friar Paul play any role whatsoever.

Let me suggest, with a measure of tentativeness, what probably took place during the disputation itself. I would be inclined to accept Nahmanides's indication that rejection of rabbinic aggadot did not, in fact, play a significant role during the actual exchanges. The Latin account does not contravene such a conclusion. Beyond this, I would also be inclined to lend credence to Nahmanides's indication of a speech in which he laid out a rationale for broader rejection of rabbinic aggadot. I would not be sure of the precise contours of this statement. As we shall see, the speech he attributes to himself is, at one and the same time, bold and restrained. It may well be that he spoke publicly in a slightly less restrained fashion. This broad speech was intended for Christian ears, in the hope of cutting away the foundations of the new missionizing. In this sense, it was very much parallel to the opening Nahmanidean statement, in which he claimed that the entire approach of Friar Paul made no sense. If the rabbis understood Christian truth, how could they have gone on living their lives as Jews? That broad thrust at the foundations of the new missionizing argumentation failed to deter the Dominicans, and the same was true of the rabbi's claim that aggadic texts were not authoritative. To be sure, it is interesting to note that Friar Raymond Martin, cognizant of this Jewish claim, went to considerable length to vitiate this line of rebuttal by including in his *Pugio Fidei* arguments based on halakhic—as well as aggadic—texts.[23] It thus seems likely that Nahmanides did attempt to derail the new argumentation by advancing a broad view of the nonauthoritative nature of aggadah, a view that might well have been somewhat overstated, although we cannot know the precise formulation of that view.

The statements that Nahmanides the author attributes to Nahmanides the disputant are not stenographic reports of what was said. Nahmanides intended his narrative, as we have seen, to serve as a vehicle of edification and encouragement for his fellow-Jews. He therefore went to considerable lengths to inform his Jewish readers of a proper stance toward aggadic statements. I suggest that a close reading of his reportage will indicate how carefully he formulates his purported statements. Again, I am suggesting that he may have expressed himself more sharply in his broad speech before the large assemblage. His reporting of that speech, however, raises almost no real difficulties for a Jewish audience. To the contrary, with but one exception, reading the Nahmanidean narrative poses no problems of discrepancy between the purported position taken by the rabbi during the disputation and that which he would have taken under other circumstances.

We might begin, in the light of the Septimus observations, by raising the issue of Nahmanides's utilization of the term *aggadah*. This term has been traditionally broad and nebulous, giving rise to much uncertainty as to its precise meaning. How, then, does Rabbi Moses use it in his narrative? The term *aggadah* generally appears, as is traditionally the case, as a foil to the term *halakhah*. Thus, in the opening exchange of the disputation, when Friar Paul introduces his first rabbinic source, which identifies the rod and the scepter of Gen. 49:10 with the exilarchs and patriarchs, the Ramban speaks deprecatingly of Friar Paul in the following manner:

> I shall show you that it was not the intention of the rabbis, of blessed memory, to interpret this verse except with reference to actual kingship. However, you fail to understand law and halakhah, [understanding] only a bit of the aggadot to which you have accustomed yourself.[24]

The same distinction is presented somewhat more fully in Nahmanides's broad statement on aggadah, which has been cited above. There, Nahmanides distinguishes three types of Jewish literature—the Bible, the Talmud (clearly identical with halakhah), and the Midrash, which he identifies with aggadah.

Now, while this is both the general and Nahmanidean sense of aggadah, we have already noted Septimus's sensitivity to a slight nuance in the Ramban's use of the term *aggadah*, a distinctly negative nuance. Septimus bases his evaluation of the Ramban's use of the term *aggadah* on its appearance in his commentary on the Torah. Following is Septimus's assessment:

> Although Nahmanides's attitude toward the non-halakhic material in classical rabbinic literature is highly complex and undoubtedly more reverent than Ibn Ezra's, he almost invariably attaches the *term* "aggadah" to those interpretations about which he seems uneasy, which make sense only when interpreted non-literally, or whose seriousness and authority he is calling into question. "Aggadah" can even be rejected in favor of kabbalistic interpretation. There is also support in Nahmanides's usage for the linkage of the term "aggadah" and popular homiletics—including one striking instance of an original interpretation proposed by Nahmanides "in the manner of

aggadah." By contrast, a position referred to by Nahmanides as "the words of our masters (*divrei rabbotenu*)" is treated with respect and seriousness of a different order. The term "*rabbotenu*" tends to suggest a somewhat more weighty consensus. Nahmanides's tendency may therefore be akin to those geonic and Andalusian authors who deny absolute authority to individual *aggadot* while recognizing the more binding character of rabbinic teachings that represent a classical consensus.[25]

Septimus's suggestion finds interesting corroboration in the Nahmanidean narrative. As we have seen, in the give-and-take that opens the third day of the disputation, Friar Paul introduces a text from Maimonides that purportedly speaks of the death of the messiah. Nahmanides portrays himself as countering that the text cited did not appear where Friar Paul claimed it did. More important, he contrasts two rabbinic views of the messiah, the second of which was, he claims, shared by him and Maimonides. The passage, which was cited above, contrasts "the opinion of the books of aggadah that he [the messiah] was born on the day of the destruction [of the Second Temple] and will live forever" with "the opinion of the straightforward exegetes [*ba'alei ha-peshat*] that he will be born close to the appointed time for redemption, that he will live many years, that he will die in honor, and that he will bequeath his crown to his son."[26] In this passage, the negative connotation identified by Septimus is very much in evidence, as the aggadic view is contrasted with what Nahmanides identifies as the straightforward view of the rabbis, espoused latterly by both Maimonides and himself. A similar contrast is drawn with respect to interpretations of the Servant of the Lord passage. On the first day of the disputation, it will be recalled, Friar Paul asked Nahmanides whether he believed that passage to refer to the messiah. The rabbi replied that "in its true meaning, it speaks only of the people of Israel in its totality." Friar Paul then indicates that he "will show from the words of their sages that it [the passage] speaks of the messiah." Nahmanides acknowledges the reality of such interpretations in the following fashion: "It is true that our sages, of blessed memory, in the books of aggadah explain it as referring to the messiah."[27] Once again the distinction between the true meaning and the explication of "the books of aggadah" suggests deprecation of the latter.[28] Thus, the first message conveyed in the careful Nahmanidean narrative is the existence of levels of rabbinic homily, with some deserving of far greater reverence than others.

Indeed, with respect to the one and only aggadah whose rejection the rabbi countenances, the grounds for this rejection are impeccable. As noted, the aggadic suggestion that the messiah was born on the day of the destruction of the Second Temple is contradicted by another aggadic tradition that speaks of the birth of the messiah close to the point of redemption. Faced with such a blatant contradiction, there is nothing to do but choose one and interpret away or reject out of hand the other. Nahmanides indicates two possibilities with respect to the view he felt compelled to reject: "Either it is not true, or it bears another explanation having to do with the mysteries of the sages."[29] None of this is in any way problematic. The reality of conflicting views and the need to choose between conflicting views is, as Fox argues, a staple of traditional Jewish thinking. Where there is a conflict as blatant as that between the views of the birth of the messiah as having taken place at the time of the destruction of the Second Temple or as yet to take place at some point close to redemption, there are indeed no alternatives other than to accept one view over the other, seeing the rejected view as either incorrect or improperly understood. For Nahmanides to assert such a position hardly shows him to be deviating from his normal stance and hardly requires positing either duress or dissembling. This was a position the rabbi could comfortably attribute to himself and comfortably propose to his readers as a reasonable and acceptable line of response to the new missionizing.

It should be noted that not all instances of conflict within the realm of aggadah necessitate rejection of one or the other of the conflicting aggadot. In the next chapter, we shall discuss at length Nahmanides's exegesis of the Servant of the Lord passage. Nahmanides believed the passage in its truest sense to refer to the people of Israel. Explaining the passage as a reference to the messiah is, for him, less appealing, yet the conflict in no sense requires his rejection of the latter view. Thus, aggadot may surely conflict. In some instances, the conflict may involve differing levels of meaning, with neither view necessarily rejected; in other instances, the conflict may be unbridgeable, necessitating the rejection of one view in favor of the other. Such rejection presents no problem whatsoever to a traditionalist position.

Slightly more problematic is the wide-ranging analysis of Jewish literature asserted by Nahmanides during his lengthy opening oration on the second day of the disputation. His statement on the Bible is unexceptionable. The Bible is, Nahmanides contends, the record of divine revelation and, as such, must be believed in its entirety by all Jews. His statement on Talmud/halakhah is similarly straightforward. He defines Talmud/halakhah as the explanation of the commandments and asserts that Jews must assent totally to its explanation of the commandments. Again, this is a perfectly proper traditionalist position. The third corpus, identified as both midrash and aggadah, is a collection of personal statements that can be believed or rejected. Herein lies the one problematic element in the Nahmanidean presentation.

Let us begin by identifying the contexts in which this broad Nahmanidean stance was taken—the contexts of both medieval Judaism and Christianity. The Jewish context is supplied by Nahmanides quite clearly, that is, recognition of the differing statuses of the Bible, the halakhic corpus, and the aggadic corpus. Such distinctions are in no sense innovative or untraditional. The Christian context is one in which the Christian equivalent of aggadic statements, that is, theological beliefs, could in many instances have obligatory status within the Church. Nahmanides alludes to this Christian sense in his portrayal of Friar Paul's outraged response to his early rejection of the statement that the messiah was born on the day of the destruction of the Second Temple: "Behold, he denies their books!"[30] Part of Nahmanides's effort at the disputation was undoubtedly to clarify for the Christian audience the difference between the Jewish view of aggadah and the Christian view of normative and obligatory theological doctrine; part of his effort in his Hebrew narrative was to clarify the same difference for his Jewish readers.

What then does Nahmanides say of the aggadah? He suggests that aggadot are the statements of individuals, written down by others;[31] he claims that belief in this corpus is not obligatory; he provides a specific example of the legitimate possibility of rejection of an aggadah. Let us examine each of these moves in turn. The first presents no problems. To identify aggadic statements as the pronouncements of individual sages that have been written down by auditors is unexceptionable. In fact, rather than diminishing the significance of aggadic statements, Nahmanides has accorded them, in medieval terms, considerable weight. By comparing Jewish aggadic statements to the sermons of bishops, he indicates the importance of such statements rather than their insignificance. The second statement constitutes the one element in the Nahmanidean formulation that is problematic. To say simply that choice may be freely exercised in the acceptance or rejection of this material is too bold. The sources that have been adduced to indicate flexibility in the reaction to aggadic materials would, I argue, never have formulated the Jewish stance to aggadah in such extreme fashion.[32] To be sure, Nahmanides, in his narrated speech, immediately proceeds to soften this bold assertion through qualification. His broad negation of the authority of aggadah is followed immediately by an example—indeed, the only example that he introduces in his entire account. Once again, Nahmanides contrasts the two statements on the birth of the messiah and indicates the right of every Jew to choose one over the other. My suggestion is that the broad formulation is indeed a carry-over from the rabbi's bold statement during the disputation itself, intended to cut away the foundation of the new line of Christian argumentation. In reporting this statement to his Jewish readers, however, Nahmanides softens it considerably, presenting a specific instance in which rejection of a given aggadah is, in fact, unavoidable. The result is to provide requisite guidance for his Jewish readers. The attentive reader will recognize that the broad statement was not intended to provide carte blanche for rejection of any or all aggadic statements. It was intended merely to formalize the limited latitude that was necessitated by the essentially unstructured nature of the aggadic corpus.

Let us pursue the matter one step further by asking what distinguishes the realm of Talmud/halakhah from that of Midrash/aggadah. The distinction clearly lies in the thorough imposition of consensus in the former and the lesser imposition of consensus in the latter. In the realm of halakhah, there certainly are individual views that turn out to be unacceptable. However, the literature itself is oriented toward debating disagreements and producing a consensus that must then be accepted. In the realm of aggadah, there is less pressure toward consensus. Unacceptable individual statements are allowed to stand, permitting a more fluid response to the body of aggadic material. The relative looseness of the realm of aggadah implies no overall rejection of the material and no denigration of its significance. It also does not signify a kind of aggadic anarchy; in the realm of aggadah also there is consensus, albeit less formal and pervasive.[33] Nahmanides makes reference to aggadic consensus, for instance, in his discussion of rabbinic interpretation of the Servant of the Lord passage, with his aforecited reference to "the true meaning" of the passage as referring to the people of Israel rather than the messiah. He goes on to say,

> However, they [the rabbis] never said that he [the messiah] would be killed by his enemies. You will never find in any book of the Jews—neither in the Talmud nor in the aggadah[34]—that the messiah son of David would ever be killed[35] nor that he would be delivered into the hand of his enemies nor that he would be buried among the wicked.[36]

Thus, despite the greater fluidity of the realm of aggadah, consensus was achieved on many issues, and anarchy was far from rampant. The rich realm of aggadah had to be properly understood, in a manner slightly different from the realm of halakhah. For Nahmanides, this meant awareness of the points of consensus and concomitant awareness of the points of legitimate divergence. Implicit throughout his narrative is the sense that Friar Paul, totally inadequate to a reading and comprehension of halakhah, is ultimately deficient in his reading of aggadah as well. He lacks the requisite sensitivity to this looser, yet valuable category of Jewish literary creativity.[37] In all of this, there is hardly a diminution of the significance of aggadah, although there is identification of that which distinguishes aggadah from the corpuses of halakhah and Scripture.

A brief summary is in order. (1) Rejection of aggadic statements does not seem to play any role whatsoever in the actual give-and-take during the disputation. (2) Nahmanides probably did make a broad statement on the nonbinding nature of aggadic material in an effort to derail the new argumentation. The precise nature of this statement cannot be determined, but it may well have been a bit extreme. (3) In his narrative, he was careful to provide guidelines for rejection of aggadic materials, guidelines that involved careful use of the term and specification of the limited circumstances under which aggadot could be responsibly rejected. (4) The subsequent divergence of opinion over his stance toward the aggadah suggests that his efforts at careful delineation of his position on this delicate matter were not altogether successful.[38]

6

Explication of the
Servant of the Lord Passage

The core of Nahmanides's effort to provide convincing rebuttal of
the new missionizing argumentation and broad reassurance to his
fellow-Jews lay in his carefully crafted report on the disputation,
which, I have argued, is a masterpiece of medieval Jewish narrative
and polemical literature. To be sure, the Barcelona disputation occasioned two other works by the rabbi as well, an explication of
the Servant of the Lord passage in Isaiah and a lengthier and more
important treatise on redemption.[1] Each of these works deserves
our attention.

On the first day of the Barcelona deliberations, discussion revolved about four important rabbinic sources. Three of these were
adduced by Friar Paul to show that the rabbis themselves recognized that the messiah had already come. The fourth—rabbinic
exegesis that identifies the Servant of the Lord of Isaiah with the
messiah—was cited to prove that according to the rabbis, the messiah was fated to suffer and die in a manner that could only be understood with reference to Jesus. The exchange around this fourth
item was perhaps the most problematic of the entire encounter
from the Jewish perspective.

For the Latin account, this exchange resulted in an unambigu-
ous admission by the rabbi. Because of the significance of the
triumphant formulation, let us cite it once more:

It was therefore asked of him whether chapter 53 of Isaiah—"Who
could have believed what we have heard"—which according to the
Jews begins at the end of chapter 52, where it is said: "Behold my
servant shall prosper," speaks of the messiah. Although he consistently claimed that this passage in no way speaks of the messiah, it
was proved to him through many authoritative texts in the Talmud
which speak of the passion and death of Christ, which they prove
through the said chapter, that the aforesaid chapter of Isaiah must
be understood as related to Christ, in which the death, passion,

burial, and resurrection of Christ is obviously contained. Indeed, forced by authoritative texts, he confessed that this section must be understood and explained as relating to Christ. From this it is clear that the messiah was to suffer.[2]

Now let us compare and contrast the Jewish account of the same exchange:

That fellow claimed: "Behold the passage [that begins] 'Indeed my servant shall prosper' indicates that matter of the death of the messiah, his delivery into the hand of his enemies, and how they put him with the wicked, as was the case with Jesus. Do you believe that this passage speaks of the messiah?"

I said to him: "According to its true sense, it [this passage] speaks only of the people of Israel in the aggregate, for thus the prophets always designate them—Israel my servant Israel, Jacob my servant."

Friar Paul said: "I shall show from the words of their sages that it [the passage] speaks of the messiah."

I said to him: "It is true that our sages of blessed memory, in the books of aggadah, explain it as referring to the messiah. However, they never said that he would be killed by his enemies. You will never find in any book of the Jews—neither in the Talmud nor in the aggadah—that the messiah son of David would ever be killed nor that he would be delivered into the hand of his enemies nor that he would be buried among the wicked. Indeed even the messiah whom you have fashioned for yourselves was not buried [among the wicked]. I shall explicate for you the passage properly and fully if you wish. There is no indication there that he [the messiah] will be killed, as happened with your messiah." But they did not wish to hear.[3]

As noted already in our earlier effort to reconstruct the major facets of the disputation, the conflicting sources clearly relate to the same basic reality, although they see it from divergent perspectives. At issue was rabbinic exegesis of the Servant of the Lord passage. From the Christian perspective, the rabbi's denial of the messianic import of this passage was refuted decisively by rabbinic texts cited by Friar Paul. In the face of these rabbinic texts, Nahmanides had to acknowledge that the Isaiah passage had messianic meaning, and, in the process, he had to acknowledge as well that the rabbis concurred with the Christian sense of a messiah fated to suffer and die. Nahmanides offers an alternative version of the exchange. Interestingly, he omits any reference to Friar Paul's citation of rabbinic texts, claiming instead that the friar made only a general observation with which he had to agree. According to Nahmanides, however, that is as far as his agreement went. Despite acknowledging that the passage had been associated by some rabbis with the messiah, he proceeded to claim that this association in no way involved espousal of the notion of a messiah slated to suffer and die. While the content of Nahmanides's depiction makes eminent sense, there is a flatness of tone that is unusual. This is the only interchange that ends on anything less than a confident and assertive note. The closing indication of an offer to explicate the passage in its totality and refusal of that offer is the closest that the entire narrative comes to a tentative tone. Clearly, this was a problematic passage and a problematic exchange.

Given the difficulties of this exchange, it is not surprising that Nahmanides saw fit to devote further consideration to this issue, through the format of an extended commentary on the Isaiah passage.[4] Prior to treating this commentary, it is worth noting explicitly a number of lines of argumentation that Nahmanides did not utilize in response to this particular thrust of Friar Paul. There is, first of all, no suggestion that Friar Paul misunderstood the rabbinic texts. Indeed, as we have noted, Nahmanides does not even mention citation of specific rabbinic texts by the friar; he suggests instead his own acknowledgment of rabbinic identification of the Servant of the Lord with the messiah. Moreover, he makes no effort to contest the validity of this rabbinic identification. By the time this exchange had taken place, Nahmanides had already established the principle of rejection of specific rabbinic sources. Nonetheless, there was no appeal to that principle in this case. The most that the rabbi permitted himself was a hierarchy of rabbinic interpretations, distinguishing between the true interpretation of the passage that refers it to the people of Israel and the "aggadic" (in a somewhat pejorative sense, as we have seen) rendering that relates it to the messiah.[5] While of lesser validity than the former, the latter interpretation was present and had to be confronted. That confrontation involved nothing less than thorough exposition of the biblical passage itself to show that rabbinic equation of the Servant of the Lord with the messiah in no way eventuated in Christological conclusions.

The essential point of the commentary and of Nahmanides's

understanding of the biblical passage is indicated in his brief introductory and concluding comments.

"Indeed, my servant shall prosper." The correct interpretation of this passage is that it refers to Israel in its entirety, as in the expression "Fear not, my servant Jacob"[6] or "He said to me: 'You are my servant in whom I glory'"[7] and many similar passages. However, according to the view of the midrash that refers it [the Isaiah passage] to the messiah, we must explicate it according to those books. This alternative view indicates that the messiah son of David concerning whom Scripture speaks will never be subjugated and will not die at the hands of his enemies. Thus the verses indicate clearly.[8]

Behold, there is no mention in the passage that he [the messiah] would be delivered into the hands of his enemies, nor that he would be killed, nor that he would be hung on a tree. Rather [it indicates] that he would see offspring and live a long life, that he would be exalted and that his kingdom would be raised to heights among the nations and that powerful kings would become his booty.[9]

Thus, Nahmanides's essential message to his fellow-Jews remains that even the midrashic understanding of the Isaiah passage as a reference to the messiah affords no support for the Christian notion of a messiah who suffered and perished on behalf of humankind. There is, in the Isaiah passage, no reference to the suffering and death of the messiah that is central to Christian teaching. To the contrary, argues Rabbi Moses to his fellow-Jews, the portrait sketched by Isaiah involves a messianic figure who, despite humble origins, ends his career with dignity and authority.

To be sure, the passage in question was not discovered by Friar Paul and, likewise, Rabbi Moses ben Nahman was not the first Jew called on to address the meaning of these important verses. It is interesting to note that Rabbi Moses's focus is strikingly—and probably consciously—limited. There are, of course, many items in the Isaiah passage which had been traditionally adduced by Christians in their argumentation with Jews. Awareness of the broad spectrum of issues involved in this important passage is reflected nicely in a speech fashioned by twelfth-century Jacob ben Reuven in his *Milḥamot ha-Shem*. The Christian protagonist in Jacob's opus quotes at length the passage and then says,

Behold all these verses, from the first letter to the last, are clear and obvious testimony that our teachings concerning our messiah are correct. It goes without saying that each and every verse reveals his [the Christian messiah's] secrets and affairs and indicates and explains the essence of those actions which he undertook. Not a single item of this testimony, which the prophecy testified concerning him, was missing.[10]

By contrast, Rabbi Moses's focus was narrowly limited. Although his comments on the passage proceed through it in its entirety, he is very heavily concerned with the precise issue that had been raised at Barcelona. He was anxious to reassure his coreligionists that rabbinic understanding of the passage as referring to the messiah, while not revealing the essential message of the prophecy, nonetheless in no way supported the Christian contention of a messiah slated to suffer and die.

Given this narrow focus, the critical verses for Nahmanides are those that seem to speak of the suffering and death of the Servant of the Lord. Nahmanides treated carefully those verses that speak of the illness and suffering of the Servant of the Lord and of the import of this illness and suffering for others. While he undoubtedly believed that these verses in their deepest sense referred to the suffering of the people of Israel, he had no real difficulty in seeing them applied to the messianic figure. Even the notion of the redemptive power of this messianic illness and suffering caused Nahmanides no major discomfort. Let us note a few of his comments in this regard.

"A man of suffering"—troubled over the sins of Israel, which cause the delay in his appearance and retard his becoming king over his people.[11]

"Familiar with disease"—for the sick person is perpetually troubled over his pain. Indeed, the term "illness" is used for the disquiet that comes from an excess of desire, as is said: "Amnon was so distraught because of his [half-] sister Tamar that he became sick."[12] Similarly, "no one becomes sick on my behalf."[13] Alternatively, [it means] that he actually becomes sick from the pain, as is the custom among people.[14]

Nahmanides consistently explains the illness and suffering in subjective, psychological terms. The messiah suffers in that he takes on himself the psychological pain associated with Israel's shortcoming and his own consequent tarrying.

"Yet it was our sickness that he was bearing"—for he is sick and troubled over our sins, over which we should be sick and troubled.

And he bears the brunt of our suffering, which we should endure, for he is troubled over them.[15]
"And by his bruises we were healed"—for the bruise, that is his pain and anguish over us, will heal us. For the Lord will forgive us on his behalf. We shall be relieved of our transgressions and the sins of our ancestors, in the sense of "it [the people of Israel] will repent and will be healed."[16]

The notion of the messiah bearing the sins of the people is seen by Nahmanides not as reflecting some sort of vicarious atonement—a notion utterly central to Christian theology in general and to Christian exegesis of this particular passage—but rather once more as the messiah's sympathetic concern for the sinning people of Israel. Even the notion of healing effected through the bruises of the messiah is still seen as a reference not to physical bruises suffered by the messiah but to his pain over the shortcomings of his people. The only element of vicarious atonement is a mild one. God, out of feeling for the messiah's empathetic pain for the people of Israel, will forgive the transgressions of that people. Throughout, Nahmanides has rejected the notion of the messiah's physical suffering and has seen the references to pain, suffering, and bruises as reflective of the messiah's total devotion to the people whom he was sent to redeem.

More critical to Nahmanides was the issue of the death of the messiah. That was the specific item with which Nahmanides was confronted at Barcelona; that was the claim that Nahmanides was most anxious to rebut; that was the contention that Nahmanides clearly felt could be most readily dismissed through a close reading of the Isaiah text. The first thrust of Nahmanides's rebuttal of the claim that the Servant of the Lord passage substantiates the Christian doctrine of a messiah fated to die was in effect a continuation of the already noted tendency to explicate the crucial verbs in the descriptive segments of the prophecy in essentially psychological terms. Thus, for example,

"Like a sheep being led to slaughter" [a widely noted verse in Christological exegesis]—he will consider in his heart: "Even if they kill me I shall complete the mission of my Creator, for that is my obligation." In the same fashion Hananiah, Mishael, and Azariah said: "But even if he does not [even if God does not save us from the burning fiery furnace], be it known to you, O king, [that we will not serve your god or worship the statue of gold that you have set up]."[17] Similarly the rabbis said: "In the cases of any one who delivers himself up in order that a miracle be effected on his behalf, a miracle is not effected on his behalf."[18] In these same terms Jeremiah said: "For I was like a docile lamb led to slaughter."[19]

"And he set his grave among the wicked"—"setting" [the Hebrew *netinah*] is used in Scripture for intention, such as "And I set my mind to study" [*natati et libi*][20] or "Do not take your maidservant for a worthless woman" [*al titen et amatekha*].[21] It is also used for speech, such as "You shall pronounce the blessing at Mount Gerizim" [*ve-natata et ha-berakhah*][22] or "And he shall put them [the sins of the people] on the head of the goat" [*ve-natan otam 'al rosh ha-sa'ir*].[23] He [the prophet] said: He shall intend that his grave be among the wicked of the nations. For he shall conclude: "They shall surely kill me and this place shall be my grave." This is the same as "O you who have hewn your tomb on high,"[24] meaning the place in which he intended to be buried when he would die, but he was not yet buried in it. Similarly: "[Be sure to bury me] in the grave which I made ready for myself,"[25] but he had not yet been buried in it.[26]

"For he exposed himself to death"—he prepared himself fully for death, that is to say that he fully intended to die, that he delivered himself over to die.[27]

Nahmanides's exegesis is thoroughly consistent. He argues again for a psychological rather than a physical meaning to the descriptive verbs. Throughout this passage, the prophet is seen as extolling the messianic figure for his willingness for self-sacrifice on behalf of his people. At no point, however, according to Rabbi Moses, is the messiah presented as actually dying or being buried. The willingness for death and burial is laudatory; the actuality of death and burial never came about. Thus, the important arguments mounted by Christians from this passage are, according to Rabbi Moses, spurious.

Rabbi Moses believes and argues that his explanation of the references to death and burial as indications of the messiah's readiness for such self-sacrifice is, in fact, necessitated by the obvious references, in the latter stages of the passage (versus 10 through 12), to a live and successful messianic figure. These references to the successes of the messiah constitute the note on which the prophecy closes. To Nahmanides, they indicate that the references to death and burial can only be understood in the subjective mode that he has proposed. Let us look briefly at a few of his comments on these verses.

"The Lord chose to crush him, to smite him with disease"—for the Lord, may he be blessed, wished to accord him merit through the pain which he suffered.[28]

"If you made himself an offering for guilt"—that he think that the guilt and sin rest with him and that, because of the paucity of his virtues, all this [the delay in redemption] has taken place. Then he will have full merit. The reason for [the expression] "if you made himself" is that they are the words of the revered and awesome Lord and his will.[29] He [God] said: "If he [the messiah] will suffer all this and if his soul will be abased, that he not carp at and criticize my qualities, then I shall grant him reward, measure for measure, [beginning with] 'He shall see offspring.' "[30]

"He shall see offspring"—thus will be fulfilled the verse: "Your sons will succeed their fathers; you will appoint them princes throughout the land."[31]

"He will enjoy length of days forever"—as is said: "He asked you for life; and granted it; a long life, everlasting."[32]

"Through him the Lord's purpose will prosper"—for he shall complete the redemption which the Lord, may he be blessed, wishes.[33]

"Assuredly I will give him the many as his portion"—all the many nations shall be his portion and his inheritance. From the [possessions of] powerful nations he shall distribute booty to this people and to his servants.[34]

The portrait that Nahmanides sees sketched in these closing verses is one of a messiah triumphant, a ruler over the Jewish people and indeed over the entire world. This ruler, for Nahmanides a human figure of unusual dimensions, would live a long and useful life, eventually passing on his power to his descendants.[35] In all of this, Nahmanides finds no hint of the Christian notions of abasement of the messiah, ending in his ignominious death. Indeed, Nahmanides finds in the Servant of the Lord passage of Isaiah the very antithesis of the Christian portrait of the messiah. Thus, Friar Paul's innovative thrust, which brought to the attention of Nahmanides and his fellow-Jews the strand of rabbinic interpretation that saw the Isaiah passage as referring to the messiah, should have, according to Rabbi Moses, no deleterious impact on Jewish belief. While he preferred the line of exegesis that proposed the Servant of the Lord as a reference to the people of Israel, Nahmanides set out to show his Jewish readers that the alternative exegetical tradition poses no problem to Jewish belief and provides no succor to Christian doctrine.

Having examined closely Nahmanides's extended explication of the Isaiah passage, let us identify the major methodological assumption on which his exegesis—and hence his reassurance to his fellow-Jews—rests. While both Christian and Jewish tradition had identified by this point a number of lines of biblical exegesis, the plane of explication on which these polemical debates had to rest was ultimately the simple and direct sense of the biblical text. While all the other levels of exegesis had their relevant roles to play in uncovering biblical truth and while Nahmanides himself was most interested in these other—indeed, deeper—levels of meaning,[36] polemical confrontation revolved about the straightforward meaning of the text. Thus, ultimately, his oral argument, as he reports it, and his more extensive written commentary seek to identify the simple and direct meaning of the Servant of the Lord passage. Since the passage clearly depicts a messiah figure who is ultimately powerful and victorious, it is necessary to seek alternative explanations for the imagery of suffering and death, explanations that relegate this imagery to the realm of psychological pain and spiritual preparedness for self-sacrifice. The key for Rabbi Moses lies in discerning the straightforward meaning of the text.

Claims of comprehension of the simple and direct meaning of Scriptures—for Jews, understanding of the *peshat* of the biblical text—are, of course, advanced regularly by both sides in the medieval Christian-Jewish religious debate.[37] These claims to straightforward comprehension of the biblical text are analogous to the parallel claims for philosophic reasonableness and moral probity. In all three cases, both sides agreed that direct and unadorned understanding of revealed truth, reasonable grasp of philosophic truth, and higher levels of moral behavior constitute evidence of religious superiority. While both parties agreed to the abstract criteria for religious superiority, they disagreed, of course, about the specifics that constitute the unadorned comprehension of the biblical text, reasonable philosophic views, and a higher level of morality. Both in his narrative and in his commentary on the Servant of the Lord passage, Nahmanides argues that contextuality is the key to straightforward comprehension of the record of revelation—or of any other text for that matter. His argument with respect to the Servant of the Lord passage is that the Christian reading distorts through its failure to treat the Isaiah prophecy in its entirety and that his own reading does treat the prophecy in its entirety.

Interestingly, one of the rabbi's most stinging rebukes to Friar Paul—at least insofar as he reports in his narrative—concerns the same issue of contextuality. In the very last interchange of the disputation, when Friar Paul argues for the divinity of the messiah by advancing the midrashic statement that explains Gen. 1:2— "the spirit of God hovered over the waters"—as referring to "the spirit of the messiah," Nahmanides portrays himself as answering scathingly:

> Woe to him who knows nothing but who thinks that he is wise and knowledgeable. Behold they [the rabbis] further said there: "'The spirit of God hovered over the waters'—that is, the spirit of Adam the first human." Did they say that he would be divine? One who does not know that which is above and below in texts distorts the words of the living God.[38]

Awareness of "that which is above and below in texts," according to Nahmanides, is the key principle for accurate understanding of both rabbinic and biblical texts. In his postdisputation writing, he was clearly anxious to remind his fellow-Jews of the importance of the principle of contextuality and to reassure them that it was their tradition that had embraced that principle consistently, in the process assuring itself of its hold on the truth.[39]

While the central message of this brief commentary on the Isaiah passage focuses on the issue of the alleged suffering and death of the messiah and the proper style for reading such key biblical texts as the Servant of the Lord passage in Isaiah, Nahmanides makes a number of important additional observations, all of them related to the issues raised by Friar Paul at Barcelona and intended to reinforce the lessons that he delivered both in his oral remarks during the disputation and through his narrative.

The first of these observations concerns the doctrine of the messiah as both divine and human, one of the agenda items at Barcelona. During the second day of those proceedings, Friar Paul had confronted Rabbi Moses with a midrash based on Isa. 52:13, which explicated the three verbs in the verse as indicating that the messiah will "rise beyond Abraham, be exalted above Moses, and be lifted beyond the heavenly angels." According to Friar Paul, midrashic suggestion that the messiah will be lifted beyond the heavenly angels reflects rabbinic awareness that the messiah was intended to be divine. As we have seen, Friar Paul attempted to argue for the messiah as a combination of human and divine, with this particular midrash serving to highlight the latter characteristic. During the disputation, Rabbi Moses had purportedly countered this reading of the midrash by arguing that Friar Paul was simply unaware of rabbinic style, that in fact the rabbis often compared humans favorably with the heavenly angels.[40] In his report on the disputation, he has himself indicating that the superiority of the messiah will lie in his achievements, not in any divine essence. The appearance of the three verbs on which the rabbinic midrash rests affords Nahmanides another opportunity to explicate this particular midrash and to explicate it once again in a manner that removes all suggestion of the messiah as in part divine.[41] Nahmanides proposes two extended explanations for the rabbinic midrash. The first, parallel to that essayed in his narrative, identifies the ascendancy of the messiah over Abraham, Moses, and the angels in his achievements, which will outstrip those of Abraham, Moses, and even the angels. The second locates the superiority of the messiah in his unparalleled knowledge of the Lord.[42] In either case, Nahmanides reinforces the message that he had already communicated in his Barcelona narrative. The midrash in no way suggests a messianic figure who is anything other than human. The distinctiveness of the messiah lies not in his divinity but in his unusual achievements or abilities.

Beyond the issues of the suffering and death of the messiah and his nature lay the issue that we have already identified as the most critical of all—whether in fact the messiah has already appeared or is yet to appear at some future date. Nahmanides utilizes the Isaiah text as the basis for identifying the claim of prior messianic advent as the most fundamental of Christian errors. He makes some trenchant observations on this purported error at the very outset of his extended commentary:

> "Indeed my servant shall understand" [*yaskil*]—for at the time of redemption the messiah shall understand and perceive the appointed end and shall know that the time of his coming has arrived and that the point at which he will appear to the community that longs for him has come. He [the prophet] used the term *yaskil*, because it is said in the Book of Daniel: "For these words are secret and sealed to the time of the end; many will be purified and purged and refined; the wicked will act wickedly and none of the wicked will understand; but the knowledgeable [*ha-maskilim*] will understand."[43] Daniel foretold that some of the wicked "will act wickedly" by abusing the steps of the messiah, because of his great tardiness, and will not believe in him at all. "None of the wicked will understand" the end, for there will be among them those who will go astray after

one who will claim that he is the messiah. "But the knowledgeable [*ha-maskilim*] will understand" the true end and will wait for him.[44]

For Nahmanides, Christianity, despite all its successes, falls simply into the category delineated by Daniel as those wicked ones who are incapable of understanding the true appearance of the promised messiah. Given the centrality of the theme of the prior advent of the messiah in the Barcelona confrontation, this represents an opportunity for Nahmanides to raise the issue once more to his fellow-Jews. Rather than allowing themselves to be convinced by the Christian argumentation that the messiah has already appeared, Jews should be aware that premature recognition of the messiah constitutes a grave error, indeed, from Nahmanides's perspective, the fundamental error of the Christian tradition. Thus, the close reading of the Isaiah text offers yet another opportunity for carrying this central message to his Jewish readers.

To negate the Christian claim that the messiah had already come was, as we have already seen, only half the goal that Nahmanides had set for himself. In his narrative account of the Barcelona proceedings, he had also made extensive efforts to reassure his fellow-Jews that their messiah would inevitably—indeed, soon—come to redeem them. This motif as well is introduced into the brief treatise on the Servant of the Lord passage; it appears in an interesting comment that looks like no more than a traditional bit of moralizing. A central theme of the Servant of the Lord passage, as we have seen, is the notion of the messiah taking on himself the sins of Israel, a theme that Nahmanides extensively and carefully explains. One of the central verses that express this theme reads:

> We all went astray like sheep,
> Each going his own way;
> And the Lord visited upon him
> The guilt of us all.

We have noted already Nahmanides's treatment of the messiah's acceptance of the guilt of Israel. Wherein, however, lie the shortcomings of Israel? The image of going astray like sheep affords Rabbi Moses an opportunity to identify the shortcomings of his contemporaries.

> He castigates Israel because, in their dispersion, they place all their concern in worldly matters. Each one places his concern in himself,

his household, and his affairs. It would be fitting for them to weep and pray before the Lord night and day that he forgive them for the iniquity of Israel and hasten the appointed time of redemption. For the messiah will come immediately as a result of repentance. If not, he will tarry until that appointed time specified in the oath [specified in Daniel], as is said: "Then he lifted his right hand and his left hand to heaven and swore by the Ever-Living One."[45]

Nahmanides's criticism of his peers concerns their excessive immersion in worldly affairs; his plea to them is for deeper concern over the repentance that would hasten the time of redemption. In this respect, he is of course in the mainstream of Jewish [and other] moralists and pietists.[46] However, the issue is more than merely pietistic. In this comment, while criticizing his coreligionists for their failure to repent with sufficient profundity, Rabbi Moses again reassures them of the inevitability of their redemption, which will be set in motion in one of two ways—either by their own repentance or alternatively by reaching that time for which God had preordained redemption.[47] The overt moral criticism is more than balanced by the reassurance of redemption.

Nahmanides's careful explication of the Servant of the Lord passage was surely an element in the rabbi's post-Barcelona activity, albeit a minor element. His major post-Barcelona composition, his narrative depiction of the disputation, allowed no room for reassuring his fellow-Jews sufficiently on the meaning of this important passage, therefore necessitating the writing of his brief but incisive commentary, again with the goal of blunting any possible impact of the new missionizing endeavor. Over and above the specific reassurance with respect to this critical passage, Nahmanides sought to impress on his Jewish readers the proper approach to biblical texts. His methodological emphasis lay in the careful contextual reading of disputed passages. For him, Christian exegesis of the Servant of the Lord passage erred fundamentally in its failure to read the passage in its entirety and in its direct and unadorned sense. In his extended commentary on this passage, the Ramban urged his fellow-Jews to remember that beyond the new missionizing effort to utilize rabbinic sources to prove Christian truth lay the old missionizing issue of proper reading of the record of divine revelation. What Nahmanides wished to urge on his fellow-Jews was that they bear firmly in mind what he perceived as the fallaciousness of Christian exegesis and the abiding appropriateness of traditional Jewish understanding of Scriptures. The correctness of Jewish reading of the Bible lay, for Nahmanides as for so many other Jewish exegetes, in its concern for literal and contextual exposition of the text. This was a message that he was anxious to communicate to his fellow-Jews, now under heavy and innovative missionizing pressure.

Inevitably, in the process of affording this guidance on the specific issue of the alleged suffering and death of the messiah and the more general matter of proper exegetical procedures, the rabbi of Gerona touched on a number of further issues as well. He attacked once more a Christian proof text for the combined divinity and humanity of the messiah and—more important—addressed the central issue in the new missionizing argumentation, the advent of the messiah. In the course of explicating the Isaiah passage, the rabbi reinforced his general message, identifying the claim of prior advent of the messiah as Christianity's most egregious error and reassuring his Jewish readers once more of the redemption that inevitably lay in store for them.

7

Messianic Redemption:
Certain and Predictable

Nahmanides's third and final post-1263 literary venture again involved a genre with which he was familiar and comfortable, the topical treatise. His post-1263 treatise, *Sefer ha-Geʾulah*, addressed the issue that was ultimately the most pressing to emerge from the new missionizing in general and the Barcelona confrontation in particular, the Christian claim of the hopelessness of Jewish circumstances and the Jewish conviction of an inevitable future redemption.[1]

Nahmanides defines the purpose of his treatise concisely but clearly at the outset:

> We are required to steady [our] loins and to brace all [our] strength[2] in order to know how to speak in timely fashion to those weary of exile the message of redemption.[3]

The numerous references throughout the treatise to the claims of Christianity indicate clearly the origins of this treatise in the missionizing campaign that began in the 1240s; the elaboration of the messianic speculation adumbrated in more limited fashion in the narrative account indicates clearly the dependence of this treatise on the Barcelona confrontation and on Nahmanides's earlier narrative report of it.

Nahmanides's goal in his *Sefer ha-Geʾulah* was to combat the Christian claim that the messiah had already come in the person of Jesus and to reassert the Jewish contention of a messianic promise both inviolable and as yet unfulfilled. Nahmanides, who was a keen student of and commentator on the Bible, based his case on a close reading of key biblical texts from all segments of the Hebrew Bible. He opened his treatise with consideration of a number of important Pentateuchal passages, particularly from Deuteronomy. He begins by noting the special quality of the Mosaic books:

It is known to all who are truly literate that our Torah [i.e., the five books of Moses] is not composed of predictions and oracles, like most of the words of the prophets and of the writings [i.e., the third and concluding segment of the Hebrew Bible], and that Moses, peace unto him, was alone the prophet of the commandments. Through him, they [the commandments] have come and reached us. No prophet is permitted to innovate with respect to them [the commandments] at all.[4] Therefore, the purpose of most of his statements was not to announce to us coming events. Rather, he indicated the calamities to come by way of warning and the benefits and consolations [to come] by way of encouragement. All of them [both the statements of calamities and consolations] were conditional: life and good when we serve him and death and evil when we rebel against him. It is true, however, that among his rebukes and his consolations he informed us, in many places, of the signs [of things to come] and revealed the future, either in allusions or explicitly.[5]

Thus, according to Nahmanides, the Torah, while the preeminent source of the commandments, with a concern for addressing the future in conditional terms, nonetheless does, at key points, make known unconditionally the future of the Jewish people.

According to Nahmanides, Deut. 4:25–31 is a passage that presents, at one and the same time, both conditional and categorical statements about the future of the Jewish people. Let us note the biblical text:

Should you, when you have begotten children and children's children and are long established in the land, act wickedly and make for yourselves a sculptured image in any likeness, causing the Lord your God displeasure and vexation, I call heaven and earth to witness against you this day that you shall soon perish from the land which you are crossing the Jordan to occupy; you shall not long endure in it, but be utterly wiped out. The Lord will scatter you among the peoples, and only a scant few of you shall be left among the nations to which the Lord will drive you. There you will serve manmade gods of wood and stone, that cannot see or hear or eat or smell.

But if you search there for the Lord your God, you will find him, if only you seek him with all your heart and soul—when you are in distress because all these things have befallen you and, in the end, return to the Lord your God and obey him. For the Lord your God is a compassionate God: he will not fail you nor will he let you perish; he will not forget the covenant which he made under oath with your fathers.[6]

For Nahmanides, this important passage is conditional, a warning to the children of Israel of what will befall them *if* they abandon the Lord and an assurance that the God who will punish them for their disobedience will also redeem them *if* they return to him wholeheartedly. At the same time, according to Nahmanides, this passage also adumbrates that which will in fact take place: the Jews were fated to sin and suffer; they are similarly fated to repent and be redeemed.[7] This is but the first of a series of Pentateuchal passages that Rabbi Moses interprets in this fashion. In all, he sees the realities of future repentance and redemption foreshadowed.[8] For the Ramban, the Pentateuchal message of ultimate redemption and salvation is presented yet more forcefully in the writings of the prophets. Again, there is a combination of conditional and unconditional statements of the future, but, according to Rabbi Moses, the unconditional element in the prophetic statements is even clearer than it is in the Pentateuch.[9] For Nahmanides, the clearest of all books of the biblical corpus in its affirmation of an unconditional redemption is of course the Book of Daniel. It contains, in his view, a series of images that allude to the actualities of world history and a series of numerical hints that, when read properly, reveal the secrets of the messianic coming.[10]

Nahmanides was well aware that the Christian world was familiar with these passages and read them differently. He therefore addressed two important Christian attacks on the message of future redemption that he was attempting to deliver to his people. The first such attack involved the suggestion that the divine promise of redemption was real but that the promised redemption had already taken place with the return from Babylonian exile in the sixth pre-Christian century. While in no way contesting the validity of the biblical message of redemption, this Christian view argued to the Jews that it had taken place and that there remained no hope for the Jewish future. The second line of Christian argumentation was that the Jews had forfeited this promised redemption, superseded by the Christians who had supplanted the Jews in their acceptability to God. Nahmanides, like many medieval Jews, argued strenuously against both these views.

Let us note first his rebuttal of the notion that redemption had already been vouchsafed to the Jews and hence no future promise of salvation remained. Since I have already cited the Ramban's use of Deut. 4:25–31, let us note his stand with respect to that important passage.

Indeed, the content [of the passage] proves that it does not refer to the redemption from Babylonia. For it [the redemption from Babylonian exile] did not take place at the end of days, rather [it took place] close to the time of their exile. Furthermore, this promise was extended to all of Israel, not to a fifth [of Israel]. However, only part of the tribe of Judah and Benjamin, along with some of the chaff, returned in the second redemption [i.e., the return from Babylonian exile], while the pure wheat remained in Babylonia.[11]

Nahmanides here combats the view that this Deuteronomic promise had already been realized. He argues once more that close reading of the text proves that the promise contained in Deut. 4:25–31 could not possibly have referred to the return from Babylonian exile and that it must perforce be understood as a reference to future redemption. The characteristics of the redemption promised in the passage—its temporal distance from exile and its inclusion of the entirety of the Jewish people—were not in evidence in the return from Babylonian exile. This promised redemption must then lie in the future.[12]

Let us note one more interesting instance of Nahmanides's wrestling with the Christian claim of a promise of redemption that has already been fulfilled. For Rabbi Moses, a further proof of unconditional redemption lies in the lengthy passages of warning in the Torah which end with promises of reacceptance by the Lord. There are two such passages, one in Leviticus and one in Deuteronomy. Nahmanides makes the following case, based on the dual passages.

When we examine closely the passages of rebuke, we shall correctly understand that the rebukes in the Torah in the reading that begins, "If [you follow] my laws,"[13] are warnings concerning the first exile and a promise of redemption from it. The warnings in Deuteronomy in the reading that begins, "When you enter the land,"[14] are a warning of this exile and a promise that we shall be redeemed from it.[15]

Nahmanides provides lengthy proof of his contention that the Leviticus passage must be seen as predictive of Babylonian exile and redemption from it, with the Deuteronomy passage referring to the later exile and the future redemption from it. For our purposes, this argument once again reflects the rabbi's awareness of the Christian contention of a prior redemption and his extensive effort to combat that damaging claim.

As already noted, there was a second Christian claim to be com-

bated as well, the contention that the Jews had forfeited their right
to redemption. Nahmanides addresses this view also. After citing
Deut. 4:25–31 as his first evidence of an unconditional promise of
redemption, Rabbi Moses next adduces Deut. 30:1–10. After explicating aspects of this passage, Nahmanides makes the following
observations.

> All this passage indicates that it refers to future redemption. But
> even to the obstinate who does not wish to acknowledge that it is
> a prediction of the future but only [that it is] a conditional statement,
> one of the conditional statements in the Torah, in any case our re-
> demption lies in our hands, in our return to God. We have not lost
> it [redemption] because of the multiplicity of our sins, nor has its
> time passed because of the length of the days of our rebelliousness.
> For indeed Moses our lord, peace unto him, threatens us with all
> forms of warning and threat which frighten us with every form of
> fright and fear, as has in fact come upon us. Yet beyond those [fear-
> ful threats], he never threatened us that, if we continue at length to
> sin, he would exchange us for another people or forget us entirely.
> The covenant between us and our God with the acceptance of his
> Torah was not established with any such condition [i.e., abrogation
> because of lengthy sinning]; rather he [God] always made it [the
> covenant] dependent upon our repentance or, in some instances,
> prior to our repentance upon [his] memory and mercy, as in the case
> of: "And I shall remember my covenant with Jacob."[16] Such is al-
> ways the conclusion of his rebukes. It is not as many, such as the
> heretics who reject the yoke [of the commandments] and the despi-
> cable people who worship a created being[17] and the rest of the faiths,
> contend against us.[18]

This passage reflects full awareness of Christian claims of the suspension of the covenant and of the promises of even conditional
redemption. Nahmanides again argues that the direct and simple
testimony of the Bible militates against such arguments.

Thus, Nahmanides set out in his *Sefer ha-Ge'ulah* to reassure his
fellow-Jews of the inevitability of redemption, whether activated
by their own repentance or by God's promise of eventual unconditional salvation. In so doing, Rabbi Moses was very much in the
mainstream of traditional Jewish reaction to Christian argumentation and, more specifically, of mid-thirteenth-century Jewish
reaction to the new Christian missionizing initiative. As was the
case in Barcelona, however, Nahmanides chose to move a step
further and to claim that he could identify with precision the date
of this future redemption. To be sure, Nahmanides could have
adequately discharged his responsibilities by rebutting the claims

of earlier fulfillment of redemptive prophecies and by arguing for a vague future redemption. Reassurance of future redemption did not require such explicit prediction of the messianic coming. Nonetheless, Rabbi Moses chose to be precise and clear-cut in identifying the date of the messianic coming. Unquestionably, such explicitness served as a more impressive buttressing of Jewish faith than would bland assertions of some undisclosed future redemption. Equally certain is the fact that others in the Jewish community might look askance at such precise predictions.[19]

Let us begin this discussion of Nahmanides's messianic calculation by recalling the striking passage in his narrative which dealt with the same issue. In his narrative, he claimed that the Book of Daniel contains but one clear indication of the date of the advent of the messiah: 1,290 years and 1,335 years found at the very close of the book. According to Nahmanides, these dates, which signal the onset and the completion of the process of redemption, must be reckoned from the destruction of the Second Temple, giving straightforward messianic dates of 1358 c.e. and 1403 c.e.[20] To gain a fuller sense of the seriousness of this reckoning, let us now note the closing sentences of the passage in which Nahmanides elucidates his messianic computation.

> Behold, there have now passed from the time of the destruction [of the Second Temple] 1,195 years [= 1263 c.e.]. Thus, there are missing from the number specified by Daniel 95 years. We hope that the redeemer will come at that time, for this explication [of the Daniel text] is correct and proper. It is fitting to believe in it.[21]

By spelling out the precise implications of his claims in terms of proximity to the onset of messianic redemption, Nahmanides makes it clear that his comments are not to be taken as intellectual ruminations but as firm statements of the obvious and inevitable dating of redemption.

Because the *Sefer ha-Ge'ulah* is fuller and more detailed than the argumentation in Nahmanides's report on the Barcelona proceedings, there are a few points that deserve special note. The first is the author's awareness of the constraints on attempting to identify precisely the date of redemption. This may well be a fuller explication of his brief observation in the Barcelona narrative that his precise predictions might offend some of his fellow-Jews. In the longer discussion in the *Sefer ha-Ge'ulah*, Nahmanides notes two objections to his enterprise. The first is the broad failure of previous efforts, and the second is explicit rabbinic condemnation of the practice.[22] Both are weighty considerations, and Nahmanides provides a parallel response to both. Let us note his response to the failure of his distinguished forebears to identify correctly the dates of the messianic coming.

> Indeed, I believe that their error was the result of God's will that the [appointed] end be obscured, as is said, "Many will range far and wide and knowledge will increase,"[23] and not because the [appointed] end is terribly hidden in this book.[24] The reason for the initial obscuring lay in the length of the exile and the distance of the [appointed] end, as is said, "Now you keep the vision a secret, for it pertains to far-off days."[25] Now behold, we in this generation—diminished in stature and ability and deprived of knowledge and intelligence—our souls suffer incessantly exile and travail, to the point that our hearts react like dead flesh that feels not the [surgeon's] knife—how can we dare open our mouths with respect to the reckoning of the [appointed] end, to know and to extract the hidden secret in this sealed book [of Daniel], concerning which the firm foundations of the earth [i.e., the great earlier figures who had erred with respect to computation of redemption] fell into error?

Not surprisingly, this note of insufficiency is succeeded by a large "however."

> However, since we are in a general way closer than they were to the [appointed] end—indeed, it is possible that we are in actual fact closer to it [the appointed end of days] in view of the great length [of time] that has already passed[26]—perhaps the [divine] decree that was enacted to obscure it [reckoning of the date of redemption] has been annulled. Indeed, the reason for it [the decree] has been eliminated, namely, the [notion of] far-off days. Because it says: "many will range far and wide and knowledge will increase," it is hinted for us that we are permitted to range after the [appointed] end in this book [Daniel] and to increase views concerning it.[27] From the statement that "the knowledgeable will understand,"[28] it can be learned that, with the approach of the [appointed] end, the knowledgeable will understand these allusions.[29]

Thus, while acknowledging prior failures in reckoning the date of redemption and the explicit prohibition of such efforts, Nahmanides makes the audacious claim that his generation's proximity to redemption makes the success of such speculation likely and removes the basis for the earlier prohibition.

Not only is Rabbi Moses more explicit in this treatise in recognizing objections to his reckoning of the end of days and in rebutting these objections but he is also fuller in making his case for redemption beginning 1,290 years after the destruction of the Second Temple, that is, in the year 1358 c.e., and concluding 45 years later. As we recall, his case at Barcelona was drawn entirely from Dan. 12:11–12. Indeed, he argued at Barcelona that this was the only point at which the Book of Daniel reveals the end of days.[30] In his *Sefer ha-Ge'ulah*, written after the Barcelona confrontation and after his narrative account, Rabbi Moses expanded his case, identifying five points in the Book of Daniel at which information on the precise date of the messiah are afforded: (1) Dan. 7:25, (2) Dan. 12:7, (3) Dan. 8:14, (4) Dan. 12:11, and (5) Dan. 12:12.[31] Rabbi Moses begins with the last two, presenting essentially the same case that we have already noted at Barcelona. For Nahmanides, these verses prove that messianic deliverance will begin with the messiah son of Joseph's arrival 1,290 years after the destruction of the Second Temple and will be completed with the arrival of the messiah son of David 1,335 years after the destruction of the Second Temple.[32] This is surely the heart of Rabbi Moses's messianic speculation.

In the *Sefer ha-Ge'ulah*, however, Rabbi Moses presents a case derived from each of the remaining three Daniel verses as well. The case from Dan. 7:25 and 12:7 both involve indication of the passage of "a time, two times, and half a time."[33] For Nahmanides, the unit involved was the paradigmatic 440 years of the first exile, that into Egypt. Three and one-half times that paradigmatic unit of 440 years gives a total of 1,540 years. For Nahmanides, this means that the predictions in Daniel correspond precisely to the combination of 206 years of Roman control over the Jews prior to the destruction of the Second Temple and the 1,335 years between the destruction of the Second Temple and the arrival of the messiah son of David predicted in Dan. 12:12.[34] What this means for Nahmanides is confirmation of the date that he had derived from Dan. 12:11 and 12:12.

In a more complex way, Nahmanides explains the 2,300 years indicated in Dan. 8:14, thereby reinforcing once more the dating first adumbrated in his Barcelona narrative. Nahmanides argues that the morning and evening of Dan. 8:14 are a reference to the first anointed king of Israel, David, and the last anointed king of Israel, the messianic redeemer. Careful calculation of the time

elapsed between David and the messiah provides, for Nahmanides, further confirmation of his claim that the messianic redemption will be completed 1,335 years after the destruction of the Second Temple.[35] Thus, according to Nahmanides, all the relevant
verses in Daniel agree on the establishment of precisely the same
years for the advent of the messiah son of Joseph and subsequently
the messiah son of David. The shift in stance from insistence in
his narrative report that only the closing verses in Daniel offer insight into the messianic advent to the fuller case made in the *Sefer
ha-Ge'ulah* is softened by Nahmanides by his indication, à la Abraham bar Hiyya, that the messages were made progressively
clearer, with full clarity offered to Daniel—and by extension to his
readers—only in the closing passages.[36]

Yet Nahmanides was not satisfied even with this internal reinforcement from the Book of Daniel. He offers a series of further
confirmations of his dating. One involves introduction of a principle of historical symmetry or, as Rabbi Moses calls it, "measure for
measure." The result of the reckoning that he proposes is that, at
the point of redemption, the Jews will have in fact passed an equal
time within their land prior to the destruction of the Second Temple and outside their land subsequent to the destruction of the Second Temple. The latter figure is, of course, his 1,290 years drawn
from Dan. 12:11. He finds this equaled by the time spent within
the Holy Land, established in the following manner: (1) 440 years
prior to the building of the First Temple; (2) 410 years of the
existence of the First Temple; (3) 19 years of return to the land
prior to the building of the Second Temple; (4) 420 years of the
existence of the Second Temple. The sum of these four periods
equals the 1,290 years that Nahmanides saw as the predicted
period between the destruction of the Second Temple and the
onset of redemption.[37]

Nahmanides closes the case for his reckoning of the date of
redemption with recourse to the system of *gematriot*, that is, the
reckoning of numbers through utilization of numerical equivalents
for the Hebrew letters. Nahmanides chooses two passages in
which to seek such numerical hints. The first is Gen. 15, the striking of a covenant between God and Abraham. Rabbi Moses notes
that this passage contains an explicit number for the first exile, the
400 years predicted in verse 13. In addition, the rabbis had derived

from the prolixity of verse 12 hints of the four empires that were eventually to subjugate the Jews.[38] All this suggested to Nahmanides that there was yet more to be gleaned from the passage. He notes that the four Hebrew words that translate "and they shall oppress them four hundred" translate numerically into 1,293, which, for Nahmanides, is evidence of the 1,290 years of exile indicated in Dan. 12:11, along with the three-year suspension of divine service prior to exile indicated in Dan. 9:27. Thus, Gen. 15, beyond its explicit indication of 400 years of Egyptian exile and its more cryptic allusion to the four empires that were to subjugate Israel, hinted numerologically, for Nahmanides, at the 1,290 years of exile that he had derived from the close of the Book of Daniel.[39]

Finally, with his customary literary flair, Nahmanides closes the circle, ending his *Sefer ha-Ge'ulah* with precisely the biblical passage with which he had begun. As we recall, the first Pentateuchal proof adduced by Nahmanides for a divine promise of unconditional redemption was Deut. 4:25–31. He closes his case for establishing the precise dating of redemption by appealing once again to that important passage. Again, he indulges in numerological computation, noting that the key seven-word Hebrew phrase, "when you [are in distress] because all these things have befallen you in the end of days," adds up to 1,291. For Nahmanides, this means that in the 1,291st year of exile, the process of redemption indicated in the next words of Deut. 4:30 will begin. Once again, Nahmanides has reinforced his earlier case for the onset of redemption 1,290 years after the destruction of the Second Temple.[40]

The result of all this is a far fuller case for the onset of redemption in the year 1358 c.e. Rabbi Moses has buttressed the initial argument made in his narrative with further explication of the Book of Daniel, with appeal to the principle of historical symmetry, and with utilization of gematriot. His case could not be more complete.[41]

To appreciate fully the innovativeness of Nahmanides's reckoning of the messianic coming, it is necessary to make some broad observations on medieval Jewish messianic thinking, a feature of medieval Jewish spiritual life that has not yet been studied in requisite detail.[42] The earlier periods of Jewish creativity bequeathed to medieval Jews a complex heritage of views on the messianic advent. The central distinction, already noted, is the discrimination between conditional messianic advent, to be controlled by Jewish behavior, and unconditional messianic advent, to be set in motion by God—irrespective of Israel's behavior—at a preordained date. The Pentateuch and prophetic books were the major repositories of teaching on the conditional advent of the messiah; the Book of Daniel was the dominant biblical source for the dating of the unconditional messianic advent. It is interesting to note a talmudic passage that identifies the psychological importance of the latter pattern of thinking. In T.B., Sanhedrin, a dispute is recorded between Rav and Samuel. The former claimed that "all the appointed times [for the messianic coming] have passed—now the matter [of messianic coming] depends only on repentance and good deeds"; the latter said cryptically, "It is enough for the mourner to remain in mourning," which is taken to mean that Israel needs the encouragement of the doctrine of eventual unconditional redemption.[43] Clearly, Nahmanides, while deeply committed to notions of repentance and good deeds, was caught up with the doctrine of an unconditional redemption and with the effort to crack the code that controlled it.

Efforts to fathom the date of this unconditional messianic advent, especially through an understanding of the Book of Daniel, cover a broad spectrum, ranging from profound skepticism regarding such understanding to ongoing efforts tempered by considerable doubt to highly optimistic assessments of the intelligibility of the messianic advent and its revelation in Daniel. The major exegetical forebears of Rabbi Moses ben Nahman—Abraham ibn Ezra the Spaniard and Rashi the Frenchman—occupy the first two of these positions, while Nahmanides is at the optimistic extreme.[44] Nahmanides's stance toward calculation of the messianic advent is expressed in a number of ways—the literary format of his calculation, the comprehensiveness of his calculation, and, most significantly, the tone of his presentation. Let us attend briefly to each of these reflections of Nahmanides's optimism and self-confidence.

Speculation on the messianic advent in the course of biblical exegesis, as undertaken by such figures as Abraham ibn Ezra and Rashi, is in large measure the result of the demands imposed by the text under study. In particular, exegesis of the Book of Daniel simply requires the addressing of the issue of messianic calculation, even if the result is a high level of skepticism, as is the case for Abraham ibn Ezra. Similarly, discussion of messianic redemption in a detailed work on Jewish theology, as undertaken by Saadia Gaon, is a reflection of the needs dictated by such a comprehensive statement of theological principles.[45] It is striking that the literary format for Nahmanides's messianic calculation is a treatise devoted solely to that issue. He was not constrained to undertake his messianic speculations by the needs of the exegetical or the theological genre. He addressed the issue out of a desire to confront precisely that issue and to clarify for his fellow-Jews what he deemed necessary. Similarly, the lengthiness of presentation is striking in Nahmanides as well. His case is longer and fuller than any of his predecessors whom we have already noted. Again, the sense conveyed is a desire to investigate thoroughly the matter of messianic advent and to clarify the issue as fully as possible.

There is one major predecessor not yet noted, who, like Nahmanides, devoted a special treatise to the messianic coming and treated the issue at even greater length. Abraham bar Hiyya's *Megillat ha-Megalleh* is the fullest medieval Jewish messianic speculation at our disposal.[46] It is a work devoted to explicating the messianic coming; indeed, its examination of the issue is considerably fuller than that of Rabbi Moses ben Nahman. More striking than the parallels in literary format and in comprehensiveness of treatment, however, is the difference in tone. *Megillat ha-Megalleh* is, above all else, an intellectual exercise; it lacks the profound conviction that lies at the core of *Sefer ha-Ge'ulah*. The intellectualist orientation of Abraham bar Hiyya's opus is proclaimed clearly in the following early statement.

> We indicate at the beginning of our comments that if we are provided with two verses—one giving for the days of the universe or for the end of redemption one number and the second giving us a different number—let this matter not disturb us or impede us from searching and investigating. Rather, let us be satisfied with such. We are indeed fortunate and blessed if we be likened and compared to our sages, of blessed memory, the pillars of the world, who commented on one matter two comments from two different verses. In line with this approach, they gave a number of messianic dates. . . .[47] Therefore, be not surprised if we emerge with diversity with respect to the number of days which we shall examine. However, if we are presented with two verses—or all the more so three—that eventuate in one dating and accord it one number, then we are justified in establishing that dating and believing in it.[48]

Clearly, this tone contrasts markedly with that of Nahmanides, whose entire endeavor is aimed at providing his fellow-Jews with a high level of certainty as to the preordained date for the messianic coming. This brief look at major predecessors serves to highlight the special quality of Nahmanides's messianic speculation. Central to his purposes was firm encouragement to his coreligionists, achieved through a rigorous and detailed analysis of key biblical testimonies. The goal of this analysis was precise establishment of *the* date of the messianic advent, unsullied by either vagueness or excessive presentation of alternatives. The Jewish reader of *Sefer ha-Ge'ulah* was to be provided with clear indication of the impending redemption.

The Ramban's views on redemption, reflected first of all in his narrative and then more fully in his *Sefer ha-Ge'ulah*, illuminate yet another facet of this fascinating figure. As already noted, Nahmanides has become the focus of intensive research over the past decade.[49] There has been much written of the ambience that spawned this creative figure, his personal predilections, and those mid-thirteenth-century developments that most influenced his behavior and thinking. The role Nahmanides played during the Barcelona disputation and his post-1263 writing can be of some assistance in shedding further light on these issues.

In the opening chapter, I drew attention to the important work of Bernard Septimus in locating Nahmanides on the rapidly changing Jewish cultural map of the thirteenth century. Differing with a number of his predecessors, Septimus argued for a more nuanced portrait of Nahmanides as a man still enormously respectful of the Andalusian tradition. I would argue that Nahmanides's position on reckoning of the time of redemption lends additional support to the Septimus thesis.

The present analysis has suggested that the thinker closest in style to Nahmanides was the Andalusian, Abraham bar Hiyya. In a classic essay, Gerson D. Cohen attempted to distinguish Ashkenazic from Sephardic patterns of messianic speculation in two ways: by linking messianic speculation to messianic activity and by distinguishing literary varieties of messianic speculation.[50] Cohen's analysis led him to an interesting distinction between aggressive and rational messianic speculation in the Andalusian tradition and weak and illuminative messianic speculation in the Ashkenazic sphere. While more work remains to be done in this area,[51] Cohen's distinction suggests a Nahmanides heavily attached to the Andalusian Jewish world. The dating supplied in the *Sefer ha-Ge'ulah* surely fits the Andalusian model identified by Cohen. Rabbi Moses's speculation is cogent and systematic, based on a number of lines of analysis that all seem to converge on the same dates. This clearly puts Nahmanides in the Andalusian ambience as depicted by Cohen. Thus, it seems fair to conclude that once more Nahmanides cannot be readily pigeonholed, that he in fact sat at the crossroads of Jewish culture in a period of critical intermingling of traditions, that his criticisms of Andalusian Jewish life must be balanced against evidence for the ongoing impact of this ambience on his thinking.

More interesting yet is the importance of our findings for an appreciation of the personality and style of Nahmanides. As the sense of his historical importance has increased, interest in his personal inclinations has increased as well. A sense of Nahmanides the person has been difficult to achieve. He has left us little in the way of distinctly personal writing. The literary genre that most attracted him was exegesis, a genre that generally yields little real sense of the personality behind the pen. The two sets of activities on which most assessments of Nahmanides the person have been based are his role in the Maimonidean crisis and his kabbalistic speculation. From this combination has emerged the sense of Nahmanides as a moderate and conservative figure, anxious to mediate between the conflicting forces in the Maimonidean controversy and equally determined to limit the expansion and diffusion of the new mystical doctrines to which he was clearly committed.

Yet the Nahmanides whom we have been examining is hardly a moderate or conservative figure, at least in his messianic reckonings. Both at the Barcelona disputation—if we are to believe Rabbi Moses's own account—and in his *Sefer ha-Ge'ulah*, the Ramban is radical, original, and open in his messianic thinking. As we have seen, rather than occupying a centrist position as he did in the Maimonidean affair, he is at the far end of the spectrum in his reading of the Book of Daniel. On messianic matters, he proceeds far beyond received tradition to read both texts and history in his own independent manner. What is more, there is no hint of reticence in communicating his innovative findings. In the *Sefer ha-Ge'ulah*, he shared openly and explicitly his messianic views, and—again, if we are to believe his own report—he was willing to communicate these matters publicly to an important Jewish and non-Jewish audience at Barcelona.[52] The same Nahmanides who was so conservative and secretive with respect to kabbalistic teachings was explosively original and open with respect to equally dangerous messianic speculations. Thus, the material that we have been considering leads us to an interesting alternative perspective on this major thirteenth-century leader.

In fact, the details of Nahmanides's messianic reckoning may serve to raise further questions with respect to the standard view of Nahmanides as a conservative kabbalist. While all experts agree on Nahmanides's commitment to maintaining these teachings in a restricted circle (unlike the openness of his messianic calculation), there has been recent disagreement as to the readiness of the rabbi of Gerona to indulge in original and innovative mystical speculation. Moshe Idel has argued the standard view of the conservativism of the Ramban, while Elliot R. Wolfson has suggested a more innovative bent.[53] To be sure, Nahmanides's pattern of thinking in the two spheres (mystical and messianic speculation) may simply diverge—conservatism in mystical matters combined with originality and innovativeness in messianic thinking. However, in his messianic thinking, there is an odd combination of conservative pronouncement with innovative flair that may illuminate his mystical stance as well.

Very early on in the *Sefer ha-Ge'ulah*, in his discussion of the first Pentateuchal passage that he adduces, Gen. 4:25–31, Nahmanides makes passing reference to the rabbinic reading of the word *venoshantem*, which was interpreted by the rabbis as a numerological reference to the number of years Israel was fated to live in its land prior to Babylonian exile. This leads Nahmanides to suggest that the same passage may eventually produce numerological hints of the date of the future redemption as well. At this point, Nahmanides makes some important and highly conservative remarks with respect to the use of gematriot or numerical equivalents.

> One may criticize me for my reliance on calculation of letters, which is called *gematria*, and it may seem to him [such a critic] that it [gematria] is vain and meaningless, since one can distort certain

verses for evil and bizarre purposes through such calculation. We reply and clarify for such a questioner the matter in a truthful manner. No one is permitted to calculate gematriot and to infer from them in arbitrary fashion. Rather, there is a tradition among our rabbis, the holy sages of the Talmud, of blessed memory, that certain gematriot were transmitted to Moses on Sinai, as a memento and symbol of matters indicated orally, along with the rest of the Oral Torah, some related to aggadah and some to that which is prohibited or permitted. . . .⁵⁴ This matter [of gematria] is like the matter of *gezerah shavah*, upon which many essential laws of the Torah are dependent. It is similarly a method with which one can infer evil things which contradict the principles of the Torah. However, they [the rabbis] indicated with respect to it [i.e., gezerah shavah] that one is not to innovate a *gezerah shavah* on his own and that it [is to be used] to buttress teachings and not to contradict them.⁵⁵

The position enunciated by Nahmanides is unimpeachably conservative. There is to be no innovative utilization of the dangerous tool of gematria, only a repetition of such reckonings earlier transmitted by the sages.

Yet, in a striking departure from his own guidelines, at the end of his treatise, Nahmanides returns to precisely the text with which he began and innovates a gematria for which he offers no hint of prior tradition. The gematria that he proposes for Deut. 4:30—as well as that which he proposes for Gen. 15:13—are advanced directly by Nahmanides, without the appeal to rabbinic tradition that he himself had stipulated as a requisite for utilization of the technique. It seems that in the area of messianic speculation, conservative guidelines and innovative thinking proceed hand-in-hand, and it may well be that the same combination is present in his kabbalistic thinking also. Whether this is so or not, the Ramban's messianic speculation is surely at odds with the moderate and conservation image projected in other spheres of his activity and thinking.

The originality and public quality of Nahmanides's messianic speculation may have been simply a quirk of Rabbi Moses's personality. Alternatively, and more compellingly, it may reflect his sense of what the times required. Much of the discussion of Nahmanides's kabbalistic teaching has emphasized its embeddedness in the particular circumstances of the thirteenth century—especially the need for a viable alternative to the philosophic reinterpretation of Judaism combined with an awareness of the dangers of rampant mystical speculation. Nahmanides was attempting, in effect, to reassure his fellow-Jews of the existence of deeper meanings to traditional Jewish practice and belief, without unduly exposing these Jews to the dangers associated with the search for these deeper levels of meaning.[56] At the same time, a second danger threatened thirteenth-century Jewry, and that was the assault from the outside, from a powerful and aggressive Christendom now deeply committed to the propagation of its belief system everywhere and among all peoples. Part of this new thrust was directed against the Jews living within the confines of Western Christendom, above all against the Jews of the Iberian peninsula. Nahmanides was in the forefront of the defensive effort against these new initiatives, parrying the thrusts of the new missionizing argumentation, attempting to convince his fellow-Jews that there was no real substance to the new claims, and striving to reassure his fellow-Jews that the historic promises with which the Jewish people had been blessed were still in effect and would some day— indeed, fairly soon—be realized. The pressure of this new missionizing led Nahmanides to take a more direct and public stance, including public discussion of the precise dating of the messianic coming. Once again, he was in the position of responding to a communal need, in this case without a sense of inhibiting restraints that might deter open discussion of the issues. Thus, what our investigation of the *Sefer ha-Ge'ulah* has ultimately led to is a fuller appreciation of the enormous pressure generated by the new missionizing campaign. To move the normally conservative Nahmanides to the radical posture that he adopted on messianic matters is most likely a reflection of his own sense of what the times demanded. His perception of the seriousness of the danger with which the Jews were confronted brought him to the more radical and public position that he adopted both in his narrative account of the Barcelona disputation and in his *Sefer ha-Ge'ulah.*

Indeed, this last point leads us to a better appreciation of the general circumstances of southern European Jewry during the second half of the thirteenth century. Not sufficiently recognized is the impact of the new missionizing campaign on the messianic predilections of this Jewry, now exposed to heavy missionizing pressure and to constant emphasis on the hopelessness of Jewish circumstances. It is easy enough to see the impact of this intensified Church assault on Jewish polemical writers of the mid- and late thirteenth century other than Nahmanides. The imprint of this Church pressure is seen clearly in the polemical writings of Rabbi Meir ben Simon of Narbonne, in whose dialogues and sermons the Christian claim of Jewish hopelessness recurs repeatedly and for whom rejection of this claim is crucial. We might note in particular the two surviving sermons of Rabbi Meir, which both focus on rebuttal of the Christian argument for Jewish hopelessness.[57] The treatise of Rabbi Mordechai ben Jehosapha of Avignon, the *Maḥazik Emunah,* affords further testimony to the same pressure and to similar efforts at reassurance of the Jews. This treatise, which is directly linked to the missionizing campaign of Friar Paul, constitutes a full and searching examination of the twin themes of exile and redemption, the purpose of which is again full reassurance to Jews buffeted by the new missionizing pressures.[58]

While these polemical works provide the most obvious reflections of the new Jewish concern with exile and redemption, recent work suggests that the same issues are strikingly attested in the nascent mystical movements of the period.[59] The newness of these mystical movements and the flexibility and elasticity of their imagery made them highly responsive to current issues of the times. Just as some of the intracommunal tension that characterized Spanish Jewish life during the second half of the thirteenth century is amply reflected in the new mystical writings,[60] so, too, the new missionizing pressures and the concerns they engendered with redemption, its inevitability, and its imminence are clearly attested in these circles.

Recent work has emphasized a dual track to the vibrant Jewish mysticism of this period—the personal prophetic mysticism represented most strikingly by Abraham Abulafia and the speculative theosophic mysticism that culminated in the *Zohar.* In both cases, the messianic theme has emerged sharply in the research of the past decade. Moshe Idel has studied exhaustively the writings and thinking of Abulafia and, in his analysis, the messianic theme plays a central role, expressing itself in sharply divergent ways.[61] On the one hand, Abulafia emphasizes the spiritual element in messianic doctrine, transposing it into a theory of ascendance of the spiritual over the material. On the other hand, there is a powerful concern with the historical theater of human affairs, with Abulafia viewing himself as the promised redeemer and involving himself in a fascinating and abortive effort to see Pope Nicholas III in what was clearly a messianic endeavor.[62] To be sure, one need not posit any outside influences on the messianic activism of Abulafia. As Idel frequently emphasizes, Abulafia's prophetic mysticism and his messianic inclinations are intimately related. The kind of mysticism he espoused could lead ineluctably to a concern with messianism. At the same time, given the messianic concerns generated in a number of spheres of Jewish creativity, it does not seem unwarranted to suggest that Abulafia also may have been reacting to the new challenges posed by a militant missionizing Christianity as well as to elements of messianic fervor broadly current on the late-thirteenth-century scene.

Perhaps most striking of all is the recent uncovering of powerful messianic elements in the theosophic kabbalism of the second half of the thirteenth century. This is a movement that in its earliest—late twelfth- and early-thirteenth-century—stages shows no evidence of messianic predisposition. Indeed, Gershom Scholem emphasized this lack of messianic orientation in all of pre–1492 kabbalah, proposing repeatedly that this Spanish kabbalah was inward in its direction, with a distinct lack of the explosive messianism that was to characterize the later Lurianic kabbalah.[63] However, the more recent work of his students, Joseph Dan and Yehuda Liebes, has identified major messianic elements in thirteenth-century Spanish kabbalah. Dan's study of Rabbi Isaac Cohen of Castile reveals powerful messianic imagery in his writing. He analyzed at some length Rabbi Isaac's opuscule on the tropes of biblical cantillation, finding in this work a recurrent central theme of mythic clash between the forces of good and evil, with heavy emphasis on the eventual victory of the forces of good. This cosmic victory would bring with it an end to the exile of Israel and reestablishment of that people to its former glory. The centrality of this theme in the smaller work of Rabbi Isaac led Dan to a fresh analysis of his major work, *The Essay on the Emanations of the Left*. There, too, he found recurrent evidence of the same dynamic messianic myth. Dan's conclusion is that Rabbi Isaac represents a considerable departure from the general tendencies of the new mysticism of the late twelfth and early thirteenth centuries, the first in the southern European Jewish mystical circles to highlight a dynamic cosmic struggle between the forces of good and evil and the implications of this struggle for an end to Jewish exile and the onset of Jewish redemption.[64]

In an extraordinary study of the classic of medieval Kabbalah, the *Zohar*, Yehuda Liebes has analyzed in great detail the centrality of messianic imagery in this crucial opus. Liebes distinguishes in his study between the bulk of those Zoharic sections written by Rabbi Moses de Leon and the special literature of the *Idrot*, the literature that focuses on the mystical convocation convened by Rabbi Simon bar Yohai. According to Liebes, in the former segment of the *Zohar*, messianic elements, while present, are not central. With respect to this body of material, Liebes proclaims himself content to accept the Scholem view of an amessianic thirteenth-century Jewish mysticism. However, according to Liebes, the body of *Idra* literature is suffused with messianic thinking, and, for Liebes, this literature represents the most profound revelation of the thinking of the author and his circle.[65] Because the Liebes study is inaccessible to so many readers, let me cite the author's own formulation of his conclusions:

> With further investigation into the *Zohar*, it has become clear to me that a distinction must be drawn between two levels: one, the vast majority of Zoharic statements; the other, the literature of the *Idrot*. With respect to the former, the conclusions of Scholem are correct; however, with respect to the latter, I claim that the heart of its concern is messianic. With respect to the messianic foundations of the *Idrot*, I shall attempt to prove that the seeds of the later kabbalistic thinking are already found in it. In the *Idra*, it is possible to find an interesting and unique combination of mystical redemption and cosmic *tikkun*, tikkun that does not represent a restoration of the universe to its original state but rather a messianic tikkun, the likes of which never existed. I shall likewise attempt to show that the *Idra* presents to us a messianic figure, who is actively occupied in the tikkun of the universe. This figure is not the messiah himself—indeed, he will appear only after the tikkun—but it paves the way to redemption and makes redemption possible. This figure is the literary persona of Rabbi Simon bar Yohai.[66]

Liebes's study is thorough and convincing; it represents a considerable reevaluation of the development of medieval, late medieval, and early modern Jewish mysticism and messianism. For our purposes, it affords a sense of late-thirteenth-century southern European Jewish mysticism as anything but removed from messianic concerns. Rather, the concern with messianic issues is revealed as the deepest involvement of the work that most identifies the Jewish mystical speculation of this period and was fated to affect most decisively the further development of kabbalah.[67]

At the conclusion of his important study, Dan raises explicitly the issue of the genesis of these messianic concerns.[68] He argues that there was no discernible persecution at this juncture, thereby reinforcing the earlier Scholem contention that persecution and messianism need not go hand-in-hand. In the absence of evidence of major persecution, Dan proposes an essentially serendipitous explanation for the arousal of these messianic concerns. He suggests that the messianic interests of Rabbi Isaac of Castile were thoroughly personal and idiosyncratic and that the appearance of messianic strains in the *Zohar* result from the chance influence of Rabbi Isaac on Rabbi Moses de Leon.

The extent to which the *Zohar* moves far beyond the imagery of Rabbi Isaac raises in and of itself some doubt with respect to this explanation. More important, I would suggest that the evidence provided by the new missionizing campaign and the remarkable messianic response on the part of Rabbi Moses ben Nahman suggest an alternative. As noted earlier, study of medieval Jewish messianic thinking is still in its infancy. Much work remains to be done on both the modalities of medieval Jewish messianic speculation and on the motivations for such speculation.[69] With respect to the latter, serious messianic thinking in Jewish circles may be generated from within Jewish tradition itself and by the impingement of outside influences.[70] Influences from the outside may be exerted in a number of ways: through the impact of physical persecution,[71] through the stimulation of widespread messianic thinking in surrounding society,[72] or through the challenge of an assault on traditional Jewish messianic doctrine. Given the clear evidence of such an assault during the middle and closing decades of the thirteenth century and of the concern on the part of Jewish polemicists with reinforcing Jewish confidence in eventual redemption, the likelihood that the young kabbalistic movements might have absorbed some of this concern seems high. Rather than reflecting an idiosyncratic aberration on the part of Rabbi Isaac of Castile and its absorption by Rabbi Moses de Leon, the messianic orientation of both may well flow from the same influences that moved the normally conservative Rabbi Moses ben Nahman to take such a public and strident position on the imminent advent of the messiah.[73]

Thus, close analysis of the Barcelona disputation and its aftermath serves in the end to advance general understanding of the potent spiritual forces at work in southern European Jewry in the second half of the thirteenth century. The clear juxtaposition of the missionizing assault, with its emphasis on the hopelessness of Jewish circumstances, and the strident messianism of Nahmanides serves to alert us to the pervasive growth of messianic thinking in late-thirteenth-century southern European Jewry and to its genesis—at least in part—from this powerful new assault on Jewish life. It is precisely the clarity of this juxtaposition in Nahmanides that serves to sensitize us to the more general relationship between aggressive Christian missionizing and heightened Jewish insistence on the inevitability and indeed the proximity of termination of the lengthy exile and on the imminent onset of divinely ordained redemption.

Sefer ha-Ge'ulah represents the third and final literary response by the Ramban to the challenge of the new Christian missionizing. This effort, of remarkable originality and interest, was vitiated by the intensity of the rabbi's commitment to succoring his community. Determined to reinforce Jewish spirits, Nahmanides was highly specific in computing the onset of messianic redemption. What he gained in reinforcement of the spirits of his contemporaries, he lost in the enduring impact of the book. As we have seen, passage of the date calculated by Nahmanides cast this important work into desuetude. The rejection of this work by subsequent generations of Jewish readers cannot, however, dim our sense of the vitality of the thought that it embodies and the sharpness of the challenge that occasioned it.

Thus, in the course of his tripartite literary endeavor, Rabbi Moses ben Nahman attempted rebuttal of the new missionizing thrusts through formats with which he was intimately familiar—commentary and the topical treatise—and through a format he tried his hand at for the first time—the narrative account—with astonishingly successful results. In these three differing literary treatments, Nahmanides addressed a broad spectrum of issues, affording wide-ranging guidance and reassurance to his beleaguered brethren. From the comprehensive response of the rabbi of Gerona to the innovative missionizing, we have emerged with a firm sense of the seriousness of the new challenge and its impact on a variety of facets of late-thirteenth-century Jewish creativity.

Epilogue

By the end of 1276, all the main protagonists in the Barcelona disputation had died. Clearly, the event played a disparate role in the life of each. For the great conquering king of Aragon, it was surely a minor episode in a lifetime of remarkable accomplishment. For the shadowy Friar Paul, it was a major achievement and a high moment. While not the undisputed victory portrayed in the Christian source, the Barcelona disputation nonetheless represented for him strong support for his innovative missionizing endeavor, an opportunity for broad public display of the new argumentation, and a chance to provide this new argumentation with the stiff challenge of capable Jewish objection. For the rabbi of Gerona, the significance of the event lay somewhere in between. Despite the richness of a lifetime that was drawing to a close, the Barcelona disputation was, for Nahmanides, hardly the incidental episode that it was for his king; at the same time, it was nothing like the crowning achievement it represented for Friar Paul. It represented yet one more instance of the aged rabbi serving his community with wisdom and distinction.

The disputation itself was, after all is said and done, not a decisive event in the history of medieval Jewry at large or even more particularly of Catalonian Jewry. It was, to be sure, an impressive event that was attended by an imposing array of dignitaries, and it generated substantial tension and discomfort. However, it changed little or nothing in the lives of the Jews of Catalonia. The king remained amenable to the pressures that they were still capable of imposing, and the missionizing appeal continued to fall on essentially deaf ears. As we have seen, the Dominicans pressed ahead with their new argumentation—refining it somewhat along the way—and the Jews retained their sense of the vacuity of both new and old Christian argumentation—likewise refining their case as well.

While not a watershed event by any means, the disputation has been worthy of our attention for a number of reasons. In the first place, it provides an unusual glimpse into some of the realities of Jewish life in Catalonia in the mid-thirteenth century. Because of its public quality, it gave rise to unusual source materials that offer us rare insights into the lives of the Jews at this critical juncture. Given the general paucity of data for this period, the opportunity to examine such an incident in depth is to be prized. Moreover, as I have argued throughout, the contradictory data allow for an unusual exercise in resolution of conflicting source perspectives. As we have seen, the data have given rise over the ages to polarized perceptions of the event, and our challenge has been to find means for mitigating this polarization. The availability of evidence and the problematics of conflicting perspectives in and of themselves make the study an absorbing one.

At another level, the disputation serves to alert us to the constellation of forces that were at work in medieval Spain. To be sure, our sense of this event in the broader context of the medieval Spanish Jewish experience reflects the advantage of historical hindsight. I suggest tentatively that a public opinion poll among the Jews of Catalonia in 1264 would probably have shown 25 percent of the respondents believing that the event was of no real significance, 25 percent believing that it reflected the ongoing power and vitality of their community, 25 percent convinced that it represented the onset of more serious threats to their physical and spiritual safety, and 25 percent asking, "Friar Paul who?" With the advantage of historical hindsight, we can now suggest that the hypothetical 25 percent who were concerned about what the future held for the Jewish community of Catalonia and of Spain at large were ultimately in the right. In that sense, the Barcelona disputation was an early harbinger of the crystallization of forces that would, over the ensuing century and a quarter, erode the material and spiritual strength of the flourishing Jewries of Spain. There was no reason to be convinced of this incipient deterioration at the moment. Knowing what we now know, however, the Barcelona disputation becomes an ominous marker along the path toward decline of Jewish circumstances.

Finally, the disputation assumes significance for what it produced in its wake, particularly, the striking literary output of the Jewish protagonist. Our investigation has revealed still further evidence of the public role of the rabbi of Gerona. Not only did he represent his fellow-Jews during the tense and dangerous disputation but he continued to afford valuable leadership in the wake of the encounter as well. Exercising his many literary talents, he composed a commentary on a particularly problematic biblical passage, a lengthy and original messianic treatise, and, most important of all, a complex and successful narrative account of the proceedings at Barcelona, a narrative account that served as a guide to the new missionizing and its rebuttal while at the same time convincing his Jewish readers in a variety of ways of the utter nullity of Christian claims new and old and of the everlasting truth of their own tradition. Our analysis has led us into the heart of the rabbi's techniques for exploiting the inherent interest of his story and building thereon an extensive and persuasive popularly directed presentation of the Jewish case against Christianity.

Indeed, our closer look at Nahmanides's postdisputation writing has provided us with deeper insight into the rich and creative spiritual milieu of mid-thirteenth-century Iberian Jewry. Buffeted by a set of internal and external pressures, the Jews of the peninsula were, at this juncture, involved in the adumbration of a series of creative responses to the challenges besetting them. In a real sense, the foreboding generated by our awareness of what the future held in store for Iberian Jewry is mitigated somewhat by admiration for the vigor with which this still vital Jewry, led by such distinguished figures as the rabbi of Gerona, responded to the pressures mounted on and against it.

Appendix:
Rabbi Moses ben Nahman,
Bonastrug de Porta, and Astrug de Porta

Much has been written of late of the communal and literary activities of Nahmanides.[1] Most recent research has focused on the Jewish source materials available for reconstructing these activities. Less valuable—but significant nonetheless—is the non-Jewish evidence as it emerges from the archives of medieval Aragon. This material has been rarely mentioned, and where it has, it has not been subjected to careful scrutiny.[2] To be sure, utilization of such archival data for reconstructing the lives of particular Jews is more than a bit problematic. Particularly vexing are the problems of identifying specific individuals. Difficulties in orthography abound, and medieval archival records often give rise to more questions than answers.[3] Reliable identification of Rabbi Moses ben Nahman in the archival sources of Aragon presents difficulties that are serious but not insuperable. When those difficulties are surmounted, the result is a somewhat extended sense of this critically important figure.

It has long been recognized that Rabbi Moses ben Nahman of Gerona and Bonastrug de Porta are one and the same.[4] This identification was made initially on the basis of the well-known document dated April 12, 1265, which speaks of "Bonastrugus de Porta" as the "magister Judeus de Gerunda."[5] Since the issue addressed in this document is the charge of blasphemy raised by a number of churchmen in the wake of the Barcelona disputation and Nahmanides's Hebrew account of that confrontation, there can be no doubt whatsoever as to this identification. Indeed, the same identification is indicated in documents of January 2, 1258, October 17, 1260, and February 25, 1265.[6] As we have seen, these documents make it clear that, in fact, royal contact with the rabbi of Gerona predated the famed disputation. The first two documents (2/2/1258 and 10/17/1260) involve royal grants to the rabbi of Gerona; the second, in particular, involves sums that are quite substantial. Unfortunately, these documents do not specify the basis for the royal largesse, which would be most interesting to know. In any case, we are informed of positive relations between the king and the rabbi well in advance of 1263. The warm depiction of King James that is so obvious in Nahmanides's Hebrew report is, at least in part, the result of the personal relations between the two.[7]

Thus far we are on firm ground. The truly difficult problem lies with the identity of Astrug de Porta,[8] who appears more frequently in the Aragonese records than does Bonastrug de Porta.[9] This is hardly surprising, since he was a member of a very prominent family in Aragonese Jewry. Particularly noteworthy is Astrug's brother, Benvenist de Porta, wealthy and high ranking in royal circles.[10] The crucial question to be posed is whether Bonastrug de Porta (= Rabbi Moses ben Nahman) and Astrug de Porta are one and the same. The implications are enormous for understanding Nahmanides. If the rabbi of Gerona belonged to the famed de Porta family, our understanding of the man and his circumstances would be altered significantly. There is good evidence both for and against this identification. I shall present both sides of the argument, suggesting eventually that Bonastrug and Astrug must be seen as two separate figures.

First, the evidence for the identification. It should be noted at the outset that the names Bonastrug and Astrug, while separate and distinct, might on occasion be conflated.[11] The separate names, in and of themselves, constitute no insuperable difficulty. The most striking evidence in favor of an identification of Bonastrug de Porta and Astrug de Porta comes from similar charges of blasphemy leveled against both and seemingly parallel punishments imposed on both. The archival evidence for such charges against Bonastrug has already been noted.[12] The evidence for the same charges against Astrug de Porta comes from three Aragonese documents.[13] The first, dated May 29, 1264, indicates that the royal punishment of exile, earlier decreed, has been remitted, although payment of a heavy fine amounting to a third of Astrug's goods remains in effect. The second royal document, dated February 22, 1265, repeats the royal remission of exile and stipulates a somewhat different—and surely lighter—fine of 2,500 Barcelona sueldos. The third, of the same date, promises royal protection for Astrug de Porta. This third document, the decree of protection, is precisely parallel to a similar decree in favor of Bonastrug de Porta, dated April 12, 1265. The conclusion enunciated by Martin A. Cohen in his important study of the Barcelona disputation surely makes much sense. After discussing at some length the evidence concerning Astrug de Porta, Cohen concludes with the following:

> The alternative to the identification of Astrug and Bonastruc is the assumption that around the same time in the realm of King James there were two Jews with nearly identical names who became involved in nearly identical discussions, who uttered nearly identical blasphemies against Jesus, and who were both punished by the king with what we would assume to be nearly identical punishments, but cannot know for sure, because when the documents speak of one they are amazingly silent about the other. The assumption of identity is at least simpler.[14]

Cohen's conclusion is certainly a reasonable one. Again, let me emphasize its significance. If we are to accept this identification, then we would have a somewhat different view of Rabbi Moses ben Nahman than that traditionally presented. We would see him as a scion of one of the wealthiest and most powerful families in Aragon. This leads us to a last argument in favor of the identification. One of the most interesting of the personal documents emanating from the pen of Rabbi Moses ben Nahman was a letter written to his son, Solomon, who was clearly entering royal service.[15] The royal service reflected in this unusual epistle would square nicely with the notion of Nahmanides as related to Benvenist de Porta, with the nephew following in the footsteps of his uncle rather than his father. While not a decisive consideration, this letter offers further support to the notion that Bonastrug de Porta and Astrug de Porta are one and the same.

Now for the negative considerations. In the first place, the likelihood of indiscriminate confusion between the names Bonastrug and Astrug is minimal. While one instance of such confusion might be readily understandable, recurrent confusion is unlikely. In fact, the documents show a high level of consistency. In all but one case, Bonastrug is carefully identified as the "magister Judeus de Gerunda."[16] Astrug de Porta is regularly identified as a Jew of Villafranca del Panades. Although Cohen suggests that the 1265 reference to Astrug de Porta in Villafranca reflects the royal penalty of exile, in fact the documents continue to identify him with that city into the 1270s.[17]

As noted, the most impressive evidence for the identification of Bonastrug and Astrug comes from seemingly parallel prosecution for seemingly identical blasphemy, with both the crime and the punishment taking place during precisely the same period. It was this juxtaposition in time and similarity in circumstances that led Cohen to his conclusion of identification of the two figures. In fact, however, there are some notable discrepancies between the two cases. It will be recalled that the royal document of April 12, 1265, which relates to Bonastrug de Porta, indicates quite clearly that a penalty of exile had been suggested by the court impaneled by the king, that the penalty had been rejected by the clerical plaintiffs, and that in fact no such penalty had ever been inflicted on the rabbi of Gerona. By contrast, the evidence concerning Astrug de Porta indicates clearly that a punishment of exile had been imposed and that this punishment had been supplemented with an extremely heavy fine, which had subsequently been mitigated. Both the reality of exile and the added fine are not present in the document depicting the circumstances of Bonastrug.

To be sure, those differences alone would hardly constitute decisive proof that the two are not to be identified. Decisive proof is available, however. The post-1263 fate of the rabbi of Gerona is well known. For reasons that are not clear, the rabbi chose to leave his native Spain and make his way to the Holy Land. Of this removal there can be no doubt whatsoever. The date of Nahmanides's death in the Holy Land has never been definitively established, but his demise clearly took place early in the 1270s, perhaps in 1270.[18] By contrast, Astrug de Porta, the Jew of Villafranca, continues to appear in royal documentation of the 1270s, long after Bonastrug had left Spain and indeed after his death as well.[19] Given the consistent pattern of specification of Astrug de Porta, the Jew of Villafranca, and the continued evidence for his presence in Spain into the late 1270s, there can be no reasonable doubt that he is in fact a different personage from Bonastrug de Porta, the rabbi of Gerona. It is quite a remarkable coincidence that both men should have been caught up in parallel accusations in the mid-1260s, but it is clear that such a coincidence did in fact occur.[20]

The differentiation of Bonastrug de Porta from Astrug de Porta, above all else, precludes the identification of Nahmanides as a member of the family of Benvenist de Porta.[21] Nahmanides was surely a man of general stature, known to the king well before the famed disputation of 1263. While he may well have been highborn and well-to-do, he was not a member of the rich and powerful family headed by Benvenist de Porta.

Notes

PREFACE

1. My first study of the Barcelona confrontation was "The Barcelona 'Disputation' of 1263: Christian Missionizing and Jewish Response," *Speculum* 52 (1977): 824–842. Chapters 5 and 6 of my *Daggers of Faith: Thirteenth-Century Christian Missionizing and Jewish Response* (Berkeley, Los Angeles, London, 1989) focus heavily on the Christian thrusts at Barcelona and the Jewish reactions. In a review of *Daggers of Faith* in the *Catholic Historical Review*, Norman Roth noted, "The chapters on Paul Christiani and the Barcelona disputation are solid, reflecting also earlier work by the author on the subject (although more remains to be said on this)." It is out of my agreement that more needed to be said on this matter that the present volume has eventuated.

2. The conference, held in Wolfenbüttel, June 11–14, 1989, was both stimulating and delightful. I am deeply appreciative of the invitation extended by the organizers, Bernard Lewis and Friedrich Niewöhner.

3. For the literature on general developments in the thirteenth-century Church, in the Crown of Aragon, and in thirteenth-century Jewish life, see chap. 1.

INTRODUCTION

1. I shall refrain from any notes to this introductory depiction of the encounter. Fully annotated discussion of the sources and the reconstruction of the main lines of the engagement will be found below, in chap. 2.

2. Heinrich Denifle, "Quellen zur Disputation Pablos Christiani mit Mose Nachmani zu Barcelona 1263," *Historisches Jahrbuch des Görres-Gesellschaft* 8 (1887): 225.

3. Cecil Roth, "The Disputation of Barcelona (1263)," *Harvard Theological Review* 43 (1950): 118.

4. Hyam Maccoby, *Judaism on Trial* (London, 1982), 11. Further major treatments of the Barcelona encounter can be found in Isidore Loeb, "La Controverse de 1263 à Barcelone entre Paulus Christiani et Moise ben Nahman," *Revue des études juives* 15 (1887): 1–18; Yitzhak Baer, "The Disputations of R. Yehiel of Paris and Nahmanides" (Hebrew), *Tarbiz* 2 (1930–1931): 172–187; José Maria Millás Vallicrosa, "Sobre las fuentes documentales de la controversia de Barcelona en el año 1263," *Anales de la Univer-*

sidad de Barcelona. Memorias y Comunicaciones 1940: 25–44; Yitzhak Baer, *A History of the Jews in Christian Spain*, trans. Louis Schoffman et al. (2 vols.; Philadelphia, 1961–1966), I: 151–159; Martin A. Cohen, "Reflections on the Text and Context of the Disputation of Barcelona," *Hebrew Union College Annual* 35 (1964): 157–192; Salo W. Baron, *A Social and Religious History of the Jews* (rev. ed.; 18 vols.; New York, 1952–1983), IX: 83–87; Chazan, "The Barcelona 'Disputation' of 1263"; Jeremy Cohen, *The Friars and the Jews: The Evolution of Medieval Anti-Judaism* (Ithaca, 1982), 108–128; Alfonso Tostado Martin, *La Disputa de Barcelona 1263* (Salamanca, 1986); Chazan, *Daggers of Faith*, 70–85, 88–103.

5. The twentieth-century traditionalist biographies of Nahmanides, cited below, chap. 1, n. 41, were all composed for a Jewish audience only and continue the earlier tradition of partisan writing for internal communal consumption. From the other side, Jeremy Cohen has noted, in *The Friars and the Jews*, 111, n. 16, the curious story that appears in the *Enciclopedia universal ilustrada europaeo-americana* (70 vols.; Barcelona, 1907–1930), VIII: 1582, that, "as a result of the disputation, Nahmanides converted to Christianity and then helped in the conversion of many of his former coreligionists." Again, this represents a view that could only be broached before a partisan and uncritical audience.

6. See the account in vol. 7 of Graetz's *Geschichte der Juden* (2d ed., Leipzig, 1873), 131–138, which is the version cited and attacked by Denifle.

7. Denifle, "Quellen zur Disputation," 225–231.

8. The paucity of specific studies written from the perspective of Aragonese or Dominican history is striking. The event was of far greater significance for the Jewish minority than for the Christian majority.

9. Loeb, "La Controverse de 1263 à Barcelone."

10. Ibid., 2.

11. Ibid., 5–7.

12. Ibid., 6–7.

13. Baer, "The Disputations of R. Yehiel of Paris and Nahmanides."

14. Ibid., 181.

15. Ibid., 184.

16. Baer, *A History of the Jews in Christian Spain*, I: 152–159.

17. M. Cohen, "Reflections on the Text and Context of the Disputation of Barcelona."

18. Ibid., 157.

19. Ibid., 158–159.

20. Ibid., 160.

21. Ibid., 161.

22. Maccoby, in *Judaism on Trial*, presents his views of the event on pp. 39–75, some observations on the Hebrew text on pp. 76–78, an introductory note on the Hebrew text on pp. 97–101, his translation of the Hebrew text on pp. 102–146, and his translation of the Latin text on pp. 147–150.

23. For the other English translations, see below, chap. 4, n. 94.
24. Maccoby, *Judaism on Trial*, 56.
25. Ibid., 57.
26. Ibid., 74.

1: SETTING AND DRAMATIS PERSONAE

1. The style of this chapter will diverge considerably from the rest of the book. Since it is my goal here to provide a broad background sketch, I shall only infrequently adduce primary sources. Instead, I shall generally cite the established findings of prior scholars in painting this background portrait.

2. Robert I. Burns, "Castle of Intellect, Castle of Force: The Worlds of Alfonso the Learned and James the Conqueror," in *The Worlds of Alfonso the Learned and James the Conqueror*, ed. Robert I. Burns (Princeton, 1985), 6.

3. For useful recent overviews, see R. W. Southern, *Western Society and the Church in the Middle Ages* (Harmondsworth, 1970); Robert Brentano, *Two Churches: England and Italy in the Thirteenth Century* (Berkeley, Los Angeles, London, 1968); Colin Morris, *The Papal Monarchy: The Western Church from 1050 to 1250* (Oxford, 1989). All three provide excellent bibliographic references.

4. See the general portrait of thirteenth-century ecclesiastical policy provided by Baron, *A Social and Religious History of the Jews*, IX: 1–134. The important study by Jeremy Cohen, *The Friars and the Jews*, advances both a broad picture of ecclesiastical policy and an innovative view of the changing theoretical stance of the Church toward the Jews. In my *Daggers of Faith* and in my essay, "The Condemnation of the Talmud Reconsidered (1239–1248)," *Proceedings of the American Academy for Jewish Research* 45 (1988): 11–30, I disagreed with aspects of Cohen's innovative view. In this brief introductory sketch of thirteenth-century ecclesiastical policy, I refrain from discussion of the Cohen thesis. I shall address it fully in my forthcoming study, *The Decline of Early Ashkenazic Jewry*.

5. For an extensive discussion of the Church's stance toward Jewish usury, see Joseph Shatzmiller, *Shylock Reconsidered: Jews, Moneylending, and Medieval Society* (Berkeley, Los Angeles, Oxford, 1990), esp. chap. 3. In my *Medieval Jewry in Northern France: A Political and Social History* (Baltimore, 1973), I studied in some detail the development of ecclesiastically inspired anti-usury enactments by the Capetian kings, Philip Augustus, Louis VIII, and Louis IX. For a more thorough treatment of these important developments, see William Chester Jordan, *The French Monarchy and the Jews: From Philip Augustus to the Last of the Capetians* (Philadelphia, 1989).

6. It is worth noting explicitly the fundamental asymmetry with respect to this issue. There were no limitations on Christian expressions with respect to Judaism, while there were stringent limitations on Jewish expressions with respect to Christianity. This reminds us that there was, during

this period, no notion of equal rights to be enjoyed by all members of society. Rather, the controlling imagery was that of ruler and ruled, of host and guest, with an emphasis on the disparate rights to be enjoyed by disparate groups.

7. The assault on the Talmud has given rise to a considerable literature. The most important studies include Baer, "The Disputations," 172–177; Baron, *A Social and Religious History of the Jews*, IX: 64–67, 79–83; Judah Rosenthal, "The Talmud on Trial," *Jewish Quarterly Review* 47 (1956–1957): 58–76, 145–169; Ch. Merhavia, *Ha-Talmud be-Re'i ha-Naẓrut* (Jerusalem, 1970), 227–360; J. Cohen, *The Friars and the Jews*, 60–76; Chazan, "The Condemnation of the Talmud Reconsidered (1239–1248)."

8. Note, in "The Condemnation of the Talmud Reconsidered (1239–1248)," my analysis of the range of allegations made by the instigator of these charges, the convert Nicholas Donin, and of the more restricted grounds on which the Talmud was eventually condemned. The latter included, beside the allegation of blasphemy, the claim that the Talmud condoned and encouraged antisocial behavior toward Christians and that it contained teachings that were in and of themselves offensive to human reason.

9. It is worth recalling the Jewish claim, in the wake of the burning of the Talmud in 1242, that prohibiting the Talmud was tantamount to prohibition of Judaism itself, that this particular limitation in fact contradicted the fundamental ecclesiastical notion of the Jewish right to existence in Christian society. It is further interesting to note that Pope Innocent IV accepted this line of reasoning and ordered that those portions of the Talmud found free of offense be returned to the Jews, so that they might continue to live according to Jewish tradition while at the same time comporting themselves in such a way as to give no offense to their Christian hosts. All of this reinforces our sense of the inherent elasticity of the notion of responsible Jewish behavior.

10. See my *Daggers of Faith*, for a full discussion of this missionizing campaign.

11. See, ibid., chap. 1.

12. This valuable text was published by Joseph Kobak, *Jeschurun* 6 (1868): Heb. sec., 1–31.

13. My essay is entitled "The Letter of R. Jacob bar Elijah to Friar Paul" and will appear in the volume in memory of Frank Talmage.

14. Kobak, *Jeschurun*, 21.

15. Ibid., 2, n. 1, and 31.

16 Isaac Lattes, "Kiryat Sefer," in *Medieval Hebrew Chronicles* (2 vols.; Oxford, 1895), II: 238.

17. See below, chap. 4.

18. Note the discussion of the fuller sources adduced by Friar Raymond in my *Daggers of Faith*, chap. 7. There I draw attention as well to the greater acuity in the argumentation of Friar Raymond.

19. Kobak, *Jeschurun*, 21–22.

20. Ibid., 21.

21. Ibid., 15–17.

22. Ibid., 1–15.

23. Ibid., 18–20. Nahmanides, in his depiction of his own opening remarks at the disputation, mentions Friar Paul's prior preaching campaign. A further aspect of Friar Paul's anti-Jewish activity mentioned in the letter of Jacob is the disinterring of Jewish corpses. For a full study of this unusual activity, see Joseph Shatzmiller, "Paulus Christianus: un aspect de son activité anti-juive," in *Hommages à Georges Vajda*, ed. Gérard Nahon and Charles Touati (Louvain, 1980), 203–217.

24. Three valuable recent surveys of the period are provided in Joseph F. O'Callaghan, *A History of Medieval Spain* (Ithaca, 1975); T. N. Bisson, *The Medieval Crown of Aragon* (Oxford, 1986); and Burns, *The Worlds of Alfonso the Learned and James the Conqueror*. All three provide extensive bibliographic guidance.

25. Here we might note also the sensitivity to ecclesiastical law, which was to have considerable impact on the Jewish population of both kingdoms. This is reflected, inter alia, in James's anti-usury legislation and in Alfonso's *Las Siete Partidas*.

26. Burns, "Castle of Intellect, Castle of Force," 21.

27. Robert I. Burns, "The Spiritual Life of James the Conqueror King of Arago-Catalonia, 1208–1276: Portrait and Self-Portrait," *The Catholic Historical Review* 62 (1976): 1–2.

28. Ibid., 1–35.

29. Ibid., 5.

30. Recall the valuable emphasis of J. Cohen, *The Friars and the Jews*, on the role of the mendicants in the evolution of thirteenth-century ecclesiastical policy concerning the Jews.

31. In a fascinating discussion in her unpublished doctoral dissertation (UCLA, 1986), "On the Western Shores: The Jews of Barcelona during the Reign of Jaume I, 'El Conqueridor,' 1213–1276," Leila Berner reinforces Burns's sense of the ambivalent spirituality of James the Conqueror. The case involved what seems to be a request by a Jewess for royal permission for her to continue living with her Christian lover and the king's positive reaction to this unusual request. In her extensive discussion of the matter, Berner cites Burns's views on James's spirituality recurrently, suggesting that the case she has discovered lends further support to the Burns portrait.

32. On the situation of the Jews in the Crown of Aragon at this juncture, see most recently, Baer, *A History of the Jews in Christian Spain*, I, chaps. 4–6, and Berner, *On the Western Shores*. Both contain full references to the prior literature. Aspects of Baer's synthesis of medieval Spanish Jewish experience have recurrently been criticized. Despite shortcomings, his synthesis remains the fullest and best documented that we possess for any medieval Jewish community.

33. Baer, *A History of the Jews in Christian Spain*, I: 138.

34. Ibid., 147.

35. Baer's equation of ecclesiastical legislation with "a rising tide of anti-Jewish feeling" may be somewhat overstated. There were surely churchmen seeking fuller limitation of Jewish behavior who were motivated by something other than anti-Jewish feeling.

36. Ibid., 147–150.

37. Ibid., 188–189.

38. Baer's sense of a recurrent swing away from and back toward "true national religious ideals" has proven problematic to some critics of his historical reconstructions.

39. Bernard Septimus, *Hispano-Jewish Culture in Transition: The Career and Controversies of Ramah* (Cambridge, Mass., 1982); idem, "'Open Rebuke and Concealed Love': Nahmanides and the Andalusian Tradition," in *Rabbi Moses Nahmanides (Ramban): Explorations in His Religious and Literary Virtuosity*, ed. Isadore Twersky (Cambridge, Mass., 1983), 11–34.

40. *She'elot u-Teshuvot ha-Ritva*, ed. Joseph Kafeh (Jerusalem, 1959), 265, #208. I am indebted to Isadore Twersky for this citation.

41. See, e.g., Aaron Yerucham, *Ohel Raḥel* (New York, 1942); Chaim Chavel, *Rabbenu Moshe ben Naḥman* (2d ed.; Jerusalem, 1973); Jacob Even-Hen, *Ha-Ramban* (Jerusalem, 1976); Isaac Unna, *Rabbi Moshe ben Naḥman* (3d ed.; Jerusalem, 1976). Special mention should be made of the more sophisticated portrait drawn by Solomon Schechter, "Nachmanides," *Jewish Quarterly Review* 5 (1893): 78–121, and Haim Hillel Ben Sasson, "Nahmanides: A Man in the Complexities of His Era" (Hebrew), *Molad* n.s., 1 (1967): 360–366.

42. Note the important observations by Isadore Twersky, in his introductory essay to *Rabbi Moses Nahmanides (Ramban)*.

43. Note, inter alia, Amos Funkenstein, "Nahmanides' Typological Reading of History" (Hebrew), *Zion* 45 (1980): 35–49 (an abridged English version of this study is available in *Studies in Jewish Mysticism*, ed. Joseph Dan and Frank Talmage [Cambridge, Mass., 1982], 129–150); David Berger, "Miracles and the Natural Order," in *Rabbi Moses Nahmanides (Ramban)*, 107–128; Bezalel Safran, "Rabbi Azriel and Nahmanides: Two Views on the Fall of Man," ibid., 75–106; Shlomo Pines, "Nahmanides on Adam in the Garden of Eden in the Context of Other Interpretations of Genesis, Chapters 2 and 3" (Hebrew), in *Galut aḥar Golah*, ed. Aharon Mirsky et al. (Jerusalem, 1988), 159–164. David Novak will soon publish a volume entitled *The Theology of Nahmanides: Systematically Presented* which will include both an analysis of the theological views of the Ramban and important texts in English translation.

44. Note, inter alia, Efraim Gottlieb, "The Ramban as a Kabbalist" (Hebrew), in *Studies in the Kabbala Literature*, ed. Joseph Hacker (Tel-Aviv, 1976), 88–95; Moshe Idel, "'We Have No Kabbalistic Tradition on This,'" in *Rabbi Moses Nahmanides (Ramban)*, 51–73; idem, an unpublished paper delivered at the Jewish Theological Seminary entitled "Nahmanides: Kabbalah, Halakhah, and Spiritual Leadership"; Elliot R. Wolfson, "'By Way

of Truth': Aspects of Nahmanides' Kabbalistic Hermeneutic," *AJS Review* 14 (1989): 103–178; idem, "The Secret of the Garment in Nahmanides," *Daat* 24 (1990): Eng. sect., xxv–xlix.

45. See below, appendix.

46. Ibid.

47. For a full description of this seal, see Isaiah Shahar, *The Seal of Nahmanides* (Jerusalem, 1972). Daniel M. Friedenberg, *Medieval Jewish Seals from Europe* (Detroit, 1987), 124, discusses this seal more briefly. He concludes with the following observation: "The seal is among the most important in its category, and its accidental discovery is so close to miraculous that a certain scepticism has been expressed regarding its authenticity. (This writer does not know whether any metallurgical tests have been employed to resolve the question.)"

48. This letter was edited, on the basis of two manuscripts, by Solomon Schechter, in the *Jewish Quarterly Review* 5 (1893): 115–117. It was reprinted in Chavel, 369–371. There is no decisive evidence, internal or external, that this letter was in fact written by Nahmanides. There is, however, broad scholarly acceptance of the authenticity of the epistle. The copyist's heading that indicates that the letter was sent to Castile can be discounted.

49. In an important essay, Bernard Septimus has argued for a powerful antiaristocratic rebellion in Barcelona of the 1230s, in which Nahmanides played a central role; see "Piety and Power in Thirteenth-Century Catalonia," in *Studies in Medieval Jewish History and Literature*, ed. Isadore Twersky (Cambridge, Mass., 1979), 197–230. I suggest tentatively that Septimus's case is not thoroughly convincing on this matter. It is based in effect on a much later (late fourteenth century) source written by a descendant of Nahmanides, which is not the strongest of evidence. The case is buttressed by a royal document of December 1241, which empowers two or three *probi homines* elected by the community to fine or even expel from the city those guilty of defaming the probi homines and to adjudicate civil cases among the Jews. This royal document hardly suggests an antiaristocratic uprising or the results of one. It is a rather standard recognition of internal autonomy in the Jewish community. In fact, the Jewish aristocracy continued to exert powerful political control in Catalonia all through the thirteenth (and fourteenth) century. For our purposes, I am interested in suggesting that we do not yet have a sure sense of Nahmanides's placement on the Jewish sociopolitical scene.

50. Note the literature indicated above in nn. 43–44. It is clear that even the rich recent literature noted does not begin to do justice to the Ramban's remarkable range of talent and achievement.

51. Septimus, "'Open Rebuke and Concealed Love.'"

52. See below, chap. 7.

53. The voluminous literature on the Maimonidean controversy regularly cites the conciliatory role played by Nahmanides.

54. Note the two studies by Moshe Idel cited in n. 44 and Wolfson, "'By Way of Truth.'" Both authors agree on the Nahmanidean conser-

vatism in maintaining kabbalistic teachings in a small and closed circle. They disagree, however, with respect to innovative interpretation on the part of Nahmanides, with Idel seeing the Ramban as highly conservative here as well and Wolfson arguing for a more dynamic hermeneutic on the part of the Ramban.

55. See below, chap. 7. The findings with respect to Nahmanides's messianic stance will tend to support Wolfson's reading of his propensity toward innovative thinking in the realm of mystical speculation.

2: THE DISPUTATION OF 1263

1. Two manuscripts of the Latin account have been preserved, one in the royal registry in Barcelona and the other in the episcopal cartulary in Gerona. The former has been published by Charles de Tourtalon, *Jacme Ier le conquérant roi d'Aragon* (2 vols.; Montpellier, 1863–1867), II: 594, #16, and by Denifle, "Quellen zur Disputation," 231–234, #1. The latter has been published by Jaime Villanueva, *Viage literario a las iglesias de España* (22 vols.; Madrid, 1803–1852), XIII: 332–335, and by Enrique Claudio Girbal, *Los judios en Gerona* (Gerona, 1870), 66–68, #2. Baer, in his study of the encounters in Paris and Barcelona, has suggested that the Gerona copy actually provides a better text; Baer, "The Disputations of R. Yehiel of Paris and Nahmanides," 178, n. 2. As an appendix to his important article, Baer reproduced the Villanueva edition of the Gerona text, with two valuable emendations based on the Barcelona manuscript. For the convenience of the reader, I shall utilize Baer's reproduction of the Villanueva edition of the Gerona manuscript and shall regularly cite it simply as Baer, with the appropriate page number.

2. See above, intro.

3. Baer, "The Disputations," 180. Vallicrosa's study, "Sobre las fuentes documentales de la controversia de Barcelona en el año 1263," includes a lengthy rebuttal of the charges leveled by Baer against the Latin record. While I have not recapitulated the arguments of Millás Vallicrosa, but have approached the issue from a somewhat different perspective, my conclusions with respect to responsible utilization of this Latin account parallel his.

4. Ibid., 185–187. During the course of this intensive look at the brief Latin account, I shall refrain from providing precise page references.

5. For further discussion of this matter, see below.

6. I would suggest that this segment of the report does not reflect poor organization but rather woeful inadequacy in depiction. The issue was, in fact, far more complex, involving Friar Paul's effort to prove that the messiah was intended to be both human and divine. For more on this matter, again see below.

7. Baer, 187.

8. This is indeed the way in which I utilized the source in *Daggers of Faith*.

9. The Hebrew text composed by Rabbi Moses ben Nahman was widely copied and read. It was first published, from a problematic manuscript, by J. C. Wagenseil, *Tela Ignea Satanae* (2 vols. in 1; Altdorf, 1681), II: 24–60. It was published from a better manuscript in the *Milḥemet Ḥovah* (Constantinople, 1710), 1–13. In 1860, Moritz Steinschneider published in Stettin a critical edition, based on the Constantinople edition with variants supplied from the Altdorf edition and two manuscripts, one from Leiden and one from Budapest. The Steinschneider edition was reproduced by Reuven Margulies (Lwow, n.d.) and by Chaim Chavel, *Kitvei Rabbenu Moshe ben Naḥman* (4th printing; 2 vols.; Jerusalem, 1971), I: 302–320. My translations will be based on the Steinschneider edition. I shall translate the text that Steinschneider provides, including material that he saw as extraneous, which he enclosed in [. . .], and material that he added, which he enclosed in (. . .). For the convenience of readers, references will be made to both the Steinschneider edition (identified simply as Steinschneider and page number) and the more readily accessible Chavel edition (identified simply as Chavel and page number). There are a number of further manuscripts available. The Institute for Microfilmed Hebrew Manuscripts of the Jewish National Library has eleven such manuscripts, including the two utilized by Steinschneider.

In his study of the Barcelona disputation, Maccoby suggests that the text that we now possess has been interpolated at a number of important points. While I shall deal with the specifics of his argument in chap. 3, his claim is prima facie extremely weak. To propose without any textual evidence that important material has been added to a source is a highly questionable procedure. Nonetheless, since a thorough scientific edition based on all extant manuscripts is not available, I decided to do a textual sounding by examining a number of manuscripts at the points proposed by Maccoby as problematic and at a number of other key points as well. The places examined were (1) the introductory passage, viewed by Maccoby as problematic (Steinschneider, 5; Chavel, 302); (2) the agenda (Steinschneider, 5; Chavel, 303); (3) Nahmanides's comment about the eventual destruction of Rome, i.e., Christendom, another passage viewed by Maccoby as an interpolation (Steinschneider, 11; Chavel, 309–310); (4) Nahmanides's suggestion that Christian emphasis on messianic redemption equaling the rescue from hell constitutes a subterfuge (Steinschneider, 11; Chavel, 310); (5) Nahmanides's slashing criticism of the Christian doctrine of Incarnation (Steinschneider, 12; Chavel, 311); (6) Nahmanides's lengthy statement rebutting on the basis of biblical texts the Christian messianic claims advanced for Jesus (Steinschneider, 12–13; Chavel, 311); (7) a second Nahmanidean statement speaking of the destruction of Christendom, also viewed by Maccoby as an interpolation (Steinschneider, 13; Chavel, 312); (8) Nahmanidean interpretation of Deut. 30:7 as a reference to the destruction of Christendom (Steinschneider, 17; Chavel, 316); (9) the depiction of the closing stages of the confrontation (Steinschneider, 21; Chavel, 320). I examined seven pre-eighteenth-century manuscripts for these passages. One of the manuscripts—Cambridge Add. 1224—has a page missing, making it impossible to check items 3 and 4 in it. In another—the Leiden ms. utilized by Steinschneider—the copyist omitted the opening sections, beginning only with the establishment of the agenda (Steinschneider, 5; Chavel, 303). Every extant section examined showed essentially the same textual tradition, with no substantive changes, additions, or deletions. This means, in general terms, that the manuscript tradition for this narrative is quite solid and that we are thoroughly justified in utilizing the Steinschneider text as the basis for this investigation. A more specific implication is dismissal of Maccoby's suggestion of textual tinkering. I shall discuss Maccoby's suggestion more fully below, chap. 3.

In his review of my *European Jewry and the First Crusade*, in *Speculum* 64 (1989): 685–688, Ivan G. Marcus raised the issue of the relationship of historical reconstruction to the providing of critical editions of important medieval texts, an issue with implications for this study also. I should therefore like to examine Marcus's views and articulate my position on this issue. Early in his review, Marcus says the following: "The texts are very problematic, and Chazan has not heeded Salo Baron's call over thirty years ago: 'a renewed scrutiny of all the available sources might justify a new truly critical edition of these chronicles.'" At the close of his review, Marcus again notes my failure to provide "the needed critical edition of the Hebrew texts." Now, in this statement, there is a fundamental ambiguity: What precisely is meant by "the needed critical edition"? I can only surmise that this expression might mean one of two things: (1) that a critical edition of the Hebrew First Crusade narratives is the highest priority of contemporary medieval Jewish studies, that providing such an edition is far more important than any effort at historical reconstruction of the events of 1096; (2) that a study of the events of 1096 could not be undertaken without such a critical edition. Let us briefly examine both possibilities and their implications for the present investigation.

The first alternative involves a very high level of subjectivity, a personal preference for one project over another. With respect to the Hebrew First Crusade narratives, such a preference is especially problematic. Marcus notes in his review that "after consulting microfilms of the manuscripts, Chazan concludes that their [Neubauer and Stern] edition 'is quite faithful and accurate in its transcription of the Hebrew texts.'" Nowhere does Marcus dispute that assertion. He only points to holes in the manuscript and erasures, the latter of which (totaling seven) might now be read through the use of ultraviolet light. The decipherment of seven erasures would hardly seem to warrant a new critical edition of these texts. A new critical edition of the Hebrew First Crusade narratives would be a useful contribution, but it is my judgment not a high priority (the quote from Baron suggests, in fact, that he did not view it as a high priority either). Given the important texts that still lie unedited, redoing a text that has been done quite well does not seem a major desideratum. With respect

to the Nahmanides narrative, the need for a new critical edition is somewhat more pressing. The Steinschneider edition does not utilize all the
available manuscripts, and a new critical edition is a serious desideratum.
It has not, however, been my intention to provide such a new critical edition, and I believe that an analysis of the 1263 disputation and its aftermath is as important as such a critical edition. I hope that no one will take
me to task for choosing to do what I have done, rather than what he or
she would have liked me to do.

I noted a second alternative for understanding Marcus's "needed critical edition," that is, that a study of the events of 1096 cannot be undertaken until a new critical edition of the texts has been prepared. I reject
this alternative as well. With respect to the 1096 texts, again my assertion
is that examination of the microfilms suggests that the Neubauer and Stern
edition is highly accurate, surely accurate enough to warrant the analysis
that I undertook, particularly when the manuscripts can be readily consulted on microfilm. To suggest that a wide-ranging analysis is vitiated by
the failure to read seven erasures seems highly exaggerated. With respect
to the Barcelona text, I similarly argue that the present critical edition can
serve as a reliable foundation for the analysis I have undertaken. The only
valid way to criticize this contention is to bring instances in which the
analysis is contravened by textual considerations. As indicated, I have
studied the manuscripts (once more in microfilm, I confess) and have
found no substantive shifts that have caused me to question the textual
basis of this study. If others can find such textual bases for doubt, I shall
welcome those findings. I reject in advance any broad assertions that the
analysis cannot be undertaken until a new critical edition is available.

10. The issue of the copy prepared for the bishop of Gerona will be
discussed below in chaps. 3 and 4.

11. See below, chap. 4.

12. See below, chap. 4.

13. See below, chap. 3.

14. Denifle, "Quellen zur Disputation," 229.

15. Baer, 187.

16. Loeb, "La Controverse de 1263 à Barcelone," 13–15. Baer, "The Disputations," 181, n. 3, rejects completely Loeb's suggestion but without
supplying any basis for this rejection.

17. Baer, 185.

18. Note Maccoby's case for the reasonableness of this depiction in
Judaism on Trial, 63–66.

19. See above, intro.

20. The fullest treatments of the Tortosa disputation can be found in
Baer, *A History of the Jews in Christian Spain,* II: 170–232; Antonio Pacios
Lopez, *La Disputa de Tortosa* (2 vols.; Madrid, 1957), I; Baron, *A Social and
Religious History of the Jews,* IX: 87–94. The key texts are the voluminous
Latin record, published by Pacios Lopez, *La Disputa de Tortosa,* II; the He-
brew account published by S. Z. H. Halberstam in *Jeschurun* 6 (1868); Heb.

sec., 45–55; and the Hebrew account found in Solomon ibn Verga, *Shevet Yehudah,* ed. Azriel Shohat (Jerusalem, 1947), 94–107. The text to which I shall frequently make reference is the contemporary account published by Halberstam.

21. See below, chaps. 3 and 4.

22. The Hebrew term is somewhat unusual, taken from Job 21:24.

23. Steinschneider, 12; Chavel, 310–311. On this issue, see the important discussion by David Berger, *The Jewish-Christian Debate in the High Middle Ages* (Philadelphia, 1979), 350–354.

24. Halberstam, *Jeschurun,* 52.

25. Baer, 185.

26. Steinschneider, 5; Chavel, 302.

27. Steinschneider, 10; Chavel, 308. For Nahmanides's purported wresting of control at this point, see below, chap. 4. Note that at the end of the rabbi's long speech, the king again identifies Friar Paul as the interrogator.

28. Steinschneider, 17; Chavel, 316.

29. Baer, 185.

30. Halberstam, *Jeschurun,* 47.

31. Ibid., 48.

32. Maccoby, *Judaism on Trial,* 74.

33. Note the 1240 edict of King James of Aragon enforcing Jewish presence at conversionist sermons, in J. Sbaralea (ed.), *Bullarium Franciscanum* (4 vols.; Rome, 1759–1768), I: 376, #90; Solomon Grayzel, *The Church and the Jews in the XIIIth Century* (rev. ed.; New York, 1966), 254–256, #105; or Shlomo Simonsohn, *The Apostolic See and the Jews: Documents, 492–1404* (Toronto, 1988), 183–185, #173. Note also Nahmanides's reference to Friar Paul's earlier preaching forays, obviously with Jewish attendance enforced; Steinschneider, 5, Chavel, 303. See my analysis of a Jewish sermon delivered in the synagogue of Narbonne in the wake of a missionizing sermon, "Confrontation in the Synagogue of Narbonne: A Christian Sermon and a Jewish Reply," *Harvard Theological Review* LXVII (1974): 437–457. See also my *Daggers of Faith,* chap. 3.

34. Steinschneider, 9; Chavel, 307.

35. Baer, 186–187.

36. Steinschneider, 9; Chavel, 307. The rabbinic text cited can be found in T.B. San., 98a.

37. I would suggest tentatively that the combination "tam per auctoritates legis et prophetarum quam per Talmuth" reflects awareness of the twin assault from rabbinic exegesis of Scriptures and from freestanding rabbinic statements.

38. Baer, 186.

39. Recall the reference in Pope Innocent IV's letter of 1247 to the plea of the rabbis that, without the Talmud, Jews could not properly observe their law. See Heinrich Denifle, *Chartularium Universitatis Parisiensis* (4 vols.; Paris, 1889–1897), I: 201, #172; Grayzel, *The Church and the Jews in*

the XIIIth Century, 274–280, #119; or Simonsohn, *The Apostolic See and the Jews*, 196–197, #187. To be sure, former Jews like Friar Paul had no need for such information to appreciate the centrality of the Talmud for Jewish life.

40. Baer, 185.

41. See below, chap. 4, for a discussion of Nahmanides's formulation of the issues.

42. I have briefly discussed above the matter of the conclusion of the disputation and will address the matter more fully at the end of this chapter. For one of the texts utilized by Friar Paul to prove the annulment of Jewish law, see Robert Chazan, "Chapter Thirteen of the *Mahazik Emunah*: Further Light on Friar Paul Christian and the New Christian Missionizing," *Michael* XII (1990) 9–26.

43. Chazan, "The Barcelona 'Disputation' of 1263," 831–832.

44. For fuller discussion of these matters, see *Daggers of Faith*, chaps. 6 and 7.

45. Steinschneider, 12; Chavel, 311. For Maccoby's reading of this passage and my rejection of that reading, see *Daggers of Faith*, 194–195, n. 49.

46. Baer, 186.

47. Steinschneider, 18; Chavel, 316.

48. Recall that this was the central Christian thrust at Tortosa.

49. To be sure, Nahmanides claims to have projected the truth of Christianity into contention. On this report and its trustworthiness, see below, chap. 4.

50. Baer, 186.

51. Steinschneider, 17; Chavel, 316.

52. Steinschneider, 5; Chavel, 303. For the reasons Nahmanides depicts himself as active in setting the agenda, for his curious formulation of the agenda, and for Nahmanides's earlier claim to receiving the right to express himself fully, see below, chap. 4.

53. Steinschneider, 12; Chavel, 310.

54. Steinschneider, 5; Chavel, 302. Recall the evidence, noted in chap. 1, of prior contact between the king and the rabbi.

55. Steinschneider, 21–22; Chavel, 319–320.

56. Steinschneider, 17; Chavel, 316.

57. Baer, 185.

58. Ibid., 187.

59. See the full depiction by Baer, cited above in n. 20.

60. On this tactic, see below, chap. 4.

61. Baer, 187.

62. For fuller treatment of the complexities of Nahmanides's stance toward aggadic teaching, see below, chap. 5.

63. Maccoby translates—*Judaism on Trial*, 133—"The Jewish community here is large." I doubt that this is the intended meaning.

64. In my translation of this phrase, I have simply followed all other translators in accepting something like the Eisenstein emendation and

reading *me-migreshe ha-ʿir*. I think it likely that the meaning of the term (however it might be vocalized) here and a few lines earlier must be something on the order of "the councilors of the city."

65. Steinschneider, 17; Chavel, 316.

66. Baer, 185.

67. See Jean Régné, *History of the Jews in Aragon*, ed. and annot. Yom Tov Assis (Jerusalem, 1978), 58–59, #319. The sum of 300 sueldos corresponds precisely to the sum indicated by Nahmanides in his narrative. See Steinschneider, 21; Chavel, 319.

3: THE AFTERMATH OF THE DISPUTATION:
BROAD PERSPECTIVES

1. Failure to recognize the irrelevance of a declaration of winner and loser constitutes, for me, one of the critical shortcomings of the position sketched out by Martin A. Cohen in his important study of the Barcelona confrontation. As I have noted in the introduction, Cohen raises a series of crucial questions and makes a number of valuable observations on the available sources. What I find problematic in his treatment of the event are the following three issues. (1) Cohen does not, it seems to me, appreciate sufficiently the missionizing context of the encounter. The critical opening sentence in his treatment of the disputation reads as follows: "The texts of the disputation point to one inescapable conclusion, that the debate was not an open discussion, but rather a demonstration of Christian intellectual superiority contrived in advance." The first part is surely correct: "the debate was not an open discussion." The notion of "a demonstration of Christian intellectual superiority" is problematic. The real issue, as we have seen, was not a demonstration of superiority but an advancing of missionizing argumentation. (2) The notion of a struggle over intellectual superiority leads ineluctably in the direction of declaring a victor and a vanquished. This leads Cohen to his claim of an obvious Christian victory, which leads him, in turn, to an unjustified denigration of the defenses erected by Rabbi Moses ben Nahman. By emphasizing intellectual superiority and victory/defeat, Cohen was drawn back into the trap of taking sides rather than acknowledging the fluidity of the event and its results. (3) This then led him to seek an understanding of the rabbi's willingness to lend himself to a preordained defeat, which Cohen explains as a political ploy on the rabbi's part. All of this, it seems to me, constitutes a misunderstanding of the event itself and its complex aftermath. Again, my disagreement with Cohen's reconstruction of the event in no way vitiates the importance of the issues that he raises or the perspectives on the texts that he advances.

2. Steinschneider, 21–22; Chavel, 319–320.

3. Steinschneider, 21; Chavel, 319.

4. See below, chap. 4.

5. Steinschneider, 21; Chavel, 320.

6. Denifle, "Quellen zur Disputation," 234–235, #2.

7. Ibid., 235–236, #4.

8. Ibid., 237, #6.

9. Ibid.

10. Chazan, *Medieval Jewry in Northern France*, 149–153.

11. Robert Chazan, "From Friar Paul to Friar Raymond: The Development of Innovative Missionizing Argumentation," *Harvard Theological Review* 76 (1983): 289–306; idem, *Daggers of Faith*, 115–136.

12. On the continuation of this line of argumentation down through the Middle Ages, see Chazan, *Daggers of Faith*, 159–169.

13. This attack on the Talmud has given rise to a considerable literature. The most important studies have been cited above, chap. 1, n. 7.

14. Note the parallel conclusion of B. Z. Kedar with respect to the use of force versus the use of persuasion by the thirteenth-century Church in his *Crusade and Mission: European Approaches toward the Muslims* (Princeton, 1984).

15. Denifle, "Quellen zur Disputation," 235, #3.

16. Steinschneider, 16–17; Chavel, 315–316.

17. See above, chap. 2, for the complexities associated with this agenda item.

18. Steinschneider, 16; Chavel, 315. The citation is from Maimonides, *Mishneh-Torah*, Hilkhot Melakhim 11:1.

19. It should be noted that Nahmanides's report of the exchange on Maimonides is somewhat strange. It occupies the entire third day of the four-day discussion; it involves the introduction of only one text, as opposed to three or four on each of the other days; and it constitutes the briefest of the depictions of the four days of discussion. It may well be that the discussion of Maimonides was more complex and problematic than indicated in the Hebrew narrative.

20. Denifle, "Quellen zur Disputation," 236–237, #5.

21. For a discussion of the range of the charges leveled during the 1230s and 1240s, see Chazan, "The Condemnation of the Talmud Reconsidered," 16–27.

22. Idem, *Medieval Jewry in Northern France*, 139–142.

23. Denifle, "Quellen zur Disputation," 238–239, #7.

24. Ibid., 243–244, #10–11; Simonsohn, *The Apostolic See and the Jews*, 233–236, #228–229.

25. Denifle, "Quellen zur Disputation," 239–240, #8.

26. Ibid., 240–243, #9; Simonsohn, *The Apostolic See and the Jews*, 230–232, #226.

27. Denifle, "Quellen zur Disputation," 239.

28. Steinschneider, 5; Chavel, 302–303.

29. Note the omission of the opening section to the narrative and the statement on pp. 309–310, which Nahmanides claims not to have uttered publicly because of its offensiveness. To be sure, he portrays himself as

uttering equally offensive statements in the list that follows. I have earlier (chap. 2) criticized methodologically the approach of Maccoby who has chosen three offensive passages in the narrative and suggested, with no manuscript basis, that they are late interpolations. More significant yet is the pointlessness of isolating those three passages without noting all the rest of the passages that I now identify.

30. Steinschneider, 11; Chavel, 310.

31. Steinschneider, 12; Chavel, 310–311.

32. Steinschneider, 12–13; Chavel, 311.

33. Steinschneider, 13; Chavel, 312. Again, this passage is no less offensive than the earlier midrash that Nahmanides purportedly refused to introduce.

34. Steinschneider, 17; Chavel, 316.

35. We might recall at this juncture the famous story told approvingly by Saint Louis about a knight's attack on a group of Jews invited to debate religious issues at the monastery of Cluny; see Jean de Joinville, *Histoire de Saint Louis*, ed. Natalis de Wailly (Paris, 1874), 30. These Jews were assaulted by the knight simply for indicating their disbelief in the doctrine of Incarnation. To be sure, that case constitutes an extreme. However, that statements of the kind indicated above could have been made with impunity before such a large Christian audience strains credulity.

Closer to home, King James himself leveled heavy penalties on a contemporary Jew, Astrug de Porta, for blaspheming. Because of the technical issues involved in clarifying the relationship of Bonastrug de Porta (= Rabbi Moses ben Nahman) and Astrug de Porta, I have deferred consideration of the matter to the appendix. My conclusion is that the two are separate personages. Here we might add the heavy punishment of Astrug de Porta as striking evidence of Christian concern (indeed, concern on the part of James I himself) with blasphemy, again reinforcing our sense that Nahmanides could not have said the abrasive things that he reports in his narrative.

36. Denifle, "Quellen zur Disputation," 239.

37. Baer, "The Disputations," 177, n. 1.

38. In one of his poems, a fairly brief poem requesting divine assistance through the dangerous sea voyage to the Land of Israel, Nahmanides beseeches that he be saved from his enemies. There is, however, no specification whatsoever as to the identity of these enemies. The poem is conveniently available in Chavel, I: 422–423.

4: THE NARRATIVE ACCOUNT OF
RABBI MOSES BEN NAHMAN

1. Note, e.g., the *Maḥazik Emunah* of Rabbi Mordechai ben Yehosapha of Avignon, composed as a response to the very same missionizing campaign. Rabbi Mordechai cogently organized his opus into thirteen topically

arranged chapters, addressed to a number of the major Christian claims in the new missionizing argumentation. While Rabbi Mordechai achieved an impressive presentation and rebuttal of the new Christian argumentation, the dry format that he chose precluded broad popular interest in the composition, which has remained unedited. For more on this important work, see Chazan, *Daggers of Faith*, chap. 6. As a parallel to the success of Nahmanides with the narrative format, we might recall the similar success of Judah ha-Levi with the same format.

2. The most valuable treatment of medieval Jewish accounts of contemporary events can be found in Yosef Haim Yerushalmi's important *Zakhor: Jewish History and Jewish Memory* (Seattle, 1982), chap. 2. Also useful are Moses A. Shulvass, "Medieval Ashkenazic Jewry's Knowledge of History and Historical Literature," *The Solomon Goldman Lectures* IV (1985): 1–27; Robert Chazan, "Representation of Events in the Middle Ages," in *Essays in Jewish Historiography* (*History and Theory*, Beiheft 27; Middletown, 1988), 40–55; idem, "The Facticity of Medieval Narrative: A Case Study of the Hebrew First-Crusade Narratives," to appear in the *AJS Review* 16 (1991). It is worth recalling the broad observation of Haim Hillel Ben Sasson in his study of medieval Jewish historiography that "all medieval historiography is tendentious"; "Concerning the Goals of Medieval Jewish Chronography and Its Problematics," in *Historyonim ve-Askolot Historyot* (Jerusalem, 1963), 29.

3. Note, e.g., the stereotyping and didactic style of *Megilat Aḥimaʾaz*. Note the important study of Reuven Bonfil on *Megilat Aḥimaʾaz* in the volume in memory of Haim Hillel Ben Sasson, *Tarbut ve-Ḥevrah be-Toldot Yisraʾel be-Yeme ha-Benavim*, ed. Reuven Bonfil et al. (Jerusalem, 1989), 99–135. In this study, Bonfil argues convincingly against dismissal of some of the problematic materials in *Megilat Aḥimaʾaz*. I am not in disagreement with Bonfil; I am simply suggesting that the historiographic stance in *Aḥimaʾaz* is highly stereotyped and blatantly didactic.

4. I have argued extensively that this was the tendency of the Hebrew First Crusade chronicles. See Chazan, *European Jewry and the First Crusade*, chaps. 2 and 5, and yet more fully in "The Facticity of Medieval Narrative."

5. To be sure, there was also more subdued narration that focused on such issues as institutional grandeur or tensions.

6. Note the traditional biographies cited above, chap. 1. This has, in fact, been the tacit assumption of all prior serious treatments of the Barcelona confrontation, except for Denifle (who saw Nahmanides as a liar), Baer, and Martin A. Cohen.

7. There is, of course, a rich and varied literature on these matters. I have found particularly useful the work of Hayden White, especially his *Metahistory: The Historical Imagination of Nineteenth-Century Europe* (Baltimore, 1973); Albert Cook, *History/Writing* (Cambridge, 1988); and Lionel Gossman, *Between History and Literature* (Cambridge, Mass., 1990). I have

also learned a great deal from the work of James Young, especially his *Writing and Rewriting the Holocaust* (Bloomington, 1988), and from extensive conversations with him.

8. To be sure, even stenographic depiction is hardly unbiased or uncontrived.

9. Note, by contrast, the extensive effort in the Latin protocols of the Tortosa disputation to provide as close to a stenographic record as possible.

10. Note the drama in all modern depictions of the Barcelona confrontation, based completely on the narrative account of Nahmanides. Note reflections of the success in arousing widespread attention indicated at the end of this chapter.

11. Steinschneider, 10, 17; Chavel, 308, 316.

12. Note, e.g., the distinct lack of dramatic tension in the twelfth-century *Sefer ha-Berit* attributed to Rabbi Joseph Kimhi, in the twelfth-century *Milḥamot ha-Shem* of Jacob ben Reuven, and in the thirteenth-century dialogues created by Rabbi Meir ben Simon of Narbonne.

13. In Judah ha-Levi's great composition, there is some measure of suspense but certainly no element of tension and threat.

14. The author of this valuable account simply lacked the dramatic flair of Nahmanides. The account abounds in caricatures and lacks totally the sense of sustained tension generated by Rabbi Moses.

15. For the text of this exchange, see above, chap. 3.

16. For a full discussion of this effort, see above, chap. 2.

17. Recall the evidence from the Tortosa encounter which showed the pope deeply offended by some of the Jewish statements. See above, chap. 2.

18. Steinschneider, 6–8; Chavel, 304–306.

19. Note the classic study by Adolph Posnanski of the exegesis of this important verse, *Schiloh: Ein Beitrag zur Geschichte der Messiaslehre* (Leipzig, 1904).

20. Note also the exchange with respect to Isa. 52–53, depicted above, chap. 2.

21. Steinschneider, 18; Chavel, 317.

22. Ibid.

23. Ibid.

24. Nahmanides argues that there were periods during which there was no political authority among the Jews at all and periods during which there was political authority exercised by leaders from tribes other than Judah. Neither phenomenon, according to Nahmanides, vitiated the divine promise that legitimate royal authority belongs to Judah.

25. Steinschneider, 7–8; Chavel, 305.

26. For more on this, see below.

27. Steinschneider, 21; Chavel, 319.

28. Loeb, "La Controverse de 1263 à Barcelone," 9.

29. On the drive for novelistic verisimilitude, there is an abundant literature. I have found particularly helpful the work of Robert Alter, including a number of his essays in *Motives for Fiction* (Cambridge, Mass., 1984) and *The Pleasures of Reading in an Ideological Age* (New York, 1989). Alter's study of emergent modern Hebrew prose, *The Invention of Hebrew Prose: Modern Fiction and the Language of Realism* (Seattle, 1988), has been especially valuable to me because of its focus on issues of Hebrew style and language.

30. There is a general lack of studies in the area of medieval Hebrew language usage. My own lack of sophistication in this area makes the following observations somewhat tentative. I hope that a researcher in Hebrew linguistics will eventually turn his or her attention to these matters.

31. Alter, *The Invention of Hebrew Prose*.

32. See above, chap. 1. As noted, the multifaceted nature of Nahmanides's oeuvre is emphasized by Isadore Twersky in his introductory essay to the volume on Nahmanides that he edited.

33. Note Alter's emphasis on the creation by the early Hebrew realists of an idiom that is both biblical and rabbinic, avoiding the rhetorical excesses of the former and the technicalities of the latter. Again, I hope that someone with expertise in Hebrew linguistics might subject the writings of Nahmanides to a more professional analysis.

34. See again the important study by Septimus, "'Open Rebuke and Concealed Love.'" We might note, in passing, that the Ramban composed two poems in Aramaic, yet a further testimony to his linguistic abilities. These poems can be found in Chavel, I: 403–406, 407–410.

35. My own work on these chronicles would have benefited from an analysis of the language style.

36. See above, chap. 1, for a fuller picture based on the available evidence. The focus here is the Nahmanidean portrait of the friar.

37. Contrast the highly negative depiction of Nicholas Donin in the *Vikuaḥ R. Yeḥiel mi-Pariz.* Contrast also the tone of the letter written to Saul/Paul by his relative, as discussed above, chap. 1.

38. See above.

39. Steinschneider, 7; Chavel, 305. See further below, chap. 5.

40. Steinschneider, 14; Chavel, 313.

41. Steinschneider, 20; Chavel, 319. See further below, chap. 6. Recall my suggestion in chap. 1 that Nahmanides's portrayal of Friar Paul may have been somewhat exaggerated.

42. To be sure, there are no real signs of profound knowledge of Christian doctrine. Recall the attack by Denifle on Nahmanides's knowledge of Christian doctrine, Baer's agreement, and Maccoby's unconvincing defense.

43. Steinschneider, 8; Chavel, 306.

44. This is seemingly an ironic slap at the judge.

45. Steinschneider, 9; Chavel, 306.

46. Fuller discussion of this assault on Christian sensitivities will follow shortly, as will consideration of the accuracy of the depiction.

47. Steinschneider, 21; Chavel, 319–320. This line of argumentation was utilized heavily by Rabbi Meir ben Simon of Narbonne in his *Milḥemet Miẓvah.* See my discussion in *Daggers of Faith,* 54–56.

48. Steinschneider, 9–10; Chavel, 307.

49. There is no suggestion whatsoever that Friar Paul or the Dominicans accorded such recognition.

50. See above, chap. 1, for a picture of the king and his reign based on the best available evidence. This discussion here is aimed at analyzing the Ramban's portrait of the king.

51. Recall that Nahmanides set up this limitation adroitly by emphasizing to the Jewish reader the utter immersion of the king in Christian life and thinking.

52. Steinschneider, 21; Chavel, 319.

53. Ibid.

54. Steinschneider, 21; Chavel, 320.

55. The reality, I have emphasized, was considerably more complex.

56. See above, chaps. 2 and 3, and further at the close of this chapter.

57. Baer, 185.

58. Steinschneider, 5; Chavel, 302.

59. Recall the parallel information from Tortosa cited above, chap. 2.

60. Note the list provided in chap. 3.

61. Steinschneider, 10–13; Chavel, 308–311.

62. Steinschneider, 11; Chavel, 310.

63. Ibid.

64. See in this connection Safran, "Rabbi Azriel and Nahmanides: Two Views on the Fall of Man," and Pines, "Nahmanides on Adam in the Garden of Eden."

65. Note Maccoby's interesting discussion with respect to this phrase, *Judaism on Trial,* 120–121, and my disagreement in *Daggers of Faith,* 194–195, n. 49.

66. Ps. 72:8. Note Nahmanides's slight alteration of the verse.

67. Jer. 31:33.

68. Isa. 11:9.

69. Isa. 2:4.

70. Isa. 11:4.

71. *Midrash Tehilim,* ed. Solomon Buber (Lemberg, 1889), Ps. 2, 13a.

72. Steinschneider, 12–13; Chavel, 311. I have added the third and final paragraph of the statement simply to show how the rabbi cleverly returned to rabbinic texts. Clearly, however, the heart of the attack is taken directly from the Bible.

73. Steinschneider, 12; Chavel, 310.

74. The full quote is given above, chap. 3.

75. See above.

76. Steinschneider, 12; Chavel, 310.

77. Note the centrality of this view among the writers who portrayed the anti-Jewish violence of the First Crusade and the resultant Jewish martyrdom; see Chazan, *European Jewry and the First Crusade*, 159–168.

78. Steinschneider, 9; Chavel, 306. See further instances of the same above, chap. 3.

79. Ezek. 28:18.

80. Isa. 27:10. The biblical text is modified slightly by Nahmanides.

81. *Pirkei Hekhalot*, ed. Solomon Wertheimer (Jerusalem, 1889), 6:2.

82. Steinschneider, 11; Chavel, 309–310.

83. Steinschneider, 14; Chavel, 312. On the standard rabbinic chronology, see, inter alia, T.B. Yoma, 9a, and ʿAvodah Zarah, 9a.

84. Steinschneider, 14; Chavel, 312.

85. Steinschneider, 14; Chavel, 313. In taking this position on the seventy weeks in Dan. 9, Nahmanides was, in fact, presenting the normative medieval Jewish stance on this chapter. For a fuller discussion of medieval Jewish exegesis of this problematic chapter, see my "Daniel 9 and Its Polemical Implications," to appear in a volume on Christian-Jewish polemics edited by Ora Limor for the Israel Academy of Arts and Sciences.

86. Dan. 12:11.

87. Steinschneider, 15; Chavel, 313–314.

88. See below, chap. 7, for fuller treatment of Nahmanides's stance on the messianic advent.

89. Again, note the more balanced Jewish depiction of the Tortosa encounter.

90. See above, chap. 3.

91. Note the reference to Barcelona in the Hebrew Tortosa account, *Jeschurun* 6 (1868), 49, 53–54, and in the later account in *Shevet Yehudah*, ed. Shohat, 102–104.

92. Denifle, "Quellen zur Disputation," 243; Simonsohn, *The Apostolic See and the Jews*, 231; Ora Limor, *The Disputation of Majorca 1286* (2 vols.; Jerusalem, 1985), 54.

93. See above, chap. 2, n. 9.

94. The Latin translation was done by Wagenseil and can be found in *Tela Ignea Satanae*, II: 24–60. The Catalan translation was done by Eduard Feliu and can be found in *Disputa de Barcelona de 1263* (Barcelona, 1985). The French translation was done by Eric Smilevitch and can be found in *La Dispute de Barcelona* (Paris, 1984). There are two German translations, one by Hermine Grossinger, "Die Disputation des Nachmanides mit Fra Pablo Christiani, Barcelona 1263," *Kairos* n.s. 19 (1977): 257–285 and 20 (1978): 1–15, 161–181, and the other by Hans-Georg von Mutius, in *Die Christlich-Jüdische Zwangsdisputation zu Barcelona* (Frankfurt am Main, 1982). The English translations were done by Morris Braude, *Conscience on Trial* (New York, 1952), 71–94; Oliver Shaw Rankin, *Jewish Religious Polemic* (Edinburgh, 1956), 178–210; Chaim Chavel, *Ramban: Writings and Discourses* (2 vols.; New York, 1978), II: 656–696; and Maccoby, *Judaism on Trial*, 102–146. This is a remarkably high number of translations for a

medieval Hebrew text. This same text was even the basis for a television drama, noted below, n. 97.

95. Twersky, *Rabbi Moses Nahmanides (Ramban)*, 8, n. 20.

96. Limor, *The Disputation of Majorca 1286*, II: 54.

97. In 1986, Channel 4 in England presented a television drama entitled *The Disputation*, written by Hyam Maccoby and based on the narrative of Rabbi Moses ben Nahman. A curious combination of accurate quotation from the Ramban's report, imaginative distortion, and sheer invention, this television drama absorbs thoroughly—indeed, even extends—the Nahmanidean portrayal of an encounter in which the Jewish protagonist emerged completely victorious. As in the Hebrew narrative, the key to this success lay in a sympathetically portrayed King James I of Aragon, who ends the presentation by requesting and receiving the rabbi's blessing.

5: THE ISSUE OF RABBINIC AGGADAH

1. Recall my rejection, in chap. 2, of Baer's argument that the Latin account was composed by an author who was not a witness to the encounter but merely stitched together a report based on an earlier written record.

2. Baer, 187.

3. Isaac Abravanel, *Sefer Yeshuᵓot Meshiḥo* (Konigsberg, 1861), 16b–17b.

4. Ibid., 17a. It is interesting to note how sophisticated the six views adduced by Abravanel are in comparison with the views of Nahmanides, which were articulated after all at the very earliest point in the development of this new challenge to Jewish thinking.

5. Note Baer, "The Disputations," 184; Roth, "The Disputation of Barcelona (1263)," 128; Ben Sasson, "Nahmanides: A Man in the Complexities of His Era," 363–364; Funkenstein, "Nahmanides' Typological Reading of History," 43–47.

6. M. Cohen, "Reflections on the Text and Context of the Disputation of Barcelona," 170–171.

7. Recall my broad methodological disagreement with Cohen, noted in the introduction and in chap. 3, n. 1. Let me add here two specific points of disagreement with issues touched on in this paragraph. In the first place, Cohen has read the reports on the give-and-take too narrowly. Nahmanides's effort to equate Jesus with the messiah had in no sense failed. It was an effective line of argumentation addressed to his fellow-Jews. In fact, the effectiveness of this tack is reflected in its assimilation by Friar Raymond Martin in his *Pugio Fidei*, where he avoids all rabbinic sources in which the discrepancy emphasized by Nahmanides is present. More important, Cohen's sense of Nahmanides's stance toward aggadah is internally inconsistent. On the one hand, he says, "Again and again we find evidence among the friends and foes of the thirteenth-century Kabbalah of the indispensable role which the ᵓAggadah, accepted literally, played among them." (ibid., 170). On the other, he says, "While the Maimonideans' troubles stemmed from their excessive reliance upon meta-

physics, the problem of the mystics lay in their exaggeration and imaginative extensions of the literal meaning of 'Aggadah to the point where they were actually measuring the physical attributes of their Maker." (ibid.). The most recent study of this issue, Wolfson's "'By Way of Truth,'" emphasizes the kabbalistic "need and desire to express new ideas in the guise of ancient authorities," indicating that someone like Nahmanides was hardly the literalist that Cohen, in part, suggests.

8. J. Cohen, *The Friars and the Jews,* 114.

9. Ibid., 119. Note another formulation of the same point, ibid., 121. Note my disagreement with Cohen's reading of the Barcelona disputation in *Daggers of Faith,* 170–173.

10. Saul Liebermann, *Shkiin* (Jerusalem, 1939), 81–83. I personally recollect, early in my studies with the late Professor Liebermann, his classroom presentation of the difference between halakhah and aggadah. As my later work drew me into the Barcelona disputation and the Ramban's narrative account of it, I realized how heavily the presentation I had heard as a student was influenced by the stance of Nahmanides.

11. Septimus, "'Open Rebuke and Concealed Love,'" 20.

12. Marvin Fox, "Nahmanides on the Status of Aggadot: Perspectives on the Disputation at Barcelona, 1263," *Journal of Jewish Studies* 40 (1989): 95–109. The issue is addressed also by Marc Saperstein, *Decoding the Rabbis: A Thirteenth-Century Commentary on the Aggadah* (Cambridge, Mass., 1980), and Septimus, "'Open Rebuke and Concealed Love.'" See also the discussion in Lester A. Segal, *Historical Consciousness and Religious Tradition in Azariah de' Rossi's Me'or 'Einayim* (Philadelphia, 1989), chaps. 6 and 7.

13. Fox, "Nahmanides on the Status of Aggadot," 98. Saperstein likewise emphasizes the heterogeneity of the corpus of aggadah.

14. Similar material is adduced also by Liebermann, Septimus, and Saperstein.

15. Fox notes that Septimus also has examined other writings of Nahmanides and has come to a parallel conclusion.

16. Fox, "Nahmanides on the Status of Aggadot," 109.

17. Recall the epistle of Jacob bar Elijah to Friar Paul, as cited in chap. 1, which is quite comfortable with the notion of teachings designed for the masses.

18. Recall the importance of this stance to the view of Jeremy Cohen.

19. Steinschneider, 8; Chavel, 306.

20. Steinschneider, 16; Chavel, 315.

21. Recall the discussion of the complexities of this issue in chap. 2.

22. Steinschneider, 10; Chavel, 308.

23. For a discussion of the use of halakhic texts in the missionizing argumentation of Friar Raymond, see chap. 7 of *Daggers of Faith* and my "Chapter Thirteen of the Maḥazik Emunah."

24. Steinschneider, 7; Chavel, 305.

25. Septimus, "'Open Rebuke and Concealed Love,'" 21–22.

26. Steinschneider, 16; Chavel, 315.

27. Steinschneider, 9; Chavel, 307.

28. In chap. 6, we shall see a parallel formulation in Nahmanides's introductory statement to his commentary on the Servant of the Lord passage.

29. Steinschneider, 8; Chavel, 306.

30. Ibid.

31. Note the etymological elements in Nahmanides's explication of the terms *midrash* and *aggadah*.

32. I do not believe that Liebermann, Septimus, and Fox, who have all argued for a complex stance on the part of the Ramban toward aggadah, would, in fact, accept this extreme formulation as reflective of his stance.

33. This point is emphasized in the Septimus study.

34. Again, note the terminology.

35. Nahmanides emphasizes the messiah son of David. On the theme of the messiah son of Joseph, who was fated to perish, see the recent study by David Berger, "Three Typological Themes in Early Jewish Messianism: Messiah Son of Joseph, Rabbinic Calculations, and the Figure of Armilus," *AJS Review* 10 (1985): 141–164, esp. 143–148.

36. Steinschneider, 9; Chavel, 307.

37. Recall Nahmanides's criticism, noted earlier, of Friar Paul as understanding "only a bit of the aggadot to which you have accustomed yourself."

38. The second of these conclusions is in agreement with the views of Baer, Roth, Ben Sasson, and Funkenstein cited above, n. 5; the third of these conclusions is in agreement with the views of Liebermann, Septimus, and Fox, discussed more fully above. In other words, my distinction between the event and the narrative account of it enables me to agree in part and disagree in part with these two groups of scholars. The very fact that it has been necessary to write this chapter and that it has been possible, indeed required, to cite so many scholarly views on the matter affords substantiation for the fourth and final conclusion.

6: EXPLICATION OF THE SERVANT OF
THE LORD PASSAGE

1. Note my study, "In the Wake of the Barcelona Disputation," *Hebrew Union College Annual* 61 (1990): 185–201. The first part of that article argues that Nahmanides's famous sermon "Torat ha-Shem Temimah" is in no sense related to the Barcelona confrontation.

2. Baer, 185–186.

3. Steinschneider, 9; Chavel, 307. The Steinschneider edition has Friar Paul saying (in his second statement), "I shall show from the words of their sages." The Chavel edition has, "I shall show from the words of your sages." Chavel does not indicate the basis for his alteration.

4. The text was first published critically by Steinschneider as an addendum to his critical edition of Nahmanides's report on the Barcelona dispu-

tation (Stettin, 1860), 23–26. It was reedited by Adolf Neubauer in *The Fifty-third Chapter of Isaiah according to the Jewish Interpreters* (2 vols.; Oxford, 1876), Heb. vol., 75–82. Chavel used the latter and better version for his *Kitvei Rabbenu Moshe ben Naḥman*, I: 322–326. I have translated from the Neubauer edition and shall cite all three, designating them simply Neubauer, Steinschneider, and Chavel.

   5. See the preceding chapter for this distinction.
   6. Isa. 44:2.
   7. Isa. 49:3.
   8. Neubauer, 75; Steinschneider, 23; Chavel, 322. There is a minor textual problem in the passage, which I have been unable to resolve. My translation certainly captures the essential point of the passage.
   9. Neubauer, 81; Steinschneider, 26; Chavel, 326. Note again Nahman-ides's insistence on introducing the specific figure of Jesus of Nazareth and the details of his story into these observations.
   10. Jacob ben Reuven, *Milḥamot ha-Shem*, ed. Judah Rosenthal (Jerusalem, 1963), 103. Note the broad lines of rebuttal reflected in Jacob's *Milḥamot ha-Shem*, in the *Sefer Yosef ha-Mekane*, and in the *Sefer Niẓaḥon Yashan*. All three can be found in *The Fifty-third Chapter of Isaiah according to the Jewish Interpreters*; they can also be found in more recent editions of the three works—the Rosenthal edition of *Milḥamot ha-Shem*, the Rosenthal edition of *Sefer Yosef ha-Mekane* (Jerusalem, 1970), and the Berger edition of *Sefer Niẓaḥon Yashan* (Philadelphia, 1979). For an important recent treatment of medieval Jewish views on this critical passage, see Joel E. Rembaum, "The Development of a Jewish Exegetical Tradition Regarding Isaiah 53," *Harvard Theological Review* 75 (1982): 289–311. For a broad survey of Jewish and Christian views of all the Servant of the Lord passages, see Christopher R. North, *The Suffering Servant in Deutero-Isaiah: An Historical and Critical Study* (2d ed.; Oxford, 1956).
   11. Neubauer, 77; Steinschneider, 24; Chavel, 323.
   12. 2 Sam. 13:2.
   13. 1 Sam. 22:8.
   14. Neubauer, 77; Steinschneider, 24; Chavel, 323–324.
   15. Neubauer, 77; Steinschneider, 24; Chavel, 324. On the moralizing element here, see below.
   16. Isa. 6:10. Neubauer, 78; Steinschneider, 24; Chavel, 324. Neubauer provides the Oxford manuscript reading of ʿaleha. The other manuscripts read ʿalenu, which makes better sense. See Neubauer, 78, n. 37.
   17. Dan. 3:18.
   18. Sifra, Emor, Perek 9, #5.
   19. Jer. 11:19. The entire passage can be found in Neubauer, 79; Steinschneider, 25; Chavel, 324.
   20. Ecc. 1:13.
   21. 1 Sam. 1:16.
   22. Deut. 11:29.
   23. Lev. 16:21.

24. Isa. 22:16.

25. Gen. 50:5.

26. Neubauer, 79; Steinschneider, 25; Chavel, 324–325.

27. Neubauer, 80–81; Steinschneider, 25–26; Chavel, 325.

28. Neubauer, 80; Steinschneider, 25; Chavel, 325.

29. Nahmanides points here to the inconsistency in usage: the verse moves from the second person verb (*tasim*) to the third person object (*'azmo*). He explains the use of the second person verb as a reflection of direct divine statement.

30. Neubauer, 80; Steinschneider, 25; Chavel, 325.

31. Ps. 5:17. The entire passage can be found in Neubauer, 80; Steinschneider, 25; Chavel, 325.

32. Ps. 21:5. The entire passage can be found in Neubauer, 80; Steinschneider, 25; Chavel, 325.

33. Ibid.

34. Ibid.

35. Similar observations can be found in Abraham ibn Ezra's commentary on these verses and in the *Milhemet Mizvah*. Both can be found in *The Fifty-third Chapter of Isaiah according to the Jewish Interpreters*, Heb. vol., 43 and 323. For an interesting modern counterpart to this medieval discussion, note the article by Baruch A. Levine, "René Girard on Job: The Question of the Scapegoat," *Semia* 33 (1985): 125–133. While the focus of the Levine study is the Book of Job, he makes some important observations on the Servant of the Lord passage. Levine, like his medieval predecessors, stresses the importance of contextual understanding, although in his case the context is expanded to the languages and customs of the Ancient Near East as well as the biblical corpus; again, like his medieval predecessors, Levine emphasizes heavily the closing imagery of the Servant of the Lord triumphant.

36. For Nahmanides's sense of multiple meanings to sacred texts, see especially the important study by Wolfson, "'By Way of Truth.'"

37. There has been much discussion of peshat in recent writings. Note the comprehensive treatment by David Weiss Halivni, *Peshat and Derash: Plain and Applied Meaning in Rabbinic Exegesis* (Oxford, 1991). Much attention has focused on the issue of peshat in the commentaries of the greatest of the medieval Jewish exegetes, Rabbi Solomon ben Isaac of Troyes. Note, inter alia, Benjamin J. Gelles, *Peshat and Derash in the Exegesis of Rashi* (Leiden, 1981), and Sarah Kamin, *Peshuto shel Mikra u-Midrasho shel Mikra* (Jerusalem, 1986). In the recently held conference, "La Culture juive en France du nord au moyen âge" (Paris-Troyes, Dec. 3–5, 1990), a striking number of the papers addressed this issue. The proceedings of this conference are scheduled for publication shortly.

38. Steinschneider, 20; Chavel, 319.

39. There is, of course, much brilliant peshat in Nahmanides's commentary to the Pentateuch. The treatise that will be examined in some detail in chap. 7, the Ramban's *Sefer ha-Ge'ulah*, shows outstanding re-

construction of the peshat of some of the historical information in the Book of Daniel and elsewhere in the Hebrew Bible.

40. I noted above, chap. 4, how Nahmanides denigrates Friar Paul for his failure to understand this text properly. Here too contextuality is involved. In this case, the context is the totality of rabbinic literature.

41. Neubauer, 80–81; Steinschneider, 23; Chavel, 323.

42. Note similar notions in the teaching of Rabbi Isaac ben Yedaiah— see Marc Saperstein, *Decoding the Rabbis*, 102–120—and in the teaching of Abraham Abulafia—see Moshe Idel, *Kitvei R. Avraham Abulafia u-Mishnato* (unpub. Ph.D. diss., Hebrew University, 1976), 395–433.

43. Dan. 12:9–10. Note Nahmanides's use of this verse to justify his own messianic speculations, as discussed below, chap. 7.

44. Neubauer, 75; Steinschneider, 23; Chavel, 322.

45. Dan. 12:7. The entire passage can be found in Neubauer, 78; Steinschneider, 24; Chavel, 324.

46. For a broad sense of the moralistic tendencies in Spanish Jewry of this period, see the chapter, "Mysticism and Social Reform," in Baer, *A History of the Jews in Christian Spain*, I: 243–305.

47. For far fuller discussion of the Ramban's teachings on redemption, see chap. 7.

7: MESSIANIC REDEMPTION:
  CERTAIN AND PREDICTABLE

1. Nahmanides's *Sefer ha-Geʾulah* has been, understandably, a highly problematic work. On the one hand, its affirmation of a future redemption for the Jewish people constitutes a popular message; on the other hand, its specific dating of the messianic advent and the failure of this prediction to materialize has made it something of an embarrassment. Only during the twentieth century has the work been printed. The first of these editions was prepared by Samuel Nahum Marat (New York, 1904), on the basis of a manuscript that the editor purchased in London; the second was prepared by Jacob Lipschitz (London, 1909), on the basis of the British Museum manuscript; the third was prepared by Joshua Moses Aaronsohn (Jerusalem, 1959), on the basis of three manuscripts—Paris, London-British Museum, and a third privately owned. Chavel's edition, found in the first volume of his *Kitvei Rabbenu Moshe ben Naḥman*, is based on the Lipschitz edition, although Chavel was aware of the Aaronsohn edition as well and its use of the Paris manuscript. Chavel also utilized a Jewish Theological Seminary manuscript. The Institute for Microfilmed Hebrew Manuscripts has copies of four manuscripts—the three already noted (London-British Museum, Paris, and New York) and a Parma manuscript as well. I shall translate on the basis of the Aaronsohn edition and will cite both that edition (simply Aaronsohn) and Chavel (simply Chavel).

In the introductory remarks to his edition of *Sefer ha-Geʾulah*, Chavel suggests that the work was in all likelihood written in 1263, as part of Nahmanides's preparation for the Barcelona encounter. It is clear, however, that the work was written in the wake of that encounter and in fact after the composition of the narrative report, with Nahmanides buttressing the limited case that he had earlier developed into a more thorough argument for dating the messianic advent.

There has been little serious study of Nahmanides's messianic calculation. The fullest to date is Louis M. Epstein, "The Eschatology of Rabbi Moses ben Nachman (Nachmanides)," *Jewish Theological Seminary Students Annual* 1914: 95–123, esp. 115–119.

2. Nah. 2:2.

3. Aaronsohn, 5; Chavel, 261. The closing words allude to Isa. 50:4.

4. This is an obvious anti-Christian note, indicating what Nahmanides, like so many other medieval Jewish polemicists, saw as one of the essential flaws of Christianity.

5. Aaronsohn, 5–6; Chavel, 261. It is interesting to note how much the missionizing pressure, despite its utilization of rabbinic literature, forced such thinkers as Nahmanides back into direct engagement with key biblical texts. The same can be readily observed with respect to Rabbi Mordechai ben Yehosapha's *Maḥazik Emunah*.

6. I have utilized here, as throughout this study, the new Jewish Publication Society translation of the Hebrew Bible. To be sure, the translation cannot capture all the nuances—in this case, all the ambiguities—of the original.

7. Aaronsohn, 6–9; Chavel, 261–263. It is interesting to note that in his commentary to the Torah, Nahmanides makes the same assertion with respect to this pericope.

8. The further Pentateuchal pericopes noted by Nahmanides are Deut. 30:1–10; Deut. 19:8–10; Deut. 31:16–32:43; Num. 24:15–19; Deut. 28:15–68.

9. Nahmanides adduces an extensive series of passages from Isaiah, Jeremiah, Ezekiel, and Obadiah.

10. Nahmanides begins, as he did in his narrative, by excluding chap. 9 of the Book of Daniel from consideration. He then analyzes the apocalyptic images of the Book of Daniel, seeking to harmonize the four beasts of chap. 7, the four metals of chap. 2, the ram and the goat of chap. 8, and the two kings of chaps. 10–12. Again, note my forthcoming study on medieval Jewish exegesis of Dan. 9, cited above, chap. 4, n. 85.

11. Aaronsohn, 8–9; Chavel, 263.

12. At the close of his discussion, Nahmanides acknowledges a serious problem in his identification of this passage as a reference to the future redemption. He notes that the rabbis saw the word *ve-noshantem* as a reference to the time spent in the Land of Israel prior to Babylonian exile. He suggests that while this might have led us to conclude that the reference to redemption should be read as applying to the return from that exile, in fact, the dispersion referred to in the pericope is to be taken more gen-

erally as a reference to all dispersions. Interestingly, in his commentary on the Torah, Nahmanides reverses himself and suggests that this passage does apply to the return from Babylonian exile. The reason for the shift may lie with the difficulty that he himself acknowledges in *Sefer ha-Ge'ulah*. Such a shift in no way harms the totality of his case, since it is based on the concatenation of a number of biblical verses.

13. These rebukes are found in Lev. 26:14–46.

14. These rebukes are found in Deut. 28:15–69.

15. Aaronsohn, 17; Chavel, 267.

16. Lev. 26:42.

17. Rejecting the yoke of the commandments is a negative reference to Islam; worshiping a created being is a negative reference to Christianity, based on Ps. 74:18.

18. Aaronsohn, 9–10; Chavel, 263.

19. Recall Nahmanides's own comment, in his narrative report, about negative Jewish reactions to his predictions; see Steinschneider, 15; Chavel, 313.

20. See above, chap. 4, for a brief discussion of this passage in the Nahmanidean narrative. The claim of Nahmanides in his narrative account that the Book of Daniel contains only one revelation of the messianic date constitutes an extreme formulation of the stance of Abraham bar Hiyya in his *Megillat ha-Megalleh*. There, bar Hiyya argues that the datings supplied in the Book of Daniel reflect increasingly articulated statements of the messianic coming, with the fullest and clearest information revealed at the close of the book. As we shall see shortly, Nahmanides, in his *Sefer ha-Ge'ulah*, espoused fully the position of bar Hiyya, positing a number of revelations of the messianic date, with each articulated in increasingly clear fashion.

It is interesting that Arnold of Villanova, in his *De cymbalis ecclesiae*, utilized much the same scheme, based on Dan. 12:11–12. Arnold's specific dating differs by eight years, due to a divergent tradition for the destruction of the Second Temple. Given the fact that Arnold spent considerable time in the court of King Peter II of Aragon and studied Hebrew as part of the circle of Friar Raymond Martin, the possibility of influence from the writings of Nahmanides cannot be summarily dismissed. As earlier Jewish thinkers had advanced much the same dating scheme (see below, n. 32), it is also possible that Arnold's general familiarity with Jewish literature may have led him to his conclusions. For broad information on Arnold and his thinking, see Harold Lee, Marjorie Reeves, and Giulio Silano, *Western Mediterranean Prophecy: The School of Joachim of Fiore and the Four-teenth-Century Breviloquium* (Toronto, 1989), 27–46, and the literature there cited. For current views on the impact of Jewish thinking on Arnold, see the literature cited in ibid., n. 8. The parallels between Nahmanidean thinking and that of Arnold of Villanova point to the utility of more fo-cused consideration of Jewish messianic thinking against the background of medieval Christian eschatological speculation. I hope to provide such a perspective in my forthcoming book on medieval Jewish approaches to the Book of Daniel.

21. Steinschneider, 15; Chavel, 314. Further evidence of the seriousness with which Nahmanides took this date is afforded in his commentary on the Torah, to Gen. 2:3. There, in establishing a correspondence of the six days of creation to the six millennia of human history, he speaks of the correspondence of the creation of Adam on the sixth day with the appearance of the messiah at the beginning of the sixth millennium, 118 years into the sixth millennium, to be exact. That is, he repeats the dating that he identified briefly in his Barcelona narrative and that he argued far more extensively in his *Sefer ha-Ge'ulah*.

22. Aaronsohn, 61–62; Chavel, 289–290.

23. Dan. 12:4.

24. Abraham bar Hiyya, in his *Megillat ha-Megalleh*, ed. Adolf Posnanski (Berlin, 1924), 2, used the same verse to justify widespread speculation concerning the messianic advent.

25. Dan. 8:20.

26. Recall the Christian emphasis on the length of Jewish exile as a negative reflection on the Jews and their fate. Here Nahmanides takes the same conclusion and turns it in a positive direction: the Jews are now much farther from the point of exile and hence much closer to the point of redemption.

27. Here Nahmanides's reading of the verse in Daniel is parallel to that of Abraham bar Hiyya.

28. Dan. 12:10.

29. Aaronsohn, 61–62; Chavel, 289–290. Recall the indication in chap. 6 of Nahmanides's condemnation of Christianity for what he saw as its erroneously precipitous claims of messianic advent.

Medieval Christian eschatological speculation likewise wrestled with the same problem of justification for findings that proceed beyond received wisdom on these matters.

30. See above, chap. 4.

31. These are the verses emphasized by all major medieval Jewish commentators on Daniel, e.g., Saadia Gaon, Rashi, and Abraham bar Hiyya. All these thinkers, like Nahmanides, deny any messianic meaning to chap. 9 of the Book of Daniel.

32. On the figure of the messiah ben Joseph, see again the recent study by Berger, "Three Typological Themes." Identification of the 1,358–1,403 combination was not an innovation on the part of Nahmanides. This was one of the major datings proposed by Abraham bar Hiyya, as we shall see shortly. The dating suggested by Rashi was not far removed from that of Abraham bar Hiyya and Nahmanides, differing only by three years. For Rashi, the reckoning of the 1,290 and 1,335 years should be begun from the institution of an idolatrous image in the sanctuary, three years prior

to its destruction. Again, recall the parallels in the thinking of Arnold of Villanova cited above, n. 20.

33. Most commentators saw these two passages as parallel. See, e.g., the commentaries of Rashi and ibn Ezra, so central to Nahmanides's own exegetical enterprise. Note, however, the treatment by Abraham bar Hiyya, who saw these two verses as grammatically distinct, as occurring at different points in Daniel's unfolding experience, and as reflecting two different reckonings. Nahmanides clearly followed the line of Rashi and ibn Ezra. Interestingly, however, he diverged from both Rashi and ibn Ezra in his reading of these verses as a reference to "a time, two times, and half a time," meaning three and one-half periods of 440 years each. Both Rashi and ibn Ezra read the verses as a reference to "a time [consisting of] two times and half a time," meaning two and one-half times some paradigmatic number.

34. Aaronsohn, 64–66; Chavel, 292. Note the one-year discrepancy between the predicted 1,540 and the actual 206 + 1,335 = 1,541.

35. Aaronsohn, 66–68; Chavel, 292–294. This reckoning has some serious problems associated with it. For Nahmanides, the verse indicates the passage of 2,300 years from King David, the instigator of the first sanctuary, to the messiah, who will be responsible for the final sanctuary. Nahmanides works out the details in two alternative fashions. In the first case, he suggests that from the kingship of David to the messianic appearance of the messiah son of David, there will elapse 2,275 years (40 years of David's kingship, 410 years of the First Temple, 490 years of exile and Second Temple, and 1,335 years from the destruction of the Second Temple to the appearance of the messiah). According to this reckoning, there is a discrepancy of 25 years, which Nahmanides explains as an indication of approximation to the coming of the messiah, not to the coming of the messiah precisely. Alternatively, he suggests that if the reckoning is begun with the birth of David (30 years prior to his kingship), then the 2,300 brings us to a point 5 years prior to the appearance of the messiah. In either case, the reckoning, while impressively close, is hardly exact.

36. See above, n. 20.

37. Aaronsohn, 68–70; Chavel, 294. Again, there is a discrepancy of one year. For symmetrical schemes in Abraham ibn Daud, see the important observations of Gerson D. Cohen in his edition of ibn Daud's *Sefer ha-Qabbalah* (Philadelphia, 1967), 189–222. Cohen emphasizes heavily the explicit statement by ibn Daud in the first book of *Sefer ha-Qabbalah:* "Behold how trustworthy are the consolations of our God, blessed be His name, for the chronology of their exile corresponded to that of their redemption. Twenty-one years passed from the beginning of their exile until the destruction of the Temple and the cessation of their monarchy. Similarly, twenty-one years passed from the time its rebuilding was begun until it was completed." Cohen proceeds to suggest further symmetries built into the chronology of Jewish history by ibn Daud. It might be noted

that historical symmetries were central to the eschatological thinking of Joachim of Fiore and the school of speculation that his writings spawned. On Joachim and this school, see, inter alia, Marjorie Reeves, *Joachim of Fiore and the Prophetic Future* (London, 1976); idem, *The Influence of Prophecy in the Later Middle Ages: A Study in Joachimism* (Oxford, 1969); Lee, Reeves, and Silano, *Western Mediterranean Prophecy*.

38. Bereshit Rabbah to Gen. 15:12. Nahmanides highlights this rabbinic interpretation in his commentary on the Torah, on the same verse.

39. Aaronsohn, 70–71; Chavel, 295. For a fuller discussion of the utilization of gematria, see below.

40. Aaronsohn, 71; Chavel, 295. Here Nahmanides notes explicitly and explains away a one-year discrepancy.

41. When I delivered a paper with some of these findings at the meeting of the European Association for Jewish Studies in Troyes during the summer of 1990, a member of the audience raised a question about Nahmanides's failure to adduce evidence from astrology, which plays a significant role in the messianic computation of many other medievals, most notably, Abraham bar Hiyya. While I had no ready answer to the question, David Novak, whose forthcoming study of the theology of the Ramban has been noted in chap. 1, indicated that his research suggests that, while Nahmanides took astrology seriously for limited personal matters, he rejected the applicability of astrology to such weighty issues as redemption of the Jewish people.

42. The study of Jewish messianic calculation is still in its infancy. The two classic works are Abba Hillel Silver, *A History of Messianic Speculation in Israel* (New York, 1927), and Joseph Sarachek, *The Doctrine of the Messiah in Medieval Jewish Literature* (New York, 1932). Much work remains to be done on explaining the modalities and motivations of medieval Jewish messianic calculation, as well as the broad intellectual and spiritual context within which it took place.

43. T.B. San., 97b. My explication of the view of Samuel follows the second of the two explanations offered by Rashi, ad loc. This distinction in types of messianic advent was noted above, chap. 6.

44. On the impact of Rashi and ibn Ezra on Nahmanides, see the introduction to Nahmanides's commentary on the Torah and the study by Septimus, "'Open Rebuke and Concealed Love.'"

45. See Saadia's important discussion in the eighth chapter of his *Sefer ha-Emunot veha-Deʿot*. On Saadia's messianic speculation, see Samuel Poznanski, "Die Berechnung des Erlösungsjahres bei Saadja," *Monatsschrift für Geschichte und Wissenschaft des Judenthums* 44 (1900): 400–416, 508–519; Henry Malter, "Saadia Gaon's Messianic Computation," *Journal of Jewish Lore and Philosophy* 1 (1919): 45–59; A. Marmorstein, "The Doctrine of Redemption in Saadya's Theological System," in *Saadya Studies*, ed. Erwin I. J. Rosenthal (Manchester, 1943), 103–118; Moshe N. Sobel, "Calculation of the Appointed End of Days and Depiction of Redemption in the

Sefer ha-Emunot veha-De'ot" (Hebrew), in *Rav Saadia Gaon,* ed. Judah L. Fishman (Jerusalem, 1943), 172–190.

46. For a fuller discussion of Abraham bar Hiyya's messianic speculation and the prior literature, see my forthcoming study of medieval Jewish views of Daniel, cited in n. 20.

47. There follows a set of rabbinic messianic calculations.

48. *Megillat ha-Megalleh,* 14–15. Note, on the one hand, Abraham bar Hiyya's rather full case for either 1,448 or 1,468 as the messianic year, based on a complex exegesis of Jer. 25 and of Dan. 8:14, and, on the other hand, his extensive arguments for 1,358 as the messianic year, based on Dan. 12:11 and complex exegesis of Dan. 7:25 and 12:7.

49. See above, chap. 1.

50. Gerson D. Cohen, "Messianic Postures of Ashkenazim and Sephardim," in *Studies of the Leo Baeck Institute,* ed. Max Kreutzberger (New York, 1967), 117–156.

51. Note Septimus's argument for more nuanced understanding of the varieties of Andalusian thought.

52. Recall my skepticism as to the facticity of this and a number of other aspects of the Nahmanidean narrative.

53. See above, chap. 1, n. 54.

54. There follows an example of rabbinic use of gematria for halakhic purposes. Nahmanides adduces this example to indicate the seriousness with which the rabbis viewed the technique of gematria.

55. Aaronsohn, 7–8; Chavel, 262. The rabbinic injunction against innovating original inference based on the *gezerah shavah* can be found in T.B., Pesahim, 66a.

56. Again, note Wolfson's important dissent.

57. See my study of one of Rabbi Meir's sermons, "Confrontation in the Synagogue of Narbonne: A Christian Sermon and a Jewish Reply," *Harvard Theological Review* 67 (1974): 437–457; for broader consideration of this theme in the work of Rabbi Meir, see my *Daggers of Faith,* 63–66.

58. See *Daggers of Faith,* 103–114.

59. In his careful study of the philosophically oriented commentary of Rabbi Isaac ben Yedaiah on the aggadah, Marc Saperstein has given considerable attention to the messianic theme in Rabbi Issac's works. Saperstein found an interesting duality in Rabbi Isaac, with some concern for messianic appearance on the historical scene and yet greater interest in transposing the issue to an altogether different level, the personal level of freedom from material concern and achievement of intellectual perfection. According to Saperstein, Rabbi Isaac exhibits this dual level of concern— the popular and simplistic, on the one hand, and the elitist and esoteric, on the other—throughout his commentary, in some instances allowing both levels to coexist and in others rejecting the popular and simplistic in favor of the more sophisticated. With respect to the messianic theme, the tendency seems to lie in the direction of coexistence, with the rich imagery

of messianic appearance before the papal court counterpointed by the emphasis on the messiah as symbol of freedom from the constraints of the senses and the perfecting of the mind. What is significant from our perspective is that this philosophically inclined author was moved to accord the issue of messianism a major place in his thinking. Whether positing a historical event of messianic redemption or reinterpretation of messianic imagery to the realm of personal inclinations, Rabbi Isaac was in effect wrestling with the issue of messianic doctrine, affording once more a sense of the impact of the new missionizing on genres of Jewish literary creativity other than polemics. To be sure, it is possible that the concern with messianic themes simply reflects the exegete's involvement with the texts he studies, rather than a temporally related preoccupation with redemption. See Saperstein, *Decoding the Rabbis*, 102–120.

60. See the classic study by Yitzhak Baer, "The Social Background of the *Ra'aya Mehemna*" (Hebrew), *Zion* 5 (1940): 1–44, and more broadly, *A History of the Jews in Christian Spain*, I: 243–305.

61. For the fullest treatment, see Idel, *Kitvei R. Avraham Abulafia u-Mishnato*, 395–433. The dualistic treatment of the messianic theme is reminiscent of the dualistic treatment by Rabbi Isaac ben Yedaiah, noted above, n. 59. Further discussion of Abulafia's messianism can be found in Moshe Idel, "Abraham Abulafia and the Pope: An Account of an Abortive Mission" (Hebrew), *AJS Review* 7–8 (1982–1983): Heb. sec., 1–17, and "Abraham Abulafia on the Jewish Messiah and Jesus," *Studies in Ecstatic Kabbalah* (Albany, 1988), 45–61.

62. Note Idel's discussion of this mission in the aforecited article in the *AJS Review*. Idel insists on the messianic element in this mission, including even the dating of the mission. He further argues that the content of the discussion with the pope was to involve Abulafia's secret teachings concerning the Divine Name. To be sure, it is difficult to understand why the pope would have gone to such lengths to prevent such a discussion and threatened death by burning as a punishment. It may well be that what was at stake here was a denunciation of Christendom and a demand for Jewish freedom. Idel calls attention also to the broad Jewish communal objection to the mission, which Idel further identifies with the messianic issue.

63. See Gershom Scholem, "The Concept of Redemption in the Kabbalah" (Hebrew), in *Devarim be-Go* (Tel Aviv, 1975), 191–216, and "The Messianic Idea in Kabbalism," in *The Messianic Idea in Judaism* (New York, 1971), 37–48.

64. Joseph Dan, "The Beginnings of the Messianic Myth in Kabbalistic Doctrine of the Thirteenth Century" (Hebrew), in *Meshihiyut ve-Askatologiyah*, ed. Zvi Baras (Jerusalem, 1983), 239–252.

65. Yehuda Liebes, "The Messiah of the *Zohar*: The Messianic Image of Rabbi Simon bar Yohai" (Hebrew), in *Ha-Ra'yon ha-Meshihi be-Yisra'el* (Jerusalem, 1982), 87–236.

66. Ibid., 87–88.

67. Note Liebes's survey of the relation of subsequent major figures to the literature of the *Idrot*, ibid., 101–118.

68. Note that Dan's study was written after that of Liebes. Thus, he is attempting to account for the messianic inclinations of both Rabbi Isaac of Castile and Rabbi Moses de Leon.

69. As indicated, I have already embarked on a study of medieval Jewish approaches to the Book of Daniel, which should elucidate some of the varying modalities in which messianic issues were treated and some of the diverse motivations that stimulated messianic speculation.

70. I do not mean to suggest that messianic speculation must be stimulated either internally or externally; clearly, complicated combinations of internal and external motivation are likely.

71. The traditional Jewish (and Christian) sense of catastrophe as a herald of the end of days certainly plays a major role in Jewish messianic speculation. Scholem's repeated emphasis on the fact that not all catastrophes lead in the direction of messianic thinking is, of course, correct. Yet the impact of catastrophic events—in certain situations—as stimuli to messianic speculation cannot be gainsaid.

72. As noted, there would be considerable benefit in setting Jewish messianic thinking in the context of majority Christian eschatological speculation. For an extremely useful study in this direction, see David Ruderman, "Hope against Hope: Jewish and Christian Messianic Expectations in the Late Middle Ages," to appear shortly in the second volume of *Galut ahar Golah*, a collection of essays in honor of Haim Beinart.

73. Note that the combination of mystical thinking and deep concern with eschatology discernible in Isaac of Castile, Moses de Leon, and Nahmanides is paralleled by a similar concatenation of ideas and interests in Joachite circles.

In a valuable study of late-fifteenth-century Jewish mystical speculation, Benjamin Gampel suggests the impact of strident Christian claims on the Jewish need to reaffirm, in the strongest possible terms, the inevitable and datable future messianic coming. Gampel presented his findings in an unpublished paper delivered at the annual conference of the Association for Jewish Studies in December 1988. I appreciate his sharing his unpublished paper with me.

APPENDIX: RABBI MOSES BEN NAHMAN, BONASTRUG
DE PORTA, AND ASTRUG DE PORTA

1. See above, chap. 1.

2. C. Roth, in his "The Disputation of Barcelona (1263)," 121, n. 7, indicates the contact between King James and Nahmanides prior to 1263; Baer, in his "The Disputations," 181, notes the royal borrowing from a Jew

of Barcelona, designed in part to pay the sum of 300 sueldos to Nahman-ides. Fullest use of this material is made by M. Cohen in his "Reflections on the Text and Context of the Disputation of Barcelona."

3. Note again the important work of Berner in her dissertation, *On the Western Shores.* Berner reconstructed a number of important family genealogies (450–458) and provided a preliminary onomasticon of Bar-celona Jewry (459–501).

4. Heinrich Graetz, in vol. 7 of his *Geschichte der Juden* (1st ed.; Leipzig, 1863), 440–441, made a strong case for the identification of Rabbi Moses ben Nahman and Bonastrug de Porta. Meyer Kayserling, "Die Disputation des Bonastruc mit Frai Pablo in Barcelona," *Monatschrift für Geschichte und Wissenschaft des Judenthums* 14 (1865): 308–313, resisted the identification. Graetz, "Die Disputation des Bonastruc mit Frai Pablo in Barcelona," ibid., 428–433, reiterated his case for the identification. Kayserling, in his review of Joseph Jacobs's *Sources of Spanish Jewish History* in the *Jewish Quarterly Review* 8 (1896): 494, reiterated his rejection of the Graetz view. However, Graetz's identification of Moses ben Nahman with Bonastrug de Porta has not been seriously questioned in subsequent literature.

5. Denifle, "Quellen zur Disputation," 239–240, #8.

6. These documents are indicated in Régné, *History of the Jews in Ara-gon*, #84, #137, #319. M. Cohen, "Reflections on the Text and Context," suggests "the appearance for the first time, in connection with the publi-cation of Nahmanides's account, of a Spanish name for the Ramban." Clearly, this is not correct, as the Bonastrug designation is noted in the documents of 1258 and 1260. As already suggested (above, chap. 2), the designation Bonastrug is obviously the regular one for the royal chancery, and the designation Moyses magister, found in the Latin report of the con-frontation, suggests a document drawn up by someone other than a reg-ular chancery official.

7. I suggested, in chap. 4, as yet another factor in the warm portrait of the king, the crucial role that he plays in the outcome of the drama created by Nahmanides.

8. The identification of Astrug de Porta with Bonastrug was suggested by Joseph Jacobs, *Sources of Spanish Jewish History* (London, 1894), 21, #289. The strongest case for this identification was made by Cohen, "Re-flections on the Text and Context," 189–191. Curiously, Kayserling, who rejected the identification of Moses ben Nahman with Bonastrug de Porta, conflated Bonastrug de Porta and Astrug de Porta in his review of Jacobs's *Sources of Spanish Jewish History.* This conflation was used by Kayserling as a further argument against the identification of Bonastrug with Moses ben Nahman. See the *Jewish Quarterly Review* 8 (1896): 494. Identification of Bonastrug de Porta and Astrug de Porta was vigorously rejected by Yit-zhak (Fritz) Baer, *Studien zur Geschichte der Juden im Königreich Aragonien* (Berlin, 1913), 34, n. 76, although without extensive evidence for the rejection.

9. See Régné, *History of the Jews in Aragon*, #262, #302, #303, #315, #316, #384, #516, #607, #673, #725.

10. Note the extensive references to Benvenist de Porta listed in the index to Régné, *History of the Jews in Aragon*, 675. Note similarly the recurrent references to Benvenist de Porta in Baer, *A History of the Jews in Christian Spain*, I.

11. In Régné, *History of the Jews in Aragon*, there are three references to a Jew of Besalu, surnamed de Porta. In two of these references (#1312 and #2318) the said Jew is designated Bonastrug; in the third (#1494), he is designated Astrug. These three documents may well refer to the same person. In general, however, the royal documentation seems remarkably precise in its differentiation of individuals. The claim of M. Cohen, "Reflections on the Text and Context," 190, that "the name Astrugus (with its variant forms Astruc, Astrug, and Astruch) is identical with the name Bonastrugus (with its variant forms Bonastruc, Bonastrug, and Bonastruch)" is too sweeping. As we shall see, in fact, the royal records are quite consistent in their treatment of our Bonastrug and our Astrug.

12. Denifle, "Quellen zur Disputation," 239–240, #8. Note also Régné, *History of the Jews in Aragon*, #324, for a related document.

13. Régné, *History of the Jews in Aragon*, #262, #315, #316.

14. M. Cohen, "Reflections on the Text and Context," 191.

15. For details on this letter, see chap. 1, n. 48.

16. The exception, as we have seen, is the Latin report of the disputation.

17. M. Cohen, "Reflections on the Text and Context," 191. For continued identification of Astrug de Porta with Villafranca, see the documents cited above, n. 9.

18. This is agreed to by all the biographers of Nahmanides, although precise evidence of the date of his death has never been uncovered.

19. Again, see the sources cited above, n. 9.

20. We might note in passing three additional names, from the closing decades of the thirteenth century, that are close to the Latin designation for Nahmanides, although they clearly identify different personages. The first is Bonastrug de Porta, the Jew of Besalu; see Régné, #1312, #1494, #2318. The second is Astrug of Gerona; see Régné, #1489, #1995. The third is Astrugus magister of Gerona; see Régné, #2098, #2102, #2106. Again, the sense is that the royal chancery was adept at distinguishing Jews, despite the limited pool of names utilized.

21. Differentiation of Astrug de Porta from Bonastrug de Porta has an important human interest significance as well. Vidalon, the son of Astrug de Porta, is a highly problematic figure. Involved in recurrent difficulties, he was eventually executed by King Peter of Aragon at the behest of the Jewish communities. The complex case against this Vidalon involved Nahmanides's distinguished student, Rabbi Solomon ben Adret. The notion of the distinguished rabbi of Barcelona involved in the execution

of the son of his mentor would be quite extraordinary. Differentiation of Astrug de Porta from Bonastrug de Porta precludes that possibility. For treatment of the remarkable case of Vidalon, see David Kaufmann, "Jewish Informers in the Middle Ages," *Jewish Quarterly Review* 8 (1896): 217–238, and Baer, *Studien zur Geschichte der Juden im Königreich Aragonien*, 42–44.

Bibliography

PRIMARY SOURCES

Abraham bar Hiyya. *Megillat ha-Megalleh.* Ed. Adolf Posnanski. Berlin, 1924.

Abraham ben Yom Tov Ishbili. *She'elot u-Teshuvot ha-Ritva.* Ed. Joseph Kafeh. Jerusalem, 1959.

Abraham ibn Daud. *Sefer ha-Qabbalah.* Ed. Gerson D. Cohen. Philadelphia, 1967.

Anonymous Hebrew account of the Tortosa disputation. Ed. S. Z. H. Halberstam. In *Jeschurun* 6 (1868). Heb. sec., pp. 45–55.

Anonymous Latin account of the Barcelona disputation. Barcelona version. Ed. Charles de Tourtalon. In *Jacme Ier le conquérant roi d'Aragon*, 2: 594. 2 vols. Montpellier, 1863–1867.

Anonymous Latin account of the Barcelona disputation. Barcelona version. Ed. Heinrich Denifle. In *Historisches Jahrbuch des Görres-Gesellschaft* 8 (1887): 231–234.

Anonymous Latin account of the Barcelona disputation. Gerona version. Ed. Enrique Claudio Girbal. In *Los judios en Gerona*, 66–68. Gerona, 1870.

Anonymous Latin account of the Barcelona disputation. Gerona version. Ed. Jaime Villanueva. In *Viage literario a las iglesias de España*, 13: 332–335. 22 vols. Madrid, 1803–1852.

Anonymous Latin account of the Barcelona disputation. Gerona version. Pub. Yitzhak Baer. In *Tarbiz* 2 (1930–1931): 185–187.

Anonymous Latin account of the Tortosa disputation. Ed. Antonio Pacios Lopez. In *La Disputa de Tortosa*, 2. 2 vols. Madrid, 1957.

Carpenter, Dwayne E., ed. and trans. *Alfonso X and the Jews: An Edition of and Commentary on Siete Partidas 7.24 "De los judios"* (*Modern Philology*, Volume 115). Berkeley, 1986.

Denifle, Heinrich, ed. *Chartularium Universitatis Parisiensis.* 4 vols. Paris, 1889–1897.

Grayzel, Solomon, ed. and trans. *The Church and the Jews in the XIIIth Century.* Rev. ed. New York, 1966.

Isaac Abravanel. *Sefer Yeshu'ot Meshiho.* Konigsberg, 1861.

Isaac Lattes. *Kiryat Sefer.* Ed. Adolf Neubauer. In *Medieval Hebrew Chronicles*, 2: 233–241. 2 vols. Oxford, 1895.

Jacob bar Elijah. *Iggeret*. Ed. Joseph Kobak. In *Jeschurun* 6 (1868). Heb. sec., pp. 1–31.

Jacob ben Reuven. *Milḥamot ha-Shem*. Ed. Judah Rosenthal. Jerusalem, 1963.

Jean de Joinville. *Histoire de Saint Louis*. Ed. Natalis de Wailly. Paris, 1874.

Judah ha-Levi. *Sefer ha-Kuzari*. Trans. Judah ibn Tibbon. Ed. Abraham Zifroni. Tel Aviv, 1964.

Meir ben Simon. *Milḥemet Mizvah*. Bib. pal. Parma, Ms. Heb. 2749.

Midrash Tehilim. Ed. Solomon Buber. Lemberg, 1889.

Mordechai ben Yehosapha. *Meḥazik Emunah*. Vatican Library, Ms. Heb. 271.

Moses ben Nahman. Account of the Barcelona disputation. Ed. J. Wagenseil. In *Tela Ignea Satanae*, 2: 24–60. 2 vols. in 1. Altdorf, 1681.

———. Account of the Barcelona disputation. In *Milḥemet Hovah*, pp. 1–13. Constantinople, 1710.

———. Account of the Barcelona disputation. Ed. Moritz Steinschneider. Stettin, 1860.

———. Account of the Barcelona disputation. Pub. Reuven Margulies. Lwow, n.d.

———. Account of the Barcelona disputation. Pub. Chaim Chavel. In *Kitvei Rabbenu Moshe ben Naḥman*, 1: 302–320. Jerusalem, 1971.

———. Account of the Barcelona disputation. Catalan trans. Eduard Feliu. In *Disputa de Barcelona de 1263*. Barcelona, 1985.

———. Account of the Barcelona disputation. English trans. Morris Braude. In *Conscience on Trial*, pp. 71–94. New York, 1952.

———. Account of the Barcelona disputation. English trans. Oliver Shaw Rankin. In *Jewish Religious Polemic*, pp. 178–210. Edinburgh, 1956.

———. Account of the Barcelona disputation. English trans. Chaim Chavel. In *Ramban: Writings and Discourses*, 2: 656–696. 2 vols. New York, 1978.

———. Account of the Barcelona disputation. English trans. Hyam Maccoby. In *Judaism on Trial*, pp. 102–146. London, 1982.

———. Account of the Barcelona disputation. French trans. Eric Smilevitch. In *La Dispute de Barcelona*. Paris, 1984.

———. Account of the Barcelona disputation. German trans. Hermine Grossinger. In *Kairos* n.s. 19 (1977): 257–285 and 20 (1978): 1–15, 161–181.

———. Account of the Barcelona disputation. German trans. Hans-Georg von Mutius. In *Die Christlich-Jüdische Zwangsdisputation zu Barcelona*. Frankfurt am Main, 1982.

———. Account of the Barcelona disputation. Latin trans. J. C. Wagenseil. In *Tela Ignea Satanae*, 2: 24–60. 2 vols. in 1. Altdorf, 1861.

———. Commentary on Servant of the Lord passage. Ed. Moritz Steinschneider. In *Vikuaḥ ha-Ramban*, pp. 23–26. Stettin, 1860.

———. Commentary on Servant of the Lord passage. Ed. Adolf

Neubauer. In *The Fifty-third Chapter of Isaiah according to the Jewish Interpreters*, Heb. vol., pp. 75–82. 2 vols. Oxford, 1876.

———. Commentary on the Servant of the Lord passage. Pub. Chaim Chavel. In *Kitvei Rabbenu Moshe ben Nahman*, 1: 322–326. 4th printing. 2 vols. Jerusalem, 1971.

———. *Kitvei Rabbenu Moshe ben Nahman*. Ed. Chaim Chavel. 4th printing. 2 vols. Jerusalem, 1971.

———. *Perushei ha-Torah le-Rabbenu Moshe ben Nahman*. 7th printing. 2 vols. Jerusalem, 1959.

———. *Sefer ha-Ge'ulah*. Ed. Samuel Nahum Marat. New York, 1904.

———. *Sefer ha-Ge'ulah*. Ed. Jacob Lipschitz. London, 1909.

———. *Sefer ha-Ge'ulah*. Ed. Joshua Moses Aaronsohn. Jerusalem, 1959.

———. *Sefer ha-Ge'ulah*. Pub. Chaim Chavel. In *Kitvei Rabbenu Moshe ben Nahman*, 1: 253–296. 4th printing. 2 vols. Jerusalem, 1971.

———. *Torat ha-Shem Temimah*. Ed. Chaim Chavel. In *Kitvei Rabbenu Moshe ben Nahman*, 1: 141–175. 4th printing. 2 vols. Jerusalem, 1971.

Neubauer, Adolf, ed. and trans. *The Fifty-Third Chapter of Isaiah according to the Jewish Interpreters*. 2 vols. Oxford, 1876.

Perarnau i Espelt, Josep, ed. "El text primitiv del *De mysterio cymbalorum ecclesiae* d'Arnau de Vilanova." *Arxiu de textos catalans antics* 7–8 (1988–1989): 7–169.

Pirkei Hekhalot. Ed. Solomon Wertheimer. Jerusalem, 1889.

Raymond, Martin. *Pugio Fidei*. Leipzig, 1687.

Régné, Jean, ed. *History of the Jews in Aragon*. Ed. and annot. Yom Tov Assis. Jerusalem, 1978.

Saadia ben Joseph. *Sefer ha-Emunot veha-De'ot*. Ed. and trans. Joseph Kafeh. Jerusalem, 1970.

Sbaralea, J., ed. *Bullarium Franciscanum*. 4 vols. Rome, 1759–1768.

Sefer Yosef ha-Mekane. Ed. Judah Rosenthal. Jerusalem, 1970.

Simonsohn, Shlomo, ed. *The Apostolic See and the Jews: Documents, 492–1404*. Toronto, 1988.

Solomon ibn Verga. *Shevet Yehudah*. Ed. Azriel Shohat. Jerusalem, 1947.

Vikuah Rabbenu Yehiel mi-Pariz. Ed. Reuven Margolies. Lwow, 1928.

SECONDARY READINGS

Alter, Robert. *Motives for Fiction*. Cambridge, Mass., 1984.

———. *The Invention of Hebrew Prose: Modern Fiction and the Language of Realism*. Seattle, 1988.

———. *The Pleasures of Reading in an Ideological Age*. New York, 1989.

Baer, Yitzhak. *Studien zur Geschichte der Juden im Königreich Aragonien*. Berlin, 1913.

———. "The Disputations of R. Yehiel of Paris and Nahmanides" (Hebrew). *Tarbiz* 2 (1930–1931): 172–187.

―――. "The Social Background of the *Ra'aya Mehemna*" (Hebrew). *Zion* 5 (1940): 1–44.

―――. *A History of the Jews in Christian Spain.* Trans. Louis Schoffman et al. 2 vols. Philadelphia, 1961–1966.

Baron Salo W. *A Social and Religious History of the Jews.* Rev. ed. 18 vols. New York, 1952–1983.

Ben Sasson, Haim Hillel. "Concerning the Goals of Medieval Jewish Chronography and Its Problematics" (Hebrew). In *Historyonim ve-Askolot Historyot*, pp. 29–49. Jerusalem, 1963.

―――. "Nahmanides: A Man in the Complexities of His Era" (Hebrew). *Molad* n.s. 1 (1967): 360–366.

Berger, David. *The Jewish-Christian Debate in the High Middle Ages.* Philadelphia, 1979.

―――. "Miracles and the Natural Order." In *Rabbi Moses Nahmanides (Ramban): Explorations in His Religious and Literary Virtuosity*, ed. Isador Twersky, pp. 107–128. Cambridge, Mass., 1983.

―――. "Three Typological Themes in Early Jewish Messianism: Messiah Son of Joseph, Rabbinic Calculations, and the Figure of Armilus." *AJS Review* 10 (1985): 141–164.

Berner, Leila. "On the Western Shores: The Jews of Barcelona during the Reign of Jaume I, 'El Conqueridor,' 1213–1276." Doctoral dissertation, UCLA, 1986.

Bisson, T. N. *The Medieval Crown of Aragon.* Oxford, 1986.

Bonfil, Reuven. "Myth, Rhetoric, History? An Examination of *Megilat Ahima'az.*" In *Tarbut ve-Hevrah be-Toldot Yisra'el be-Yeme ha-Benavim*, ed. Reuven Bonfil et al., pp. 99–135. Jerusalem, 1989.

Brentano, Robert. *Two Churches: England and Italy in the Thirteenth Century.* Berkeley, Los Angeles, London, 1968.

Burns, Robert I. "The Spiritual Life of James the Conqueror King of Arago-Catalonia, 1208–1276: Portrait and Self-Portrait." *The Catholic Historical Review* 62 (1976): 1–35.

―――. "Castle of Intellect, Castle of Force: The Worlds of Alfonso the Learned and James the Conqueror." In *The Worlds of Alfonso the Learned and James the Conqueror*, ed. Robert I. Burns, pp. 3–22. Princeton, 1985.

―――― (ed.). *The Worlds of Alfonso the Learned and James the Conqueror.* Princeton, 1985.

Chavel, Chaim. *Rabbenu Moshe ben Nahman.* 2d ed. Jerusalem, 1973.

Chazan, Robert. *Medieval Jewry in Northern France: A Political and Social History.* Baltimore, 1973.

―――. "Confrontation in the Synagogue of Narbonne: A Christian Sermon and a Jewish Reply." *Harvard Theological Review* LXVII (1974): 437–457.

―――. "The Barcelona 'Disputation' of 1263: Christian Missionizing and Jewish Response." *Speculum* 52 (1977): 824–842.

―――. "From Friar Paul to Friar Raymond: The Development of Innovative Missionizing Argumentation." *Harvard Theological Review* 76 (1983): 289–306.

———. *European Jewry and the First Crusade*. Berkeley, Los Angeles, London, 1987.

———. "The Condemnation of the Talmud Reconsidered (1239–1248)." *Proceedings of the American Academy for Jewish Research* 45 (1988): 11–30.

———. "Representation of Events in the Middle Ages." In *Essays in Jewish Historiography* (*History and Theory*, Beiheft 27), pp. 40–55. Middletown, 1988.

———. *Daggers of Faith: Thirteenth-Century Christian Missionizing and Jewish Response*. Berkeley, Los Angeles, Oxford, 1989.

———. "Chapter Thirteen of the *Maḥazik Emunah*: Further Light on Friar Paul Christian and the New Christian Missionizing." *Michael* 12 (1990): 9–26.

———. "In the Wake of the Barcelona Disputation." *Hebrew Union College Annual* 61 (1990): 185–201.

———. "The Facticity of Medieval Narrative: A Case Study of the Hebrew First-Crusade Narratives." *AJS Review* 16 (1991).

Cohen, Gerson D. "Messianic Postures of Ashkenazim and Sephardim." In *Studies of the Leo Baeck Institute*, ed. Max Kreutzberger, pp. 117–156. New York, 1967.

Cohen, Jeremy. *The Friars and the Jews: The Evolution of Medieval Anti-Judaism*. Ithaca, 1982.

Cohen, Martin A. "Reflections on the Text and Context of the Disputation of Barcelona." *Hebrew Union College Annual* 35 (1964): 157–192.

Cook, Albert. *History/Writing*. Cambridge, 1988.

Dan, Joseph. "The Beginnings of the Messianic Myth in Kabbalistic Doctrine of the Thirteenth Century" (Hebrew). In *Meshiḥiyut ve-Askatologiyah*, ed. Zvi Baras, pp. 239–252. Jerusalem, 1983.

Denifle, Heinrich. "Quellen zur Disputation Pablos Christiani mit Mose Nachmani zu Barcelona 1263." *Historisches Jahrbuch des Görres-Gesellschaft* 8 (1887): 225–244.

de Tourtalon, Charles. *Jacme Ier le conquérant roi d'Aragon*. 2 vols. Montpellier, 1863–1867.

Epstein, Louis M. "The Eschatology of Rabbi Moses ben Nachman (Nachmanides)." *Jewish Theological Seminary Students Annual* 1914: 95–123.

Even-Hen, Jacob. *Ha-Ramban*. Jerusalem, 1976.

Fox, Marvin. "Nahmanides on the Status of Aggadot: Perspectives on the Disputation at Barcelona, 1263." *Journal of Jewish Studies* 40 (1989): 95–109.

Friedenberg, Daniel M. *Medieval Jewish Seals from Europe*. Detroit, 1987.

Funkenstein, Amos. "Nahmanides' Typological Reading of History" (Hebrew). *Zion* 45 (1980): 35–49.

———. "Nahmanides' Symbolical Reading of History." In *Studies in Jewish*

Mysticism, ed. Joseph Dan and Frank Talmage, pp. 129–150. Cambridge, Mass., 1982.

Gelles, Benjamin J. *Peshat and Derash in the Exegesis of Rashi*. Leiden, 1981.

Girbal, Enrique Claudio. *Los judíos en Gerona*. Gerona, 1870.

Gossman, Lionel. *Between History and Literature*. Cambridge, Mass., 1990.

Gottlieb, Efraim. "The Ramban as a Kabbalist" (Hebrew). In *Studies in the Kabbala Literature*, ed. Joseph Hacker, pp. 88–95. Tel-Aviv, 1976.

Graetz, Heinrich. "Die Disputation des Bonastruc mit Frai Pablo in Barcelona." *Monatschrift für Geschichte und Wissenschaft des Judenthums* 14 (1865): 428–433.

———. *Geschichte der Juden*. 1st ed. 11 vols. in 12. Leipzig, 1853–1876.

Idel, Moshe. *Kitvei R. Avraham Abulafia u-Mishnato*. Doctoral dissertation. Hebrew Univ., 1976.

———. "Abraham Abulafia and the Pope: An Account of an Abortive Mission" (Hebrew). *AJS Review* 7–8 (1982–1983): Heb. sec., pp. 1–17.

———. "'We Have No Kabbalistic Tradition on This.'" In *Rabbi Moses Nahmanides (Ramban): Explorations in His Religious and Literary Virtuosity*, ed. Isadore Twersky, pp. 51–73. Cambridge, Mass., 1983.

———. "Abraham Abulafia on the Jewish Messiah and Jesus." In *Studies in Ecstatic Kabbalah*, pp. 45–61. Albany, 1988.

Jacobs, Joseph. *Sources of Spanish Jewish History*. London, 1894.

Jordan, William Chester. *The French Monarchy and the Jews: From Philip Augustus to the Last of the Capetians*. Philadelphia, 1989.

Kamin, Sarah. *Peshuto shel Mikra u-Midrasho shel Mikra*. Jerusalem, 1986.

Kaufmann, David. "Jewish Informers in the Middle Ages." *Jewish Quarterly Review* 8 (1896): 217–238.

Kayserling, Meyer. "Die Disputation des Bonastruc mit Frai Pablo in Barcelona." *Monatschrift für Geschichte und Wissenschaft des Judenthums* 14 (1865): 308–313.

———. Review of Joseph Jacobs, *Sources of Spanish Jewish History*. *Jewish Quarterly Review* 8 (1896): 486–499.

Kedar, B. Z. *Crusade and Mission: European Approaches toward the Muslims*. Princeton, 1984.

Lee, Harold, Marjorie Reeves, and Giulio Silano. *Western Mediterranean Prophecy: The School of Joachim of Fiore and the Fourteenth-Century Breviloquium*. Toronto, 1989.

Levine, Baruch A. "René Girard on Job: The Question of the Scapegoat." *Semia* 33 (1985): 125–133.

Liebermann, Saul. *Shkiin*. Jerusalem, 1939.

Liebes, Yehuda. "The Messiah of the *Zohar*: The Messianic Image of Rabbi Simon bar Yohai" (Hebrew). In *Ha-Raʿyon ha-Meshihi be-Yisraʾel*, pp. 87–236. Jerusalem, 1982.

Limor, Ora. *The Disputation of Majorca 1286*. 2 vols. Jerusalem, 1985.

Loeb, Isidore. "La Controverse de 1263 à Barcelone entre Paulus Christiani et Moise ben Nahman." *Revue des études juives* 15 (1887): 1–18.

Maccoby, Hyam. *Judaism on Trial*. London, 1982.

Malter, Henry. "Saadia Gaon's Messianic Computation." *Journal of Jewish Lore and Philosophy* 1 (1919): 45–59.

Marcus, Ivan G. Review of Robert Chazan, *European Jewry and the First Crusade. Speculum* 64 (1989): 685–688.

Marmorstein, A. "The Doctrine of Redemption in Saadya's Theological System." In *Saadya Studies,* ed. Erwin I. J. Rosenthal, pp. 103–118. Manchester, 1943.

Merhavia, Ch. *Ha-Talmud be-Re'i ha-Nazut.* Jerusalem, 1970.

Millás Vallicrosa, José Maria. "Sobre las fuentes documentales de la controversia de Barcelona en el año 1263." *Anales de la Universidad de Barcelona, Memorias y Comunicaciones* 1940: 25–44.

Morris, Colin. *The Papal Monarchy: The Western Church from 1050 to 1250.* Oxford, 1989.

North, Christopher R. *The Suffering Servant in Deutero-Isaiah: An Historical and Critical Study.* 2d ed. Oxford, 1956.

O'Callaghan, Joseph F. *A History of Medieval Spain.* Cornell, 1975.

Pacios Lopez, Antonio. *La Disputa de Tortosa.* 2 vols. Madrid, 1957.

Pines, Shlomo. "Nahmanides on Adam in the Garden of Eden in the Context of Other Interpretations of Genesis, Chapters 2 and 3" (Hebrew). In *Galut ahar Golah,* ed. Aharon Mirsky et al., pp. 159–164. Jerusalem, 1988.

Posnanski, Adolph. *Schiloh: Ein Beitrag zur Geschichte der Messiaslehre.* Leipzig, 1904.

Poznanski, Samuel. "Die Berechnung des Erlösungsjahres bei Saadja." *Monatsschrift für Geschichte und Wissenschaft des Judenthums* 44 (1900): 400–416, 508–519.

Rembaum, Joel E. "The Development of a Jewish Exegetical Tradition Regarding Isaiah 53." *Harvard Theological Review* 75 (1982): 289–311.

Reeves, Marjorie. *The Influence of Prophecy in the Later Middle Ages: A Study in Joachimism.* Oxford, 1969.

———. *Joachim of Fiore and the Prophetic Future.* London, 1976.

Rosenthal, Judah. "The Talmud on Trial." *Jewish Quarterly Review* 47 (1956–1957): 58–76, 145–169.

Roth, Cecil. "The Disputation of Barcelona (1263)." *Harvard Theological Review* 43 (1950): 117–144.

Roth, Norman. Review of Robert Chazan, *Daggers of Faith. The Catholic Historical Review* 76 (1990): 119–121.

Safran, Bezalel. "Rabbi Azriel and Nahmanides: Two Views on the Fall of Man." In *Rabbi Moses ben Nahman (Ramban): Explorations in His Religious and Literary Virtuosity,* ed. Isadore Twersky, pp. 75–106. Cambridge, Mass., 1983.

Saperstein, Marc. *Decoding the Rabbis: A Thirteenth-Century Commentary on the Aggadah.* Cambridge, Mass., 1980.

Sarachek, Joseph. *The Doctrine of the Messiah in Medieval Jewish Literature.* New York, 1932.

Schechter, Solomon. "Nachmanides." *Jewish Quarterly Review* 5 (1893): 78–121.

Scholem, Gershom. "The Messianic Idea in Kabbalism." In *The Messianic Idea in Judaism*, pp. 37–48. New York, 1971.

———. "The Concept of Redemption in the Kabbalah" (Hebrew). In *Devarim be-Go*, pp. 191–216. Tel Aviv, 1975.

Segal, Lester A. *Historical Consciousness and Religious Tradition in Azariah de' Rossi's Me'or 'Einayim.* Philadelphia, 1989.

Septimus, Bernard. "Piety and Power in Thirteenth-Century Catalonia." In *Studies in Medieval Jewish History and Literature*, ed. Isadore Twersky. Cambridge, Mass., 1979.

———. *Hispano-Jewish Culture in Transition: The Career and Controversies of Ramah.* Cambridge, Mass., 1982.

———. " 'Open Rebuke and Concealed Love': Nahmanides and the Andalusian Tradition." In *Rabbi Moses Nahmanides (Ramban): Explorations in His Religious and Literary Virtuosity*, ed. Isadore Twersky, pp. 11–34. Cambridge, Mass., 1983.

Shahar, Isaiah. *The Seal of Nahmanides.* Jerusalem, 1972.

Shatzmiller, Joseph. "Paulus Christianus: un aspect de son activité anti-juive." In *Hommages à Georges Vajda*, ed. Gérard Nahon and Charles Touati, pp. 203–217. Louvain, 1980.

———. *Shylock Reconsidered: Jews, Moneylending, and Medieval Society.* Berkeley, Los Angeles, Oxford, 1990.

Shulvass, Moses A. "Medieval Ashkenazic Jewry's Knowledge of History and Historical Literature." *The Solomon Goldman Lectures* IV (1985): 1–27.

Silver, Abba Hillel. *A History of Messianic Speculation in Israel.* New York, 1927.

Sobel, Moshe N. "Calculation of the Appointed End of Days and Depiction of Redemption in the *Sefer ha-Emunot veha-De'ot*" (Hebrew). In *Rav Saadia Gaon*, ed. Judah L. Fishman, pp. 172–190. Jerusalem, 1943.

Southern, R. W. *Western Society and the Church in the Middle Ages.* Harmondsworth, 1970.

Tostado Martin, Alfonso. *La Disputa de Barcelona 1263.* Salamanca, 1986.

Twersky, Isadore (ed.). *Rabbi Moses ben Nahman (Ramban): Explorations in His Religious and Literary Virtuosity.* Cambridge, Mass., 1983.

Unna, Isaac. *Rabbi Moshe ben Nahman.* 3d ed. Jerusalem, 1976.

Weiss Halivni, David. *Peshat and Derash: Plain and Applied Meaning in Rabbinic Exegesis.* Oxford, 1991.

White, Hayden. *Metahistory: The Historical Imagination of Nineteenth Century Europe.* Baltimore, 1973.

Wolfson, Elliot R. " 'By Way of Truth': Aspects of Nahmanides' Kabbalistic Hermeneutic." *AJS Review* 14 (1989): 103–178.

———. "The Secret of the Garment in Nahmanides." *Daat* 24 (1990): Eng. sect., pp. xxv–xlix.

Yerucham, Aaron. *Ohel Rahel*. New York, 1942.
Yerushalmi, Yosef Haim. *Zakhor: Jewish History and Jewish Memory*. Seattle, 1982.
Young, James. *Writing and Rewriting the Holocaust*. Bloomington, 1988.

Index

Abraham bar Hiyya, 180, 182–184; *Megillat ha-Megalleh*, 183
Abraham ibn Ezra, 182–183
Abravanel, Isaac, 143; on Nahmanides's approach to aggadah, 143; on unacceptable approaches to aggadah, 143
Abulafia, Abraham, 189–190
Abulafia, Meir ha-Levi, 35
Aggadic texts, 142–157; Abravanel on, 143; on birth of messiah, 153; J. Cohen's views on, 144; M. A. Cohen's views on, 143–144; conflict in realm of, 153–154; consensus and, 155–156; Fox's views on, 145–146; versus halakhah, 151, 155–156; interpretation of Servant of the Lord passage and, 160–161; Latin account of Barcelona disputation on, 142–143, 146–147, 150; Liebermann's views on, 145; Nahmanidean stance on, 142–157; Septimus's views on, 145, 151–152
Alfonso the Learned, king of Castile, 17–18; Burns on, 29
Alter, Robert, 110–111
Aquinas, St. Thomas, 19
Aragon, archival records of, 199–202
Aragonese Jewry, 18, 28, 32–35; James the Conqueror and, 1, 29–30, 32–34, 82–83, 85–87; lobbying against sermons by, 85–86
Arnold of Segurra, 31, 90; complaints lodged against Nahmanides by, 93–95, 99

Babylonian exile, and redemption, Nahmanides on, 174–175, 186
Baer, Yitzhak, 11, 14, 98; on Barcelona disputation, 7–8; *History of the Jews in Christian Spain*, 8; on James the Conqueror's policy toward Jews, 33; on Latin account of Barcelona disputation, 39–40, 42, 43–44, 47; on Nah-

manidean account of Barcelona disputation, 50; on Nahmanides, 36; on Paris disputation of 1240, 7
Barcelona disputation of 1263, 1–79; accounts of, 39–79; aftermath of, 80–99; agenda of, 41–42, 65; analysis of, 39–79; Christian argumentation, 62–63; Christian control of proceedings of, 50–54, 63–64, 65, 78; conclusion of, 75–78; divergent views of, 2–12; James the Conqueror and, 32, 33, 51, 66; literary materials resulting from, 196, 197; methodology of present study of, 12–16; as missionizing endeavor, 1–2, 3, 13, 24, 51, 55–56, 87–88; potential outcomes of, 81–82; prior historiography on, 4–12; reconstruction of events of, 50–79; role of, in lives of participants, 195; setting of agenda for, 65; significance of, 2–4. *See also* Latin account of Barcelona disputation; Nahmanidean account of Barcelona disputation
Barcelona synagogue, missionizing visit to, 82–83
Burns, Robert I., 17–18, 29; on thirteenth century, 17–18

Catalonian Jewry, 17, 18; awareness of intellectual power of Christian world, 58–59; Barcelona disputation and, 64, 195, 196; effect of ecclesiastical and secular policies on, 32–35; James the Conqueror and, 1, 29–30, 32–33, 78, 82–83. *See also* Aragonese Jewry
Censorship, of rabbinic literature, 89–92, 99
Christian-Latin account of Barcelona disputation. *See* Latin account of Barcelona disputation
Clement V, pope, letter on Nahmanidean narrative, 93
Cohen, Gerson D., 184–185

253

76, 77–78; as crafted record, 102–103; Denifle on, 6–7, 14; on denigration of Paul Christian, 68, 69, 70; dissemination of, 138–139; distortions in, reasons for, 123–124; Dominican reaction to, 93–99; embellishment in, 93, 111, 147; exaggeration in, 112, 147; Graetz on, 5, 11; intended audience of, 97–98; James the Conqueror as portrayed in, 119–120; James the Conqueror on, 93–94; Jewish perspective of, 92–93, 147; Loeb on, 7; Maccoby on, 10–11; on missionizing argumentation of Paul Christian, 68, 69; on Nahmanides, 79, 114–120; on Nahmanides's stance on aggadic statements, 147–157; narrative format of, 45, 101–112, 136–137; on opening stages of disputation, 94–95; Paul Christian as portrayed in, 25, 26, 27, 113–114, 138, 156; popularity of, 138–140; purposes of, 45, 87, 101, 123–135, 150; as refutation of Christianity, 123–135; reliability of, 45–50, 136, 140; self-portrayal in, 79, 114–120; suspense and tension in, 105, 121–122; tone of, 73; wittiness of, 118–119

Nahmanides, Moses (Moses ben Nahman), rabbi of Gerona, 34, 35, 195; Abravanel on, 143; on aggadic texts, 142–157; Andalusian Jewish world and, 184–185; on Barcelona disputation (*see* Nahmanidean account of Barcelona disputation); choice of, as spokesman in disputation, 65–66, 67–68; M. A. Cohen on, 10, 143–144; death, 202; defensive position of, in disputation, 51, 52; disputation with Paul Christian (*see* Barcelona disputation of 1263); distortion of account of Barcelona disputation, 123–124; Dominican proceedings against, 93–99; emigration from Aragon, 98–99; environment of, 36–37; on establishment of agenda for debate, 65; exile to Holy Land, 202; explication of Servant of the Lord passage in Isaiah, 158–171; Fox on, 145–146; identification of, in archival sources of Aragon, 199–203; importance of, 35–36; James the Conqueror and, 1, 4–5, 66, 67, 130, 199–200, 203; and kabbalah, 36, 37–38, 185, 187–188; language facility of, 111; Latin account on, 42, 43, 79; letter to son, Solomon, 36, 201; literary abilities of,

45, 101, 103–112, 122–123, 141; Loeb on, 7; Maccoby on, 11; Maimonidean controversy and, 185; on messianic advent, 38, 42–43, 60–62, 65, 71–73, 116, 117–118, 124–125, 126–128, 130–133, 134, 168–169, 172–186, 193; personality and style of, 37–38, 185; public role of, 197; religious and spiritual interests of, 36; self-portrayal in, 114–119; Septimus on, 145, 184; settlement in Holy Land, 98–99; socioeconomic circumstances of, 36; on Torah, 149, 151, 154, 173

Paris disputation of 1240, 3, 111–112
Paul Christian, 17, 24–27; complaints lodged against Nahmanides by, 93–95, 99; as convert from Judaism, 25, 26; Jewish scholarship of, 25–26; on midrashic statements about messiah, 167–168, 171; missionizing argumentation of, 1–2, 24, 27, 55–64, 85–87, 113–114, 189, 195; Nahmanides's portrayal of, 25, 26, 27, 113–114, 138, 156; offensive position of, in disputation, 51–53, 76; pre-1263 activities of, 24–27; sources of information about, 24–25; on Talmud, 26–27; use of rabbinic exegesis by, 57
Peter of Genoa, 130
Proselytizing. *See* Missionizing, by Dominican Order
Pugio Fidei (Raymond Martin), 86, 150

Rabbinic texts: Church concern over, 88–89; use of, in Dominican missionizing argumentation, 25–26, 27, 41, 53–54, 57, 58–59, 61–63, 88–89, 159, 170–171. *See also* Aggadic texts
Rashi, 182
Raymond Martin, 25; *Pugio Fidei*, 86, 150
Raymond of Penyafort, 31, 82–83, 90; complaints lodged against Nahmanides by, 93–95, 99; missionizing sermons of, 117
Reconquest, Baer on, 33–35
Roman Catholic church: concerns regarding effects of Jewish behavior on Christian society, 20–27; ecclesiastical policies and programs of, in thirteenth century, 17, 18–27; and heresy, 19; James the Conqueror and, 19, 20, 23–24, 30–31, 32, 55, 82–86, 117; Paul Christian and, 24–27; stance towards Jews, in thirteenth century,

Designer: U. C. Press Staff
Compositor: Prestige Typography
Text: 10/13 Palatino
Display: Palatino
Printer: Bookcrafters
Binder: Bookcrafters